Y0-EKQ-684

Taste of Humanity

Tammy Hotsenpiller

Graphic design by Doreen Mazur
Photos from Photos.com and Shutterstock.com

Library of Congress Cataloging-in-Publication Data
Hotsenpiller, Tammy, 1957-
Taste of Humanity/Tammy Hotsenpiller
p. cm.
ISBN: 978-0-9792880-0-5 (hardcover)
1. Cookery, International. 2. Dinners and dining. 3. Menus. I. Title.
TX725.A1H5885 2008
641.59–dc22
2008000828

Printed in Singapore, 2009

08 09 10 11 12 — 5 4 3 2 1

To my family: Phil, Jeremy, Josh, Jen, Kim and Erin.
I told you I could cook! You are the joy of my life.
May you always aspire to your highest dreams.

I love you,
Mom

Contents

Acknowledgments

Just as the countries featured in this book are diverse, so are the people who assisted in its creation. I started with an idea, a really great idea, and it quickly became much bigger than I. Friends, church members, neighbors, and family all rallied around me to make this vision become a reality. Dreams and visions only enlarge when you share them with another.

I want to thank my Jersey Girls who piloted the first few dinners with me: Jamie Longo, Marita Dowell, Diane Magee, Vivian Gemian, JoAnne Lotorto, Lynn Slagter, Gloria Hubner, and Christine Sakdalan. I will always remember the good times and value all the lessons learned on the East Coast.

Thank you to Diane Cline for keeping me focused and inspired. Your positive words were my inspiration many a night.

Thank you to my recipe consultant and culinarian, Heidi Ferris—you spice up my life. Your talent and training are evident in each recipe. I look forward to working with you on the next edition of *Taste of Humanity.*

Thank you to my West Coast church family, Marlene Tafoya, June Rush, Staff Fieldhouse, Jill Fieldhouse, Carol Williams, Kay Bye, Wendy Lee, Janet Allen, Karen Beamish, Janet Woessner, Sue Scherlers, Lydia Martinez, Judy Aase, Summer Teal, and Sue Coventon. Your talents, abilities, passion, and assistance helped to make this book become reality.

Thank you to Marlene Tafoya. Your research made my life much easier. Your love and passion for life are evident in each step you take.

Thank you, Mom, for teaching me at a young age about such a diverse world.

Thank you to my family who supported and encouraged me to reach for something bigger than myself.

Thank you to my fantastic husband who has taken me around the world and back. My love for culture began with you.

Thank you to Andy Collins for assisting me with the initial manuscript layout.

Thank you to Elaine Khodorkovsky, my great neighbor and librarian, who is determined to have Russian recipes in the next volume!

Thank you to Doreen Mazur, my designer. Your eye for detail and color has allowed the reader to experience firsthand the culture, cuisine, and costumes of each magnificent country.

Thank you to Jennifer Greenstein for a wonderful job editing this book. Your gifts and talents are evident throughout the book.

Thank you, God, for giving me the gift of vision and creativity. May I always use my gifts and abilities for You.

Thank you to each reader, host, and organization that uses this book. Your enjoyment is my utmost goal.

Introduction

Taste of Humanity was written with you in mind. Whether you are a whiz in the kitchen or a novice, this book will be a great resource. Culture, cuisine, costume, and customs—it's all in here.

Our view of the world is constantly changing! Every day brings a new layer of culture from around the world. These cultures influence the way we dress, think, eat, and interact with one another. No culture is good or bad—just delightfully different. These cultural differences are what make life interesting and exciting.

When I was a young girl growing up in the Midwest, my local church hosted an international mission night once a month that highlighted the culture and cuisine of the world. I made a decision then to visit as many countries as possible and to experience their culture firsthand.

I have kept that promise. I have had the privilege of traveling worldwide, and through my travels I have become a student of culture.

Moving to the East Coast and dining in some of the greatest restaurants in Manhattan taught me that we are truly a global village.

One way to understand culture is to experience it through the art of entertainment. This allows you a glimpse into the hearts and minds of the wonderful world of people.

To fully enjoy the many dimensions of this book, you must leave your inhibitions and fears at the door. As you embrace the customs and traditions of each particular country, you will find a new appreciation for that culture.

Taste of Humanity will become the coveted event planner for anyone hoping to host the perfect party. As you follow the evening's agenda and serve each course, you will be praised for your knowledge and expertise. It is my hope that you will use this book as both a cookbook for fantastic recipes from around the world and as an entertainment guide to be enjoyed with family and friends—but most of all as a bridge into the lives of people from around the world. Enjoy your meal, *buon appetito, buen provecho, manman chi!*

Ways You Can Use This Book

You may enjoy the challenge of creating a foreign dish or searching for the perfect costume. You may use this book as a teaching tool for family members. Or you may be the romantic sort who will love the Dinner and a Movie option. However you choose to use this book, I guarantee you will find new insights to faraway lands you have never explored. You may become so intrigued by one of the many lovely countries highlighted in this book that you plan a trip there.

I have included several ways to enjoy this book, along with the directions. Allow this book to stretch you beyond your natural comfort zone, to a place of understanding and knowledge. My hope is that you will enjoy learning about these special countries that so many call home.

Monthly dinner club: A group of six to eight individuals rotate monthly from house to house. Each participant selects a course (appetizer, salad, side dish, entrée, dessert, or drink) to bring for the next month's dinner party. The host or hostess decorates the home in the theme of the country.

Girls' night out: Enjoy the costume ideas—from French maids to geisha girls—and share cuisine with close friends as you discover new truths about one another through discussions inspired by the theme. This will be a night to remember.

Family activity: Include the family in cooking and costumes while experiencing the cultures of faraway lands. This is a perfect way to teach your family the traditions and convictions of other countries as you taste, smell, and sometimes even feel foreign foods.

Couples dinner: Enjoy an intimate evening with your friends as you host an authentic international evening. This is a great opportunity for couples to dress in costume and experience the culture, romance, and intrigue of a foreign land.

Date night: Enjoy preparing a meal with your date and choose a movie from the movie selections provided.

Take-out: Skip the cooking and pick up take-out, and enjoy the activities in the book (dinner questions, icebreaker quizzes, music, and more) for a rewarding international evening.

Dinner party: Whether you are having six or sixteen, all the information you need to host an international dinner party is included. From recipes to dinner questions, your party is guaranteed to be a success.

International night: Each participant selects a different country to represent at the party. He or she dresses in the costume of that culture and brings a dish prepared from the recipes provided for that country. Each guest chooses a question to share from the dinner questions of the selected country.

What This Book Provides

Here is what each chapter includes for the ten countries this book explores:

Hostess tips: Begin by previewing the hostess tips several weeks before your event. This will allow you to begin planning and preparing for your party. You may choose to consult the Internet for additional decoration ideas or typical costumes of the country.

Agenda: Next comes setting the agenda for the evening. Following this step-by-step process will ensure your party runs smoothly. This will be your personal event planner.

Language: Here you will find key words, phrases, and greetings. Review these before your guests arrive to set the mood for an international experience.

Table settings/etiquette/traditional cooking: This includes tips or background information on place setting, table etiquette, or cuisine to help you understand the culture and customs of each individual country.

Costumes: As host or hostess, you can encourage your guests to participate in the evening by dressing in costume, and can share these costume ideas and tips with them in advance. This has proven to be one of the highlights of the evening. Participants may choose to make or assemble the costumes themselves, or purchase or rent them from a local costume store.

Movies: You can choose one of the recommended movies in each chapter for your personal understanding of the country and its particular culture, or as a date night option. Enjoy making dinner with a loved one and relaxing with a good meal and a movie.

Activities: Whether it's matching questions, limbo, or belly dancing you are sure to start the evening off right with these party icebreakers.

Music: You may select one from these recommendations of music selections or choose to play something of your own. (You can always check out the offerings at your public library.) Either way, music sets the pace and ambiance for your international evening.

Dinner questions: The most entertaining part of the evening comes with the dinner questions. The questions have been designed to encourage discussion, revelation, and sometimes surprise. Conversation is a big part of most cultures, and what better time than over dinner? Some questions will stimulate intriguing conversation; some will reveal your passion and others will tell your story. As the host or hostess, you will facilitate the dialog and keep the conversation moving.

Topics of interest: Each chapter offers various topics of interest relevant to the country, such as trivia, a historical event, or a glossary of terms. These give the host or hostess the opportunity to learn more about the country's background and to share this information with guests.

Recipes and menu: Last you will find the recipes, with a recommended menu as well as several other options. As you review the menu selection, keep in mind your guest list and any dietary restrictions any of your guests may have. If you are participating in the monthly dinner club, you will want to select recipes that your guests will enjoy preparing.

This book has been designed with you, the host or hostess, in mind. Everything you need to have an exciting international dinner party has been provided. Of course, in distilling a country or culture down to a chapter in a book, I have given only a general overview and focused on selected facets. I hope that you, in planning your own dinner parties, will be motivated to learn even more about these countries and fully appreciate the richness and diversity within each. Although some of the movies (especially older ones) and costume ideas may reflect a stereotypical or one-dimensional view of a culture, they are included because they offer familiar images that can be worked into the dinner party theme in a fun or interesting way. And they are also wonderful starting points for discussions. Enjoy the education you will receive as you plan, prepare, and participate in an evening to remember!

BRAZIL

UNDER THE INFLUENCE OF MANY CULTURES, BRAZIL HAS BECOME A COUNTRY OF A VARIETY OF RHYTHMS AND DANCES. "You sleep only in order to dance again," writes John Krich, author of a 1993 travelogue about Brazil. Brazilian cuisine is famous for its eclectic flare and is influenced and nurtured by its varied regional backgrounds: Indian, African, Portuguese, Italian, German, Syrian, Lebanese, and Asian. The national cuisine is a collection of five unique regional styles within Brazil: northern, northeast, central-west, southeast, and southern. Staple ingredients in Brazilian recipes are rice, beans, coconut, dried shrimp, codfish, lemon, and dendi oil (oil from a Brazilian palm tree).

In Brazil you can see hundreds of miles of white sandy beaches as well as magnificent mountain ranges and the wonders of the Amazon. You can see firsthand the wildlife of the Pantanal wetland or the awesome power of Iguaçu Falls. You can experience the historical charm of old cities such as Ouro Preto, or enjoy the music, cuisine, and heritage of Brazil's 500-year-old culture. It doesn't matter if you are drawn by the allures of Rio de Janeiro or simply want to kick back and enjoy the delights of a freshly made Brazilian drink. Brazil is a big country, with diverse places, people, and things, and something to interest everyone.

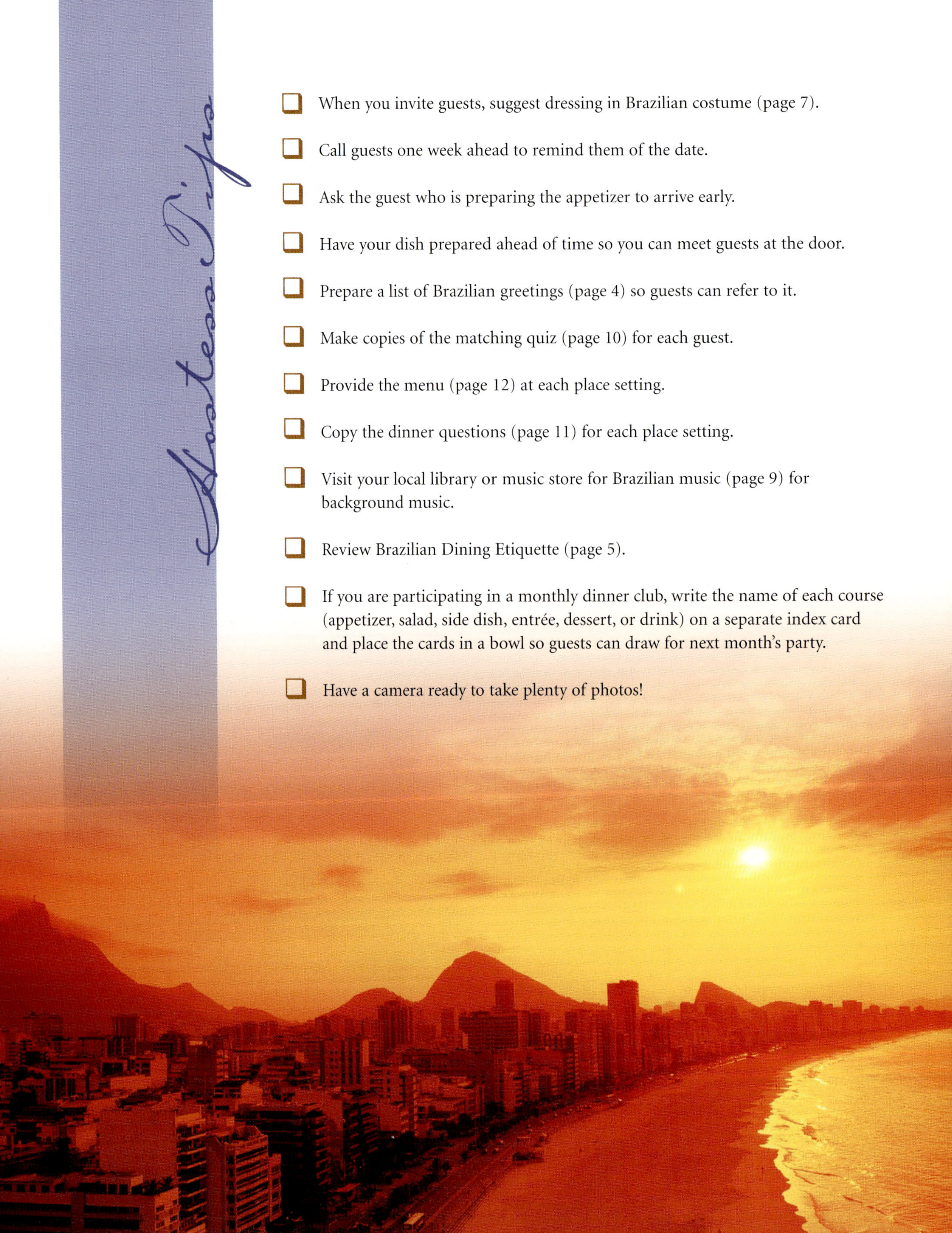

Hostess Tips

- ❑ When you invite guests, suggest dressing in Brazilian costume (page 7).
- ❑ Call guests one week ahead to remind them of the date.
- ❑ Ask the guest who is preparing the appetizer to arrive early.
- ❑ Have your dish prepared ahead of time so you can meet guests at the door.
- ❑ Prepare a list of Brazilian greetings (page 4) so guests can refer to it.
- ❑ Make copies of the matching quiz (page 10) for each guest.
- ❑ Provide the menu (page 12) at each place setting.
- ❑ Copy the dinner questions (page 11) for each place setting.
- ❑ Visit your local library or music store for Brazilian music (page 9) for background music.
- ❑ Review Brazilian Dining Etiquette (page 5).
- ❑ If you are participating in a monthly dinner club, write the name of each course (appetizer, salad, side dish, entrée, dessert, or drink) on a separate index card and place the cards in a bowl so guests can draw for next month's party.
- ❑ Have a camera ready to take plenty of photos!

Before Dinner

Welcome guests with *olá,* which is hello in Portuguese, the official language of Brazil. Men should shake hands, while women kiss each other on the cheeks, starting with the left cheek. If a woman wishes to shake hands with a man, she should offer her hand. Hugging and backslapping are common greetings.

Invite guests to enjoy the appetizer, music, and conversation. Ask them to participate in the matching quiz.

Dinner

After you have enjoyed the appetizer and matching quiz, seat your guests around the dinner table and begin serving the meal.

Invite guests to read and discuss the dinner questions. As the host or hostess, you are the discussion leader. Encourage each person to participate.

Serve dinner by passing each item around the table. Ask guests to continue discussing the dinner questions as you begin to clear the table.

After Dinner

Serve dessert first and then take coffee orders. Coffee is called *cafezinho* in Brazil; it is offered after dessert and served very strong and sweet.

If you are participating in a monthly dinner club, invite guests to draw names of courses (appetizer, salad, side dish, entrée, dessert, or drink) from a bowl for next month's party, and decide who will host.

As guests leave for the evening, shake their hands or kiss them good-bye.

Hello	*Olá*
Hi	*Oi*
Good evening	*Boa noite*
How are you?	*Tudo bom?*
I'm fine	*Estou optimo*
Please	*Por favor*
Thank you	*Obrigado (to a male)* *Obrigada (to a female)*
You're welcome	*De nada*
Yes	*Sim*
No	*Não*

Dining Etiquette

Do not touch anything with your fingers. In Brazil using the hands is considered ill-mannered and unhygienic. Use utensils for all foods, including those you may normally hold in your hand, such as pizza, sandwiches, fruit, and chicken.

When not being held, the knife rests with the handle on the table and the tip on the side of the plate. Never use the fork to cut anything.

When talking, rest the silverware on the plate. When finished, place the utensils horizontally on the plate. Eat Continental style, with the fork in the left hand and cutting with the right hand.

Brazilians keep both hands above the table while eating. The American habit of keeping one hand on the lap strikes them as very odd and may spark jokes.

Wrap finger foods carefully with a napkin when picking them up. Fruit is most often served in a dish or sliced and eaten from a napkin.

Wipe your mouth after every sip of drink.

Always offer to share your food. Even if the amount of food is clearly not sufficient to share, make the offer.

When offered something to eat, reply "yes" or "please" if you want the food. The phrase "Thank you" indicates a refusal, and "No, thank you" is considered rudely blunt. Always give an explanation when you refuse an offer, so that the person who offered is not offended.

Breakfast is the only meal served with coffee, which is served with milk. Coffee is served at the end of all other meals. Music and long, animated conversation are a Brazilian pastime. When conversing, interruptions are viewed as passionate conversation. Brazilians enjoy joking, informality, and authentic friendships.

Burping and then excusing oneself is particularly repulsive to Brazilians. Brazilians consider burping highly offensive, and to call attention to the burp after the fact is considered embarrassing for all. The same goes for sneezing and coughing; one should leave the table or at least turn completely away from the group.

Toothpicks *(palitos)* may be used at the table, but the mouth must be covered with hand or napkin.

Brazilians do not drink directly from the bottle or the can; they always use a glass.

Acceptable conversation topics at the dinner table include Brazil's beaches, soccer, family, and children. Unacceptable conversation topics include Argentina, politics, poverty, religion, and cutting down areas of the rain forest.

Never wear the colors green and yellow together, which should be reserved for the Brazilian flag.

Flicking the fingertips underneath the chin indicates that you do not know the answer to a question.

Cocktails are served in the salon or living room along with a variety of crackers, cheese, fruits, nuts, and light sweets. A cart is often wheeled in and you may help yourself.

Table Settings

Place all forks at left of plate with prongs up.

Place napkins folded in squares or rectangles to the left of the forks. Place knives to the right of the plate, and the spoon above the plate.

Place silver one inch from the edge of the table in a straight line. Place no more than three pieces of silver on each side of the plate.

Arrange flat silver at each place setting in the order of its use for the various courses, with the outside pieces to be used first.

Place the water glass or goblet just above point of the knife, and place the bread and butter plate just above the forks.

Keep table decorations below eye level. Candles may be slightly higher.

Carmen Miranda: Miranda was a famous singer and dancer who appeared in many movies in the 1940s. Wear a fruit-covered headdress. For the top, wear a bodysuit, multicolored blouse, or a sequined stretch top with multicolored cuffs; you can add arm ruffles as an extra touch. Wear a wrap-around skirt or a multicolored ruffled skirt. Accessorize with a belt and ropes of large pearls, a scarf of bronze silk, and bronze-colored slippers.

Daiane dos Santos: Dos Santos, Brazil's most successful female gymnast, won the gold medal in floor exercises in the 2004 World Cup competition. Wear a leotard and tights with slippers; accessorize with a jacket, with the words "2004 World Cup Winner" on it, and wear a gold metal attached to a ribbon around your neck.

Female flamenco dancer: Wear a black velvet dress with a fishtail back, a mantilla comb headpiece, and handcrafted jewelry. Accessorize with a fan and shawl.

Male flamenco dancer: Wear a white dress shirt, tight black pants, and a short jacket. Accessorize with a flat Cordoban hat.

Pelé (Edson Arantes do Nascimento): This Brazilian soccer player is considered one of the greatest players of all time. Wear soccer shorts with a soccer shirt with the name Pelé on the back (you can cut letters out of felt and glue them on), with long soccer socks, shin guards, and soccer shoes.

Traditional Brazilian dress: Wear a simple white skirt *(saia rodada)* and a blouse *(bata)* similar to a gypsy's top, worn off the shoulder. Wear a large scarf with jewels as a head wrap. Accessorize by carrying fruit in a simple basket or flowers in your hands.

Who Was Carmen Miranda?

Carmen Miranda was born in 1909 in Portugal, and grew up in Brazil. She began her career singing on a local radio station at age nineteen. In 1929, she recorded her first song *Samba Não vá Simbora.* She later got a recording contract with RCA Victor and started her career recording *Dona Balbina* and *Triste Jandaia.* She made several films in Brazil before coming to the United States in 1939, and appeared in the movie *Down Argentine Way* with 20th Century Fox in 1940. Thus began a busy and successful movie career, and her fruit hat became her famous trademark. She died of a heart attack at age forty-six.

Brazil Film Festival

Black Orpheus
Starring Breno Mello and Marpessa Dawn
Directed by Marcel Camus, 1959

Bye Bye Brazil
Starring Jose Wilker and Betty Faria
Directed by Carlos Diegues, 1979

O Cangaceiro
Starring Paulo Gorgulho and Alexandre Paternmost
Directed by Anibal Massaini Neto, 1997

Carmen Miranda: Bananas Is My Business
Starring Carmen Miranda, Cynthia Adler, and Cesar Romero
Directed by Helena Solberg, 1995

Dona Flor and Her Two Husbands
Starring Sonia Braga and Jose Wilker
Directed by Bruno Barreto, 1978

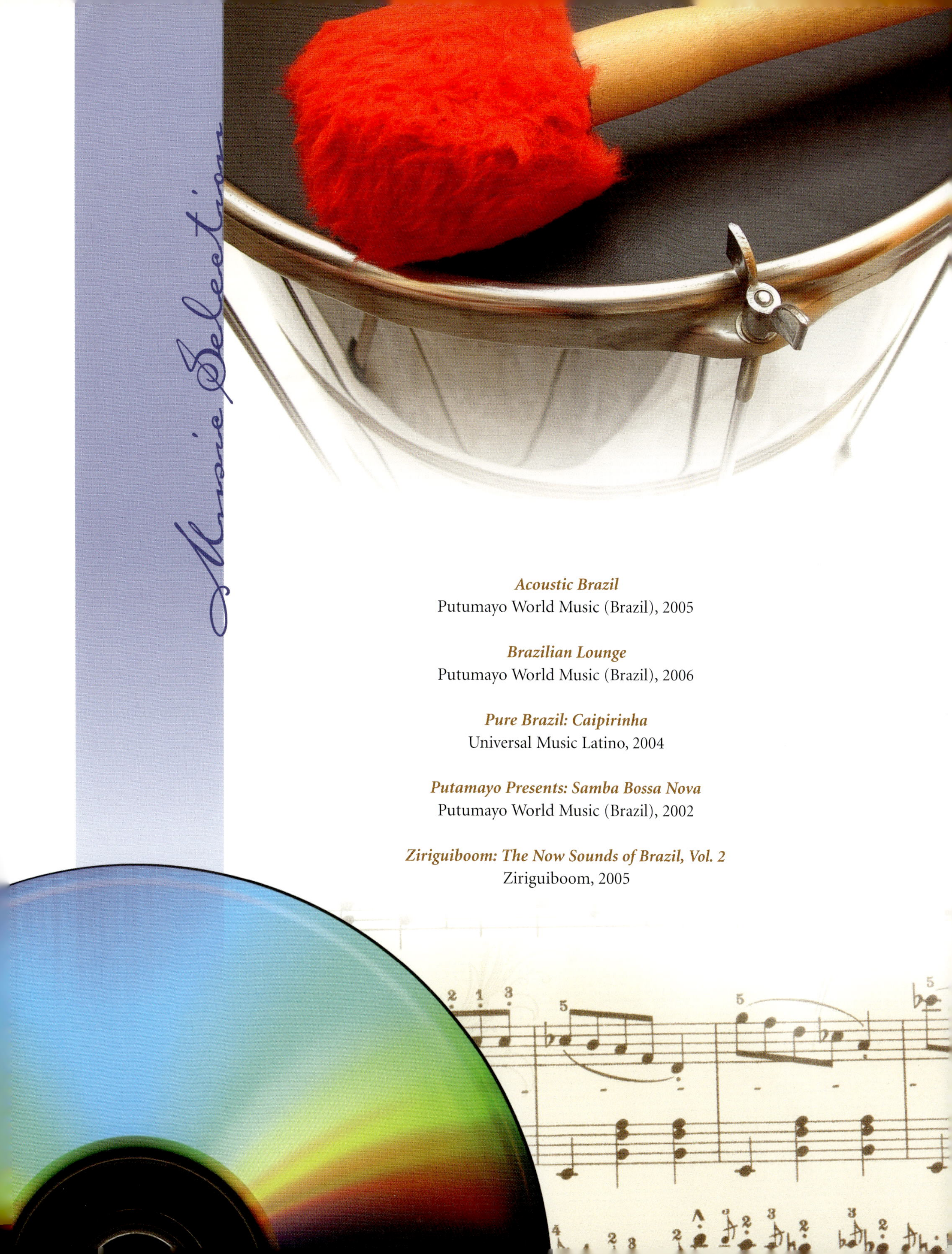

Music Selection

Acoustic Brazil
Putumayo World Music (Brazil), 2005

Brazilian Lounge
Putumayo World Music (Brazil), 2006

Pure Brazil: Caipirinha
Universal Music Latino, 2004

Putamayo Presents: Samba Bossa Nova
Putumayo World Music (Brazil), 2002

Ziriguiboom: The Now Sounds of Brazil, Vol. 2
Ziriguiboom, 2005

Icebreaker: Matching

Match the term on the left with the correct phase on the right:

1. ____ Boto	a.	big city slums
2. ____ Piranhas	b.	Brazilian cowboy
3. ____ Brazil nut	c.	meat-eating fish
4. ____ São Paulo	d.	pre-Easter season of Lent
5. ____ Amazon	e.	beef grilled on skewers
6. ____ Capybara	f.	folk song
7. ____ 1494 Treaty	g.	meat and bean stew of Tordesillas
8. ____ Iguaçu Falls	h.	100-pound rodent
9. ____ Favelas	i.	seeds encased in a heavy pod
10. ____ Carnaval	j.	industrial and financial hub
11. ____ Capoeiro	k.	16 percent of all fresh water flows through this body of water into the Atlantic Ocean
12. ____ Feijoada	l.	Afro-Brazilian martial arts
13. ____ Gaucho	m.	Spain and Portugal divide the New World
14. ____ Churrasco	n.	2.5 miles wide by 300 feet deep
15. ____ Corde	o.	pink dolphin

ANSWER KEY

1-o, 2-c, 3-i, 4-j, 5-k, 6-h, 7-m, 8-n, 9-a, 10-d, 11-l, 12-g, 13-b, 14-e, 15-f

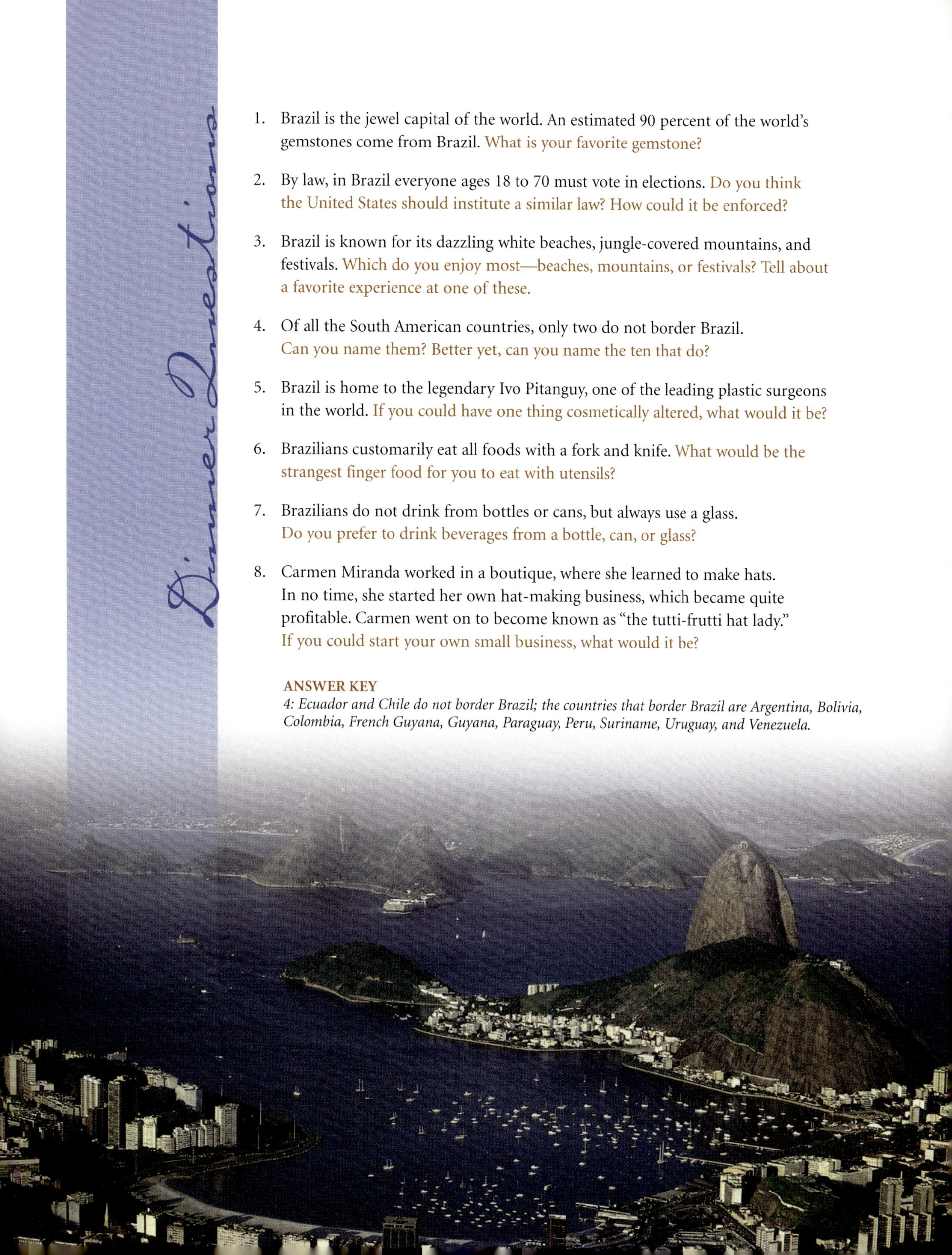

Dinner Questions

1. Brazil is the jewel capital of the world. An estimated 90 percent of the world's gemstones come from Brazil. What is your favorite gemstone?

2. By law, in Brazil everyone ages 18 to 70 must vote in elections. Do you think the United States should institute a similar law? How could it be enforced?

3. Brazil is known for its dazzling white beaches, jungle-covered mountains, and festivals. Which do you enjoy most—beaches, mountains, or festivals? Tell about a favorite experience at one of these.

4. Of all the South American countries, only two do not border Brazil. Can you name them? Better yet, can you name the ten that do?

5. Brazil is home to the legendary Ivo Pitanguy, one of the leading plastic surgeons in the world. If you could have one thing cosmetically altered, what would it be?

6. Brazilians customarily eat all foods with a fork and knife. What would be the strangest finger food for you to eat with utensils?

7. Brazilians do not drink from bottles or cans, but always use a glass. Do you prefer to drink beverages from a bottle, can, or glass?

8. Carmen Miranda worked in a boutique, where she learned to make hats. In no time, she started her own hat-making business, which became quite profitable. Carmen went on to become known as "the tutti-frutti hat lady." If you could start your own small business, what would it be?

ANSWER KEY

4: Ecuador and Chile do not border Brazil; the countries that border Brazil are Argentina, Bolivia, Colombia, French Guyana, Guyana, Paraguay, Peru, Suriname, Uruguay, and Venezuela.

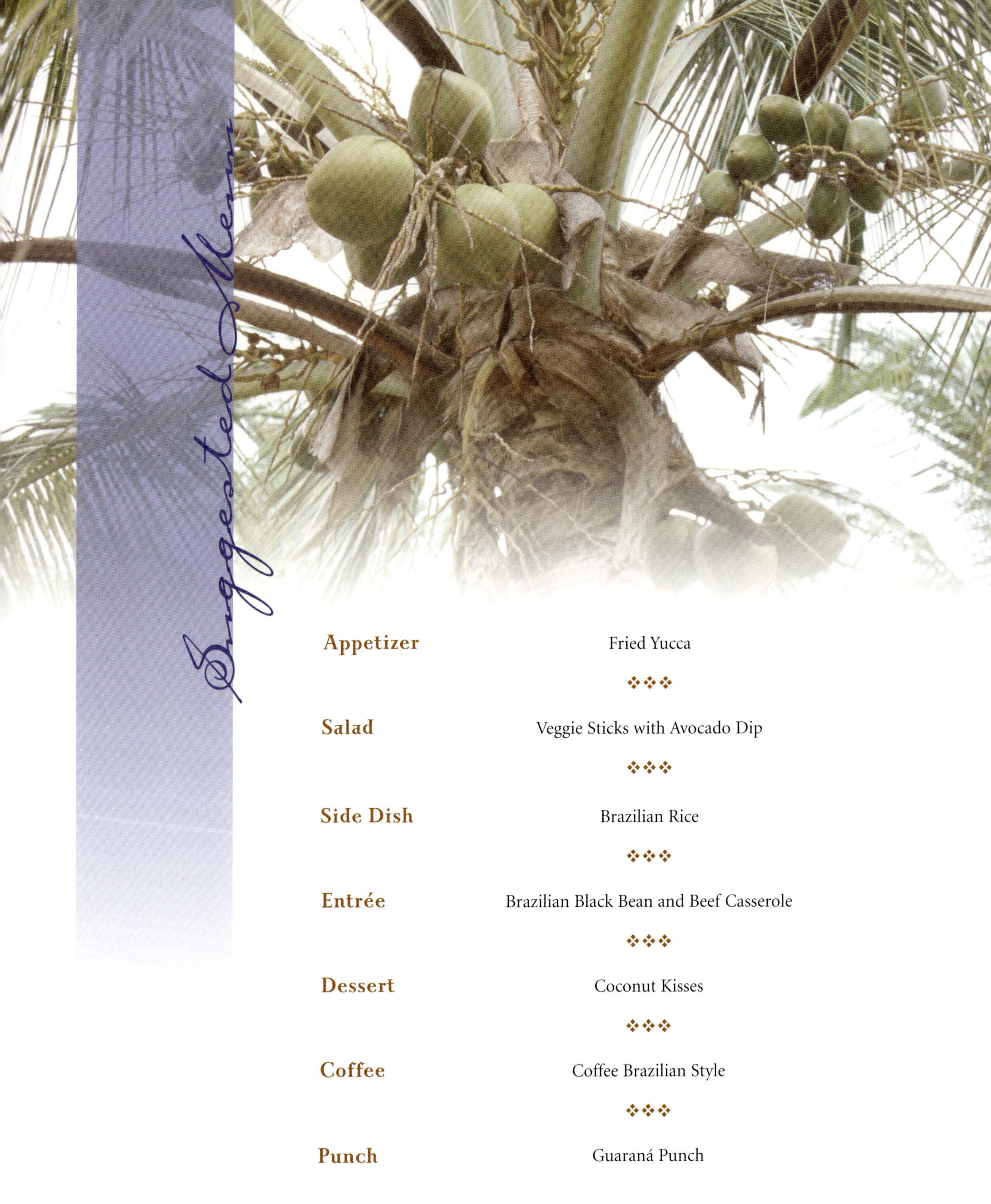

Suggested Menu

Appetizer	Fried Yucca
Salad	Veggie Sticks with Avocado Dip
Side Dish	Brazilian Rice
Entrée	Brazilian Black Bean and Beef Casserole
Dessert	Coconut Kisses
Coffee	Coffee Brazilian Style
Punch	Guaraná Punch

Fried Yucca

1 (24-ounce) package fresh yucca, cut into ½-inch wedges (see note)
4 cups vegetable oil
1 teaspoon garlic salt
1 teaspoon finely chopped fresh parsley
1 teaspoon paprika

Combine the yucca in a deep pan and cover with 1 inch of water. Bring the water to a boil, and slowly simmer the yucca for 20 to 30 minutes, or until tender. In a large skillet on medium-high heat or an electric fryer set to 325 degrees, heat the oil and fry the yucca in a few batches for 3 minutes, or until golden brown. Transfer the fried yucca onto paper towels. In a small bowl, combine the garlic salt, parsley, and paprika, and sprinkle over the yucca pieces.

Makes 6 servings.

Note: You can find fresh yucca at your local Latin grocery store.

Veggie Sticks with Avocado Dip

5 garlic cloves, crushed
1 cup cooked and chopped spinach
2 medium red chiles, chopped
2 cups diced avocado
1 tablespoon warm water
1 tablespoon white vinegar
2 teaspoons ketchup
1 tablespoon Tabasco sauce
1 tablespoon Worcestershire sauce
1 teaspoon ground mustard
1 tablespoon sugar
1 teaspoon salt
1 cup red bell pepper slices
1 cup green bell pepper slices
1 cup carrot sticks
1 cup zucchini sticks
1 cup celery sticks
1 cup jicama sticks

Combine the garlic, spinach, chiles, and avocado in a food processor until smooth. Combine the water, white vinegar, ketchup, Tabasco sauce, Worcestershire sauce, ground mustard, sugar, and salt in a large bowl. Combine the two mixtures in the large bowl. Chill for 1 hour. Serve with red pepper and green pepper slices, and the carrot, zucchini, celery, and jicama sticks.

Makes 8 servings.

Hearts of Palm Empanadas

❖❖❖

2 tablespoons butter
1 cup chopped white onion
1 tablespoon all-purpose flour
1¼ cups milk
1 cup chopped hearts of palm
1 cup cooked shrimp
2 tablespoons chopped fresh parsley
½ teaspoon paprika
½ teaspoon ground cardamom
⅛ teaspoon white pepper
1 teaspoon salt
2 medium hard-cooked eggs, diced
1 package pastry dough, defrosted
3 egg yolks, whisked

In a large saucepan over medium heat, melt the butter and sauté the onions until soft. Whisk in the flour and cook for 3 minutes. Add the milk and whisk. Combine the hearts of palm, shrimp, parsley, paprika, cardamom, white pepper, salt, and hard-cooked eggs with the milk and onion mixture. Cut the pastry dough into circles 4 inches in diameter. Brush a very small amount of egg yolk around the edges of each circle of dough. Scoop out 1 tablespoon of the hearts of palm mixture onto the center of each circle of dough. Fold the dough in half so the edges meet, and pinch and fold the edges until completely sealed. Preheat the oven to 425 degrees. Brush the top of each empanada with a small amount of the egg yolk, and bake for 10 minutes.

Makes 6 servings.

Brazilian Rice

3 tablespoons vegetable oil
5 garlic cloves, crushed
4 cups rice
1¼ cups sliced onion
1¼ cups chopped tomato
4 cups boiling water
1½ tablespoons salt

Heat the vegetable oil in a medium-size skillet over medium heat. Add the garlic, rice, and onion, and sauté for about 15 minutes until the rice sizzles. Add the tomato, boiling water, and salt. Bring the garlic, rice, onion, tomato, and water mixture to a boil; cover and cook for 20 minutes, or until the rice is fully cooked.

Makes 6 servings.

Brazilian-Style Collard Greens

5 bunches collard greens
1 tablespoon butter
2 tablespoons olive oil
½ cup diced onion
1 teaspoon coarse sea salt
1 teaspoon freshly ground pepper

Remove the stems and center ribs of the greens. Rinse and roll the leaves tightly together, and slice into very thin strips. In a skillet over medium heat, melt the butter and add the olive oil. Sauté the diced onion, slowly add the greens, and cook until the greens are tender. Stir constantly for about 5 minutes, and add the salt and pepper.

Makes 6 servings.

Cornmeal Mush

1 tablespoon olive oil
2 garlic cloves, minced
½ cup finely chopped onion
2 cups cold water
½ cup finely stone-ground cornmeal
1 teaspoon salt
1 teaspoon freshly ground pepper

Put the olive oil in a large skillet, and sauté the garlic and onion over medium heat for 3 minutes. Combine the water and cornmeal, stirring constantly to avoid clumps. Pour the cornmeal mixture into the skillet with the garlic and onion, reduce the heat to low, and gently simmer 6 minutes. Season with the salt and pepper. Pour the mixture into a small loaf pan, and let cool thoroughly in the refrigerator.

Makes 6 servings.

Entrée

Brazilian Black Bean and Beef Casserole

- 1 cup olive oil
- 1 cup chopped celery
- ¾ cup grated carrots
- 1 cup chopped onion
- 2 tablespoons minced garlic
- ½ cup chopped green bell pepper
- 1 teaspoon minced orange zest
- 1 (14-ounce) can stewed tomatoes
- 1 pound stew beef, cut into ½-inch cubes
- 6 slices bacon, cut into ½-inch pieces
- 2 (15-ounce) cans black beans, rinsed
- 1 teaspoon salt
- 1 teaspoon freshly ground black pepper

Heat the olive oil in a skillet, and sauté the celery, carrots, onions, garlic, and green pepper over medium heat. Simmer for 6 minutes, stirring occasionally. Add the orange zest, tomatoes, beef, and bacon. Cover and simmer for 25 minutes. Add the black beans, and cook for 25 minutes more. When completely cooked, add the salt and pepper.

Makes 8 servings.

Sweet Sausage and Broccoli

❖❖❖

2 tablespoons vegetable oil
1 pound chorizo
5 tablespoons butter, divided
3 cups broccoli florets
2 tablespoons water
3 cups whole corn kernels
1½ teaspoons salt
1½ teaspoons freshly ground pepper

Heat the vegetable oil on medium in a large skillet. Add the chorizo, cover, and heat until fully cooked. Remove from the skillet, and drain on paper towels to remove any excess oil. Slice the chorizo into ½-inch pieces. Add 4 tablespoons butter to the large skillet and melt slowly. Add the broccoli, and cook for 3 minutes. Add the water, cover, and cook until the broccoli is tender. Transfer the broccoli and chorizo into a large covered dish, and keep warm. Place the corn in a blender and purée. Melt the remaining butter in a medium saucepan, add the puréed corn, and cook until thoroughly heated. Pour the corn mixture over the broccoli and chorizo, and add the salt and pepper.

Makes 6 servings.

Walnut Candy

1 (14-ounce) can or 1½ cups sweetened condensed milk
3 tablespoons powdered chocolate, divided
3 tablespoons butter
2 cups chopped walnuts
Cooking spray

Heat the sweetened condensed milk and 1½ tablespoons powdered chocolate in a heavy saucepan. Add the butter. When the butter is melted, add the walnuts. Cook on low heat, stirring constantly until the mixture thickens. Pour the mixture onto a cookie sheet lined with parchment paper. Let cool completely. Wash and spray your hands with cooking spray. With a spoon, scoop out about 1 tablespoon of the mixture, and roll it into a ball with your hands. Repeat with the remaining mixture. Roll the balls in the remaining 1½ tablespoons chocolate powder to serve.

Makes 12 servings.

Coconut Kisses

❖❖❖

1 (14-ounce) can or 1½ cups sweetened condensed milk
2 egg yolks
2 teaspoons vanilla
2 tablespoons soft butter
Cooking spray
3 cups flaked coconut
3 tablespoons powdered sugar

Heat the sweetened condensed milk in a heavy saucepan on low heat. In a small bowl, whisk the egg yolks, vanilla, and butter, and add to the milk. Heat slowly until thickened. Pour the mixture onto a cookie sheet lined with parchment paper. Let completely cool. After washing your hands, spray them with cooking spray. Take a spoon and scoop out about 1 tablespoon of the mixture, and roll into a ball with your hands. Roll the balls in flaked coconut and powdered sugar to serve.

Makes 12 servings.

Coffee Brazilian Style

4 cups water
2 tablespoons sugar
4 tablespoons finely ground espresso beans
6 twists of orange rind

Bring the water to a boil in a medium saucepan over high heat. Add the sugar and stir until completely dissolved. Fill a coffee filter with the ground espresso beans, and place on top of a coffee carafe. Slowly pour the boiling water and sugar mixture over the ground espresso beans. Pour the coffee into an espresso cup. Serve with a twist of orange rind.

Makes 6 servings.

Punch

Guaraná Punch

❖❖❖

3 cans guaraná soda (see note)
3 cups grape juice
½ cup water
1 cup pineapple chunks
3 cups sparkling wine

Combine the guaraná soda, grape juice, water, and pineapple chunks in a large pitcher. Slowly add the sparkling wine, and refrigerate for 1 hour. Serve over ice in a tall glass.

Makes 8 servings.

Note: Guaraná, a tropical plant with small red fruit, has a high caffeine content. People in the Amazon region of Brazil chew the seeds for energy, and some drink guaraná powder mixed with water. It is also a very popular soft drink flavor in Brazil. You can find guaraná in powdered form in some health food stores, and most Brazilian and Latino stores in the U.S. carry the soda, which tastes a bit like cream soda. If guaraná soda is not available for this recipe, you can substitute cream soda.

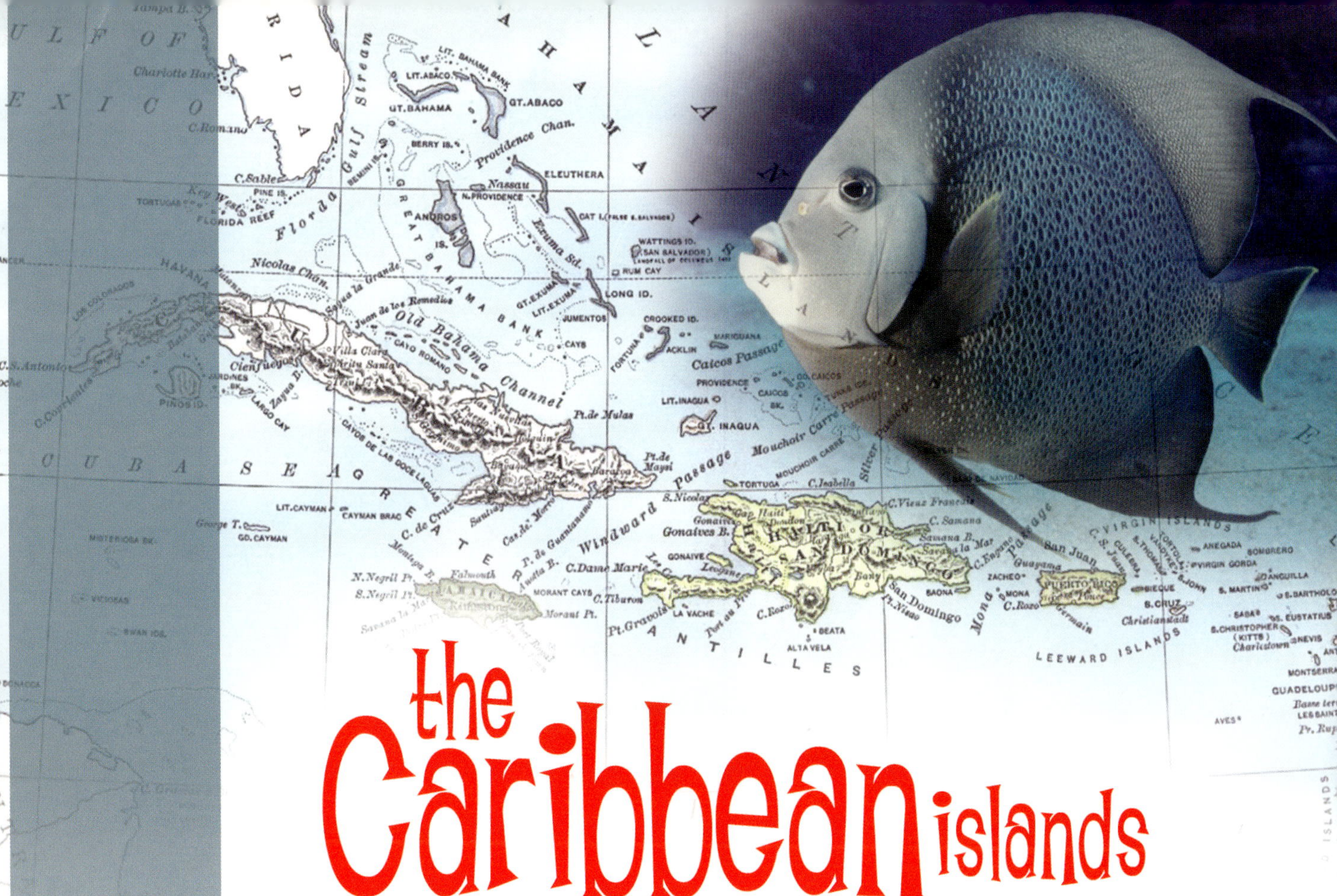

the Caribbean islands

THE CARIBBEAN ISLANDS FEATURE MANY WONDERFULLY DIVERSE DESTINATIONS. Jamaica, the Bahamas, the Cayman Islands, and Aruba all offer white sand beaches, ancient marvels, luxurious resorts, and charming local shops. From the moment you arrive, the atmosphere of reggae, calypso, steel drums, and laughter will fill you with excitement. The rhythms, food, and architecture all reflect the history of the islands.

The turquoise-colored Caribbean Sea is one of the world's most beautiful and biologically rich bodies of water, and the home of such famous beaches as Trunk Bay and Magens Bay.

The cuisine of the Caribbean can be described as a "patchwork quilt." Each patch represents culinary customs from a variety of nationalities that live on the islands. The most common seasoning is "jerk," which is made with hot peppers and a variety of other ingredients, and is mainly used in chicken or pork dishes. Bold flavors and distinct aromas are typical of Caribbean cooking.

From delicious cuisine to activities such as water sports, bird-watching, or off-road biking, the Caribbean Islands can provide something special for every visitor.

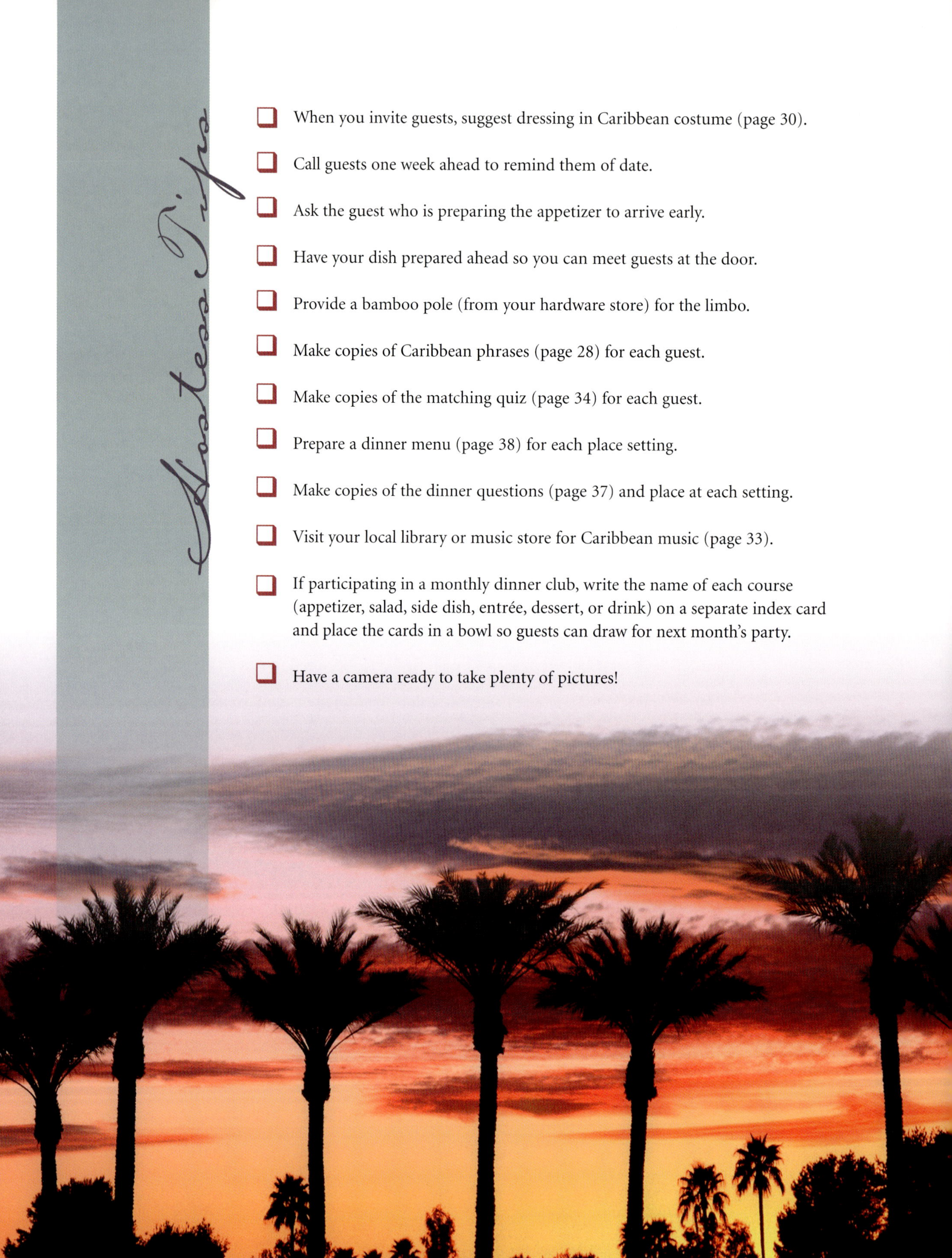

Hostess Tips

- When you invite guests, suggest dressing in Caribbean costume (page 30).
- Call guests one week ahead to remind them of date.
- Ask the guest who is preparing the appetizer to arrive early.
- Have your dish prepared ahead so you can meet guests at the door.
- Provide a bamboo pole (from your hardware store) for the limbo.
- Make copies of Caribbean phrases (page 28) for each guest.
- Make copies of the matching quiz (page 34) for each guest.
- Prepare a dinner menu (page 38) for each place setting.
- Make copies of the dinner questions (page 37) and place at each setting.
- Visit your local library or music store for Caribbean music (page 33).
- If participating in a monthly dinner club, write the name of each course (appetizer, salad, side dish, entrée, dessert, or drink) on a separate index card and place the cards in a bowl so guests can draw for next month's party.
- Have a camera ready to take plenty of pictures!

Before Dinner

Turn on Caribbean music to set the mood for an authentic Caribbean evening. Set table buffet style for guests to enjoy a relaxed evening. See table tips (page 29).

Welcome guests and invite them to enjoy the appetizer, music, and conversation. Invite guests to join you in making piña coladas or other Caribbean drinks. Discuss with guests whether they have been to the Caribbean islands and where. Give each guest a copy of the matching quiz. After the guests finish the matching questions, invite them to try the limbo (page 35).

Dinner

After the appetizer and dinner drinks, ask guests to help themselves to the buffet, or to be seated at the table. Serve all courses at the same time.

Invite guests to read and discuss the dinner questions. As the host or hostess, you are the discussion leader. Encourage each person to participate.

After Dinner

After the meal is complete, begin to collect the plates and clear the table. Ask guests to continue their conversation. You may begin to serve the dessert at this time. Serve coffee and tea if desired.

If you are participating in a monthly dinner club, invite guests to draw names of courses (appetizer, salad, side dish, entrée, dessert, or drink) from a bowl for next month's party, and decide who will host.

Greetings & Phrases

English is spoken throughout much of the Caribbean, but many islands have their own unique expressions. Here are some common Jamaican phrases and gestures.

When asked a yes or no question, the response is typically *ya mon.* If everything is good with you, and someone asks, "How are you?" reply *Irie (i-re) mon.* Always ask in return, "How are you?"

Every ting criss is the equivalent of "Everything's cool."

When you pass a person or friend and want to acknowledge them, a chin nod can be used as the standard response.

"No problem" is the answer to just about every request made of a Jamaican.

Wa gwan means "What is going on?"

Dining Etiquette & Table Settings

Table manners are relatively informal. Meals are often served buffet-style and conversation is encouraged.

Because of the European influence on the Caribbean, the table etiquette is often Continental, with the fork held in the left hand and the knife in the right while eating.

Wait for the host or hostess to invite you to begin eating.

Decorating for a Caribbean-themed dinner party is relatively simple. Place coconuts, pineapples, and mangos in a large bowl as a centerpiece. Drape your table with roped nets, seashells, and fresh flowers. Provide sunglasses, maracas, and seashell necklaces for each guest. Your local craft store will have birds, such as flamingos and parrots, paper fish cutouts, or even tropical piñatas. Write each guest's name on a sand dollar and use as place settings.

Costume Ideas

Arawaks or Txcariana: These are indigenous natives of the Caribbean. Women should wear a plain white linen dress with a beaded apron and a wide scarf tied in the back of the head. Men should wear a loincloth or shorts and carry a bamboo spear. They can accessorize with face and body paint: the natives painted their legs red up to the knee and painted their faces with black and white dots to blend with the forest. Both men and women should go barefoot.

Captain Jack Sparrow: This movie pirate was immortalized by Johnny Depp in *Pirates of the Caribbean*. Wear a loose long-sleeved white shirt with a vest, two wide black belts with large square buckles, and black loose pants. Accessorize with a pair of black boot covers, pirate hat and bandanna with beaded braids. Don't forget the sword!

Tango or salsa dancer: Men should wear a white or black silk loose-sleeved shirt and gaucho or straight black pants. Women should a wear plain dance dress, mid-length with a flowing effect, and a flower in the hair. Both can accessorize with castanets and black dance shoes.

Traditional Caribbean woman: Wear a floral print peasant blouse and white sarong skirt with a brightly colored head wrap or turban. Accessorize with sandals and plenty of jewelry.

Trivia

The Spanish explorer Juan Ponce de Leon was the first to discover the Turks and Caicos Islands when he sailed with Columbus on his second voyage.

Barbados was the only foreign country George Washington ever visited. He visited with his older half-brother for seven weeks in 1751 and recorded his impressions in his diary.

Christopher Columbus discovered the Virgin Islands in the northeast Caribbean in 1493, and named them after Saint Ursula and the 11,000 virgins.

Only about 2 percent of the Caribbean's numerous islands are inhabited.

The Greater Antilles includes Cuba, Haiti, Dominican Republic, Jamaica, and Puerto Rico. The Lesser Antilles includes the Leeward Islands, the Windward Islands, and Trinidad and Tobago.

The Windward Islands include Grenada, St. Vincent and the Grenadines, St. Lucia, Martinique, and Barbados. The Leeward Islands include Dominica, Guadeloupe, St. Martin, Marie-Galante, St. Barths, Montserrat, Antigua, Barbuda, St. Kitts, Nevis, Anguilla, the SSS Islands, and the Virgin Islands. Eastern Caribbean often refers to the nine-member Organization of Eastern Caribbean States (OECS): Anguilla, Antigua and Barbuda, British Virgin Islands, Commonwealth of Dominica, Grenada, Montserrat, St. Lucia, St. Kitts and Nevis, and St. Vincent and the Grenadines. They share a common currency, the East Caribbean dollar.

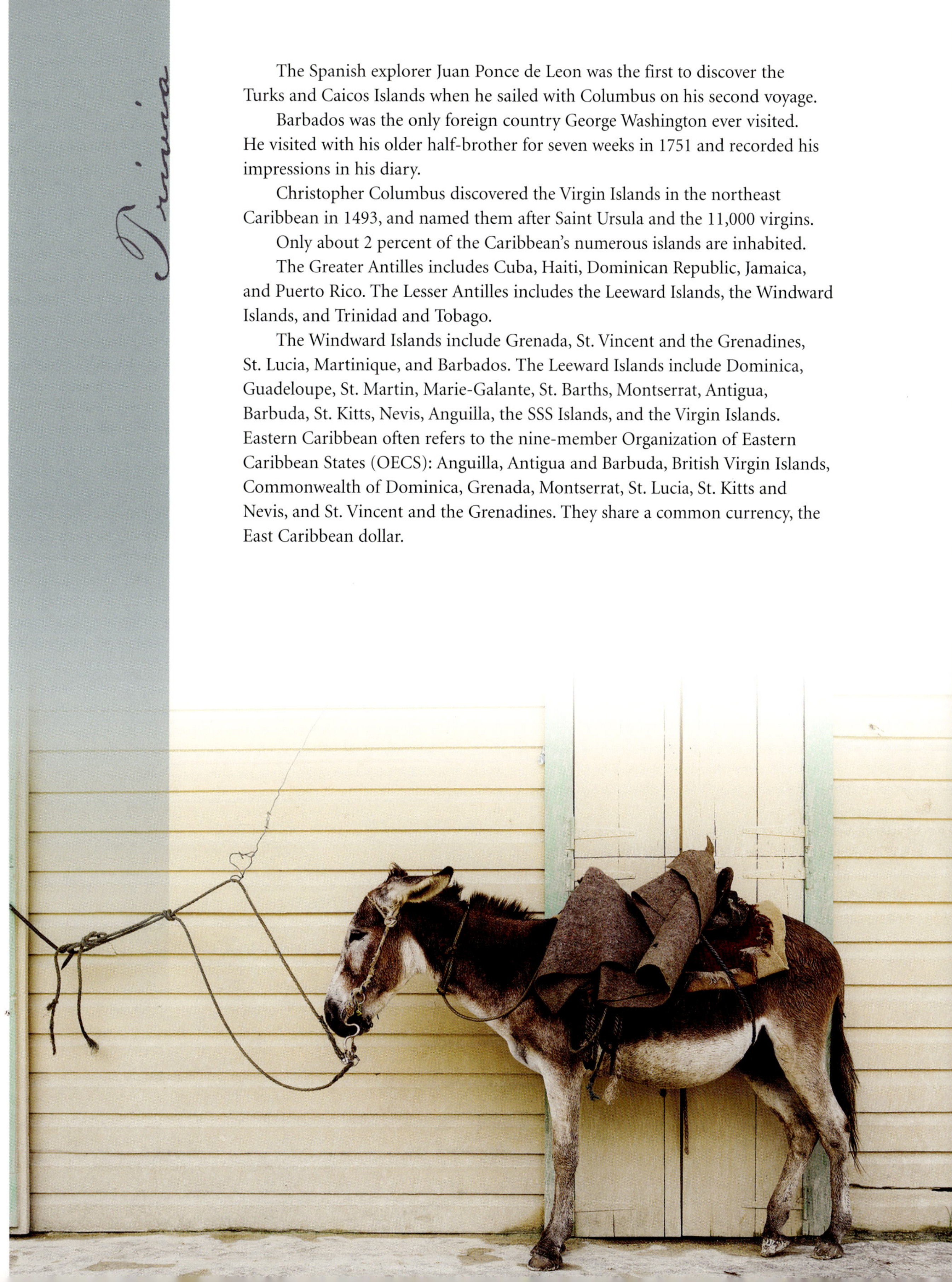

Caribbean Film Festival

The Caribbean Mystery
Starring James Dunn
Directed by Robert D. Webb, 1945

Islands in the Stream
Starring George C. Scott, Hart Bochner, and Claire Bloom
Directed by Franklin J. Schaffner, 1977

Pirates of the Caribbean: The Curse of the Black Pearl
Starring Johnny Depp, Geoffrey Rush, Orlando Bloom, and Keira Knightley
Directed by Gore Verbinski, 2003

Swiss Family Robinson
Starring John Mills, Dorothy McGuire, James MacArthur, and Janet Munro
Directed by Ken Annakin, 1960

Music Selection

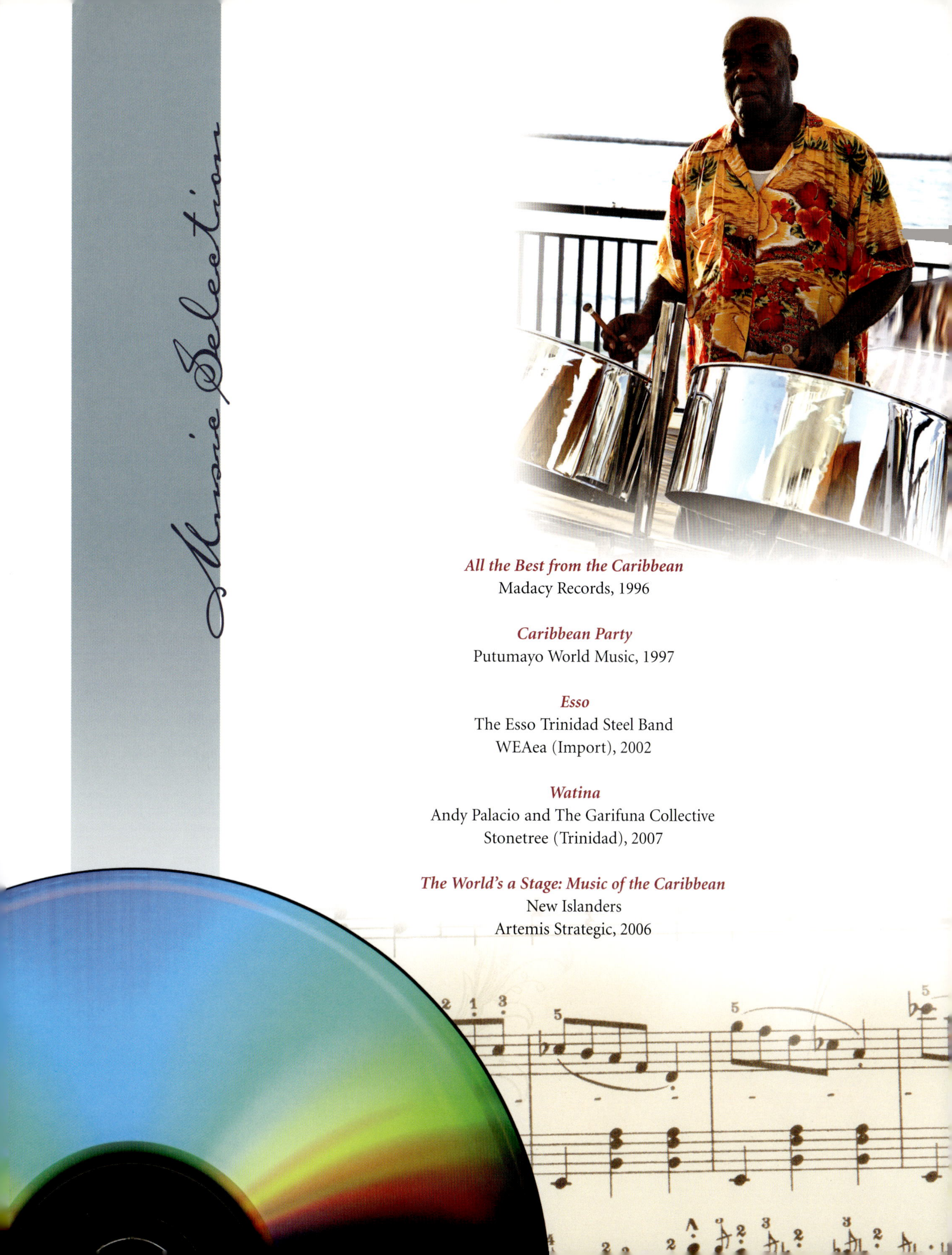

All the Best from the Caribbean
Madacy Records, 1996

Caribbean Party
Putumayo World Music, 1997

Esso
The Esso Trinidad Steel Band
WEAea (Import), 2002

Watina
Andy Palacio and The Garifuna Collective
Stonetree (Trinidad), 2007

The World's a Stage: Music of the Caribbean
New Islanders
Artemis Strategic, 2006

Icebreaker: Matching

Can you match each island with its official language? Check the correct box for each one.

	DUTCH	ENGLISH	FRENCH	SPANISH
Aruba	❑	❑	❑	❑
Bahamas	❑	❑	❑	❑
Barbados	❑	❑	❑	❑
Belize	❑	❑	❑	❑
Bermuda	❑	❑	❑	❑
British Virgin Islands	❑	❑	❑	❑
Cayman Islands	❑	❑	❑	❑
Cuba	❑	❑	❑	❑
Dominica	❑	❑	❑	❑
Dominican Republic	❑	❑	❑	❑
French Guiana	❑	❑	❑	❑
Grenada	❑	❑	❑	❑
Guadeloupe	❑	❑	❑	❑
Guyana	❑	❑	❑	❑
Haiti	❑	❑	❑	❑
Jamaica	❑	❑	❑	❑
Martinique	❑	❑	❑	❑
Netherlands Antilles	❑	❑	❑	❑
Puerto Rico	❑	❑	❑	❑
St. Lucia	❑	❑	❑	❑
Suriname	❑	❑	❑	❑
Trinidad and Tobago	❑	❑	❑	❑
Turks and Caicos	❑	❑	❑	❑

ANSWER KEY

Dutch: *Aruba, Netherlands Antilles, Suriname*
English: *Bahamas, Barbados, Belize, Bermuda, British Virgin Islands, Cayman Islands, Dominica, Grenada, Guyana, Jamaica, St. Lucia, Trinidad and Tobago, Turks and Caicos*
French: *Haiti, French Guiana, Guadeloupe, and Martinique*
Spanish: *Cuba, Dominican Republic, and Puerto Rico*

Icebreaker: Limbo

Music and dance permeate every aspect of life in the Caribbean. From calypso and reggae to rumba and mambo, you are sure to get a great physical workout. Try your flexibility at another Caribbean move: limbo! How low can you go?

To begin, ask two of your guests to hold a bamboo pole horizontally, starting at chest level. One by one, invite each remaining guest to begin the limbo dance.

Each dancer arches his or her back to go under the pole, while swinging to the music and making sure not to touch the pole. Guests continue in single file. The pole is gradually lowered until only one dancer can successfully go under without touching. Consider playing "Limbo Rock" by Chubby Checker or a Caribbean jazz CD.

Terms to Know

Adobo: Spanish for "seasoning"; this includes garlic, oregano, and other spices.

Casabe: Flat, unleavened bread dating back to the Arawaks Indians, made from cassava root.

Chorizo: Spicy Spanish sausage made from pork.

Hearts of palm: Tender inner core of the palm tree.

Plantain: Similar to the banana but slightly bigger, covered by a hard green skin, and used as a vegetable.

Sofrito: A spicy mix of tomatoes, roasted peppers, garlic, onions, and herbs used to complement other dishes.

Yucca: Similar to the potato in texture, the yucca is high in starch and used to make tapioca or ground and made into bread. Also know as manioc or cassava.

Dinner Questions

1. In the Bahamas you will find Paradise Island, home to the famed Atlantis resort, where you can arrange a time to swim with the dolphins. Would you like to swim with dolphins? If not, why not? What is the strangest thing you have swum with?

2. Some people prefer to take a cruise to the Caribbean Islands rather than fly. Which do you prefer and why? What would be enjoyable about a cruise?

3. When we think of the Caribbean we think of leisure and relaxation. What does relaxation mean to you? What are your favorite ways of relaxing?

4. The Caribbean suggests exciting activities and adventure. What are some of your experiences with boating, diving, sailing, scuba, waterskiing, hiking, kayaking, or the spa?

5. In *Treasure Island,* Robert Louis Stevenson wrote of the Caribbean Island known as Dead Man's Chest, where pirates were abandoned by their mates. If you were stranded on an island with someone other than your spouse or family member, who would you choose?

6. The popular 1960s sitcom *Gilligan's Island* featured seven people stranded on a tropical island. Which character from the show would people say you are most like?
   Gilligan (carefree, lighthearted)
   The Skipper (looking out for everyone)
   The Professor (analytical)
   Ginger (movie star, glamorous)
   Mary Ann (cute, everyone loves you)
   Mr. Howell (rich, arrogant)
   Mrs. Howell (spacey, flighty)

7. Legend says that the native Tai'no people saw no special importance in gold so they traded it with Columbus for Spanish trinkets. Do you prefer white or yellow gold?

8. From British influence, cricket is a popular sport in the Caribbean. Have you ever played cricket? Have you ever seen it played? What is your favorite sport to watch?

Suggested Menu

Appetizer — Caribbean Guacamole

❖❖❖

Soup — Mango Soup

❖❖❖

Salad — Coconut Ginger Salad

❖❖❖

Side Dish — Caribbean Rice

❖❖❖

Entrée — Jerk Chicken with Grilled Pineapple-Chipotle Salsa

❖❖❖

Dessert — Dark Caribbean Fudge Pie

❖❖❖

Caribbean Drinks — Piña Colada, Caribbean Punch,
Tropical Treasures, Individual Caribbean Soda

Caribbean Guacamole

- 5 tablespoons lime juice, divided
- 3 teaspoons sugar
- 1 teaspoon crushed red pepper flakes
- 2 ripe papayas
- 2 ripe avocados
- 1 cup flaked coconut
- 1 (12-pack) Hawaiian sweet rolls
- Cooking spray

Combine 4 tablespoons lime juice, sugar, and crushed red pepper in a large bowl. Cut 1 papaya in half lengthwise and discard the seeds, leaving the halves intact. From 1 papaya half, cut 2 long slices. Slice the second papaya in half, discard the seeds, and dice with the remaining half of the first papaya. Cut 1 avocado in half lengthwise and discard the pit. From 1 half, cut 2 long slices. Slice the remaining avocado in half, discard the pit, and dice with the remaining half of the first avocado. Sprinkle the papaya and avocado slices with 1 tablespoon lime juice and keep them separated. Very gently combine the diced papaya and diced avocado with the lime juice mixture, and refrigerate.

Preheat the oven to 400 degrees. Sprinkle the coconut onto a baking sheet, and place in the oven until the coconut is lightly browned. Remove the pan from the oven, and place the coconut in a small bowl. Slice each Hawaiian sweet roll from top to bottom into 3 slices. Arrange the 36 slices on two baking sheets and lightly toast for 7 minutes. Remove from the oven, and cover to keep warm.

Spray the inside of a 1-cup measure with cooking spray. Spoon half of the avocado/papaya mixture into the cup, and pack to level. Place the cup upside down on the center of the serving dish, and gently shake until the contents come out in a neat mound. Repeat the process with the remaining avocado/papaya mixture, placing the second mound next to the first. Place the two papaya slices on top of one mound and the two avocado slices on top of the other mound. Sprinkle with the coconut. Serve with toasted roll slices.

Makes 6 servings.

Mango Soup

❖❖❖

5 cups diced mangoes
½ cup cubed avocado
5 cups chicken broth
1 cup coconut milk
2 tablespoons orange juice
½ cup sugar
¼ teaspoon ground cinnamon
½ teaspoon curry
¼ teaspoon cayenne pepper
½ teaspoon ground ginger
¼ teaspoon ground nutmeg
2 tablespoons finely chopped cilantro

Put the mangoes, avocado, chicken broth, coconut milk, orange juice, sugar, cinnamon, curry, cayenne pepper, and ginger in a large saucepan. Cook over medium heat, and reduce the liquid until one-fourth of the original liquid has evaporated. Then pour the mixture, in parts if necessary, into a blender or food processor, and blend until smooth. Cool and refrigerate for 1 hour. Pour the soup into individual bowls, and garnish with a sprinkle of nutmeg and cilantro.

Makes 6 servings.

Caribbean Corn Chowder

❖❖❖

4 slices bacon, cooked and chopped
3 tablespoons butter
1 cup chopped onion
½ cup diced green bell pepper
1 cup diced red bell pepper
½ cup diced celery
1 tablespoon minced garlic
1 teaspoon dried thyme
1 teaspoon dry tarragon
1 bay leaf
5½ cups low-sodium chicken broth
4 tablespoons flour
2 cups corn kernels
½ teaspoon sugar
¾ cup heavy cream
1 teaspoon salt
1 teaspoon freshly ground pepper

Put the cooked bacon and the butter in a large saucepan. Cook over medium heat until the butter melts. Add the onion, green peppers, red peppers, celery, garlic, thyme, tarragon, and bay leaf; sauté for 7 minutes. Add the chicken broth and flour, stirring to mix, and bring the mixture to a boil. Add the corn and sugar, reduce the heat to a simmer, cover, and cook for 20 minutes, stirring the chowder occasionally. Add the cream, salt, and pepper. Using a hand mixer, beat the chowder for 2 minutes.

Makes 6 servings.

Coconut Ginger Salad

❖❖❖

3 tablespoons olive oil
½ cup lime juice
½ cup toasted and flaked coconut
½ cup chopped red onion
1 tablespoon grated fresh ginger
½ cup chopped cilantro
¼ teaspoon allspice
4 cups watercress
2 (14-ounce) cans hearts of palm, cubed
2 large tomatoes, cubed
3 cups cubed mango
1 lime, cut into 6 wedges

In a large bowl, whisk together the olive oil, lime juice, toasted coconut, red onion, ginger, cilantro, and allspice. Add the watercress to the bowl, and toss gently until the watercress is well coated with the dressing. Refrigerate until chilled. Arrange the dressed watercress on a serving platter. In a medium bowl, add the hearts of palms, tomatoes, and mango, and gently toss. Arrange the watercress on a platter, and top with the hearts of palm, tomatoes, and mangos. Garnish with the lime wedges. Cover and refrigerate until ready to serve.

Makes 6 servings.

Spicy Tomato Salad

½ cup extra-virgin olive oil
2 tablespoons lime juice
1 tablespoon minced lime zest
1 tablespoon soy sauce
1 teaspoon crushed red pepper flakes
1 teaspoon ground ginger
½ teaspoon ground coriander
1 teaspoon pepper
2 teaspoons salt
5 cups diced tomatoes
1½ cups diced white onion
1½ cups diced red onion

Combine the olive oil, lime juice, lime zest, soy sauce, crushed red pepper, ginger, coriander, pepper, and salt in a large bowl. Gently fold in the tomatoes and the white and red onions. Chill in the refrigerator for ½ hour.

Makes 8 servings.

Caribbean Rice

- 1 tablespoon olive oil
- ½ cup diced onion
- ½ cup grated carrot
- 2 garlic cloves
- 4 cups rice
- 2 cups chicken broth
- 2 cups coconut milk
- ½ cup unsweetened grated coconut
- 1 cup mandarin orange sections
- 1 cup crushed pineapple
- ½ cup chopped red bell pepper
- ½ cup toasted slivered almonds
- ⅓ cup sliced green onions
- ½ cup diced mango
- ¼ teaspoon ground ginger

Preheat the oven to 350 degrees. In a large saucepan, heat the olive oil, and sauté the onion, carrot, and garlic. Add the rice, chicken broth, and coconut milk, and bring to a boil. Cover and simmer for 15 minutes, or until the rice is fully cooked. On a baking sheet, spread the grated coconut evenly, and bake in the oven for 5 minutes, or until toasted. In a large skillet, heat the oranges, pineapple, red pepper, almonds, toasted coconut, green onions, mango, and ginger. Add the cooked rice, and fold into the skillet mixture. Serve hot.

Makes 8 servings.

Caribbean Sweet Potatoes

- 1 cup peeled and diced carrots
- 7 cups peeled and diced sweet potatoes
- ½ cup coconut milk
- 3 tablespoons melted butter
- 3 tablespoons honey
- 2 tablespoons fresh lime juice
- 1 teaspoon ground cinnamon
- 1 teaspoon white pepper
- 1 teaspoon sea salt
- 2 tablespoons olive oil

Boil the carrots for 3 minutes, add the sweet potatoes, and boil an additional 10 minutes. Drain the cooked carrots and sweet potatoes. In a large bowl, combine the coconut milk, butter, honey, lime juice, cinnamon, white pepper, and salt. Toss in the carrots and sweet potatoes, and fold them in until well coated. Pour the olive oil evenly over a baking sheet, and spread the carrots and sweet potatoes out in a single layer. Drizzle with any remaining sauce. Bake for 20 minutes.

Makes 8 servings.

Jerk Chicken with Grilled Pineapple-Chipotle Salsa

❖❖❖

½ cup diced green onions
2 tablespoons brown sugar
2 tablespoons garlic powder
1 tablespoon ground allspice
1 teaspoon ground cinnamon
½ teaspoon ground nutmeg
1 teaspoon ground thyme
1½ teaspoons ground sage
½ teaspoon cayenne pepper
2 tablespoons salt
1½ teaspoons black pepper
3 tablespoons olive oil
2 tablespoons soy sauce
¼ cup white vinegar
½ cup orange juice
¼ cup fresh lime juice
6 skinless, boneless chicken breasts
Grilled Pineapple-Chipotle Salsa (recipe follows)

In a large bowl, combine the green onions, brown sugar, garlic, allspice, cinnamon, nutmeg, thyme, sage, cayenne pepper, salt, and black pepper. In a small bowl, whisk the olive oil, soy sauce, vinegar, orange juice, and lime juice. Add the olive oil mix to the seasoning mixture and combine. Reserve 1 cup of the marinade and refrigerate. Place the chicken breasts in a dish, and pour the remaining marinade over the chicken; cover and refrigerate for at least 3 hours.

To cook, grease and heat the grill. Place the marinated chicken breasts on the grill, and cook for 6 minutes on each side, or until fully cooked. Discard the remaining marinade that the chicken breasts have touched. Use the refrigerated 1 cup marinade to drizzle on top of the cooked chicken. Serve with Grilled Pineapple-Chipotle Salsa.

Makes 6 servings.

Grilled Pineapple-Chipotle Salsa

4 tablespoons olive oil, divided
1 pineapple, peeled and sliced
4 chipotle peppers, minced
1 cup seeded, diced tomato
1 cup diced mango
1 green bell pepper, diced
1 red bell pepper, diced
½ cup diced white onion
½ cup diced red onion
¼ cup chopped cilantro
1 tablespoon lime juice
½ cup sugar
2 teaspoons chili powder
2 teaspoons coriander
2 teaspoons ground cumin
2 teaspoons salt
1 teaspoon minced garlic

Heat a grill, and grease with 2 tablespoons olive oil. Place the pineapple slices on the grill next to each other, and grill for 3 minutes on each side. Dice the pineapple slices, and place them in a large bowl. Add the chipotle peppers, tomato, mango, green pepper, red pepper, white onion, red onion, and cilantro. Combine the remaining olive oil, lime juice, sugar, chili powder, coriander, cumin, salt, and garlic in a small bowl. Add to the grilled pineapple mixture and refrigerate.

Makes 8 servings.

Entrée

Cinnamon Chicken

2 teaspoons ground cinnamon
½ teaspoon ground nutmeg
1 teaspoon curry
1 teaspoon crushed red pepper flakes
2 teaspoons salt
2 teaspoons pepper
1 teaspoon soy sauce
1 tablespoon garlic powder
1 tablespoon ground ginger
1½ tablespoons allspice
1½ teaspoons dried thyme
3 tablespoons olive oil
2 tablespoons apple cider vinegar
3 tablespoons brandy
4 tablespoons honey
8 chicken leg-thigh pieces, not separated

In a large glass bowl, combine the cinnamon, nutmeg, curry, crushed red pepper, salt, pepper, soy sauce, garlic, ginger, allspice, thyme, olive oil, vinegar, brandy, and honey. Add the chicken to the marinade, and cover and refrigerate overnight. Preheat the oven to 375 degrees. Place the marinated chicken pieces on a baking sheet, and brush them with the extra marinade. Bake for 55 minutes, or until cooked thoroughly.

Makes 8 servings.

Dark Caribbean Fudge Pie

❖❖❖

2 tablespoons butter
¾ cup firmly packed brown sugar
3 eggs
1½ cups semi-sweet chocolate chips, melted and cooled
½ cup dark chocolate chips
1½ teaspoons finely ground espresso beans
1 teaspoon rum flavoring
¼ cup all-purpose flour
1 cup coarsely chopped pecans
1 unbaked 9-inch pie shell
8 pecan halves

Preheat the oven to 375 degrees. In a medium bowl, cream together the butter and brown sugar. Add the eggs, semi-sweet chocolate, dark chocolate, ground espresso, and rum flavoring, and combine well. Stir in the flour, and fold in the chopped pecans. Pour the mixture into the unbaked pie shell. Arrange the 8 pecan halves to mark each slice of the pie. Bake for 25 minutes.

Makes 8 servings.

Drinks

Piña Colada

For a nonalcoholic drink, omit the rum.

3 to 4 cups ice
18 ounces pineapple juice
18 ounces coconut cream
6 ounces rum
Cherries
Pineapple slices
Paper umbrellas, if desired

In a blender, blend the ice while gradually adding the pineapple, coconut cream, and rum. Serve in a tall glass with a straw. Garnish with a cherry and a pineapple slice. Insert a paper umbrella for a tropical touch.

Makes 6 servings.

Caribbean Punch

Juice from ½ lime
8 ounces pineapple juice
8 ounces orange juice
6 ounces banana liqueur
14 ounces dark rum
4 cups crushed ice

In a punch bowl, combine the lime juice, pineapple juice, orange juice, banana liqueur, and dark rum in a punch bowl. Mix well and add the crushed ice.

Makes 6 servings.

Tropical Treasures

½ cup pineapple chunks
½ cup banana chunks
16 ounces pineapple juice
16 ounces orange juice
4 ounces water
¾ cup crushed ice
6 pineapple slices

Combine the pineapple chunks, banana chunks, pineapple juice, orange juice, water, and ice in a blender. Pour the mixture into six decorative cups, and garnish each cup with a pineapple slice.

Makes 6 servings.

Individual Caribbean Soda

Try this for a refreshing nonalcooholic treat.

4 ounces seltzer
2 ounces fruit juice

Serve the seltzer mixed with fresh juices such as orange, pineapple, grapefruit, or banana.

Makes 1 serving.

CHINA

AT THE CLOSE OF THE NINETEENTH CENTURY, CHINA WAS KNOWN AS THE SICK MAN OF ASIA because it had been defeated by Western and Japanese powers. However, the nation rebounded through trade and commerce that turned the economy around. About the size of the United States, China has a population five times larger than that of America and is home to one-fifth of the world's population.

Originating in China, silk was so acclaimed that a 4,000-mile trade route across Western Asia and China was called the Silk Road. Silk, when first discovered, was so desired by international merchants that it was traded extensively, and so coveted that visiting monks smuggled silkworms out of the country in the hollows of their walking sticks.

While silk has long been a valued product of China, Chinese cuisine is also enjoyed by many Americans today. The Chinese believe that the preparation of a dish is an art and food is not simply a source of nourishment. The food is to be cut into small bite-sized pieces and seasoned to perfection with the proper blend of ingredients before serving. Knives are never to be used at the table. Not only is plate presentation important, but nutrition as well. Chinese cuisine focuses on foods that provide many health benefits, such as ginger, which can be a remedy for an upset stomach or even a cold. Because Chinese cooking relies heavily on wholesome foods such as steamed vegetables, fish, and rice, it is considered one of the healthiest cuisines in the world.

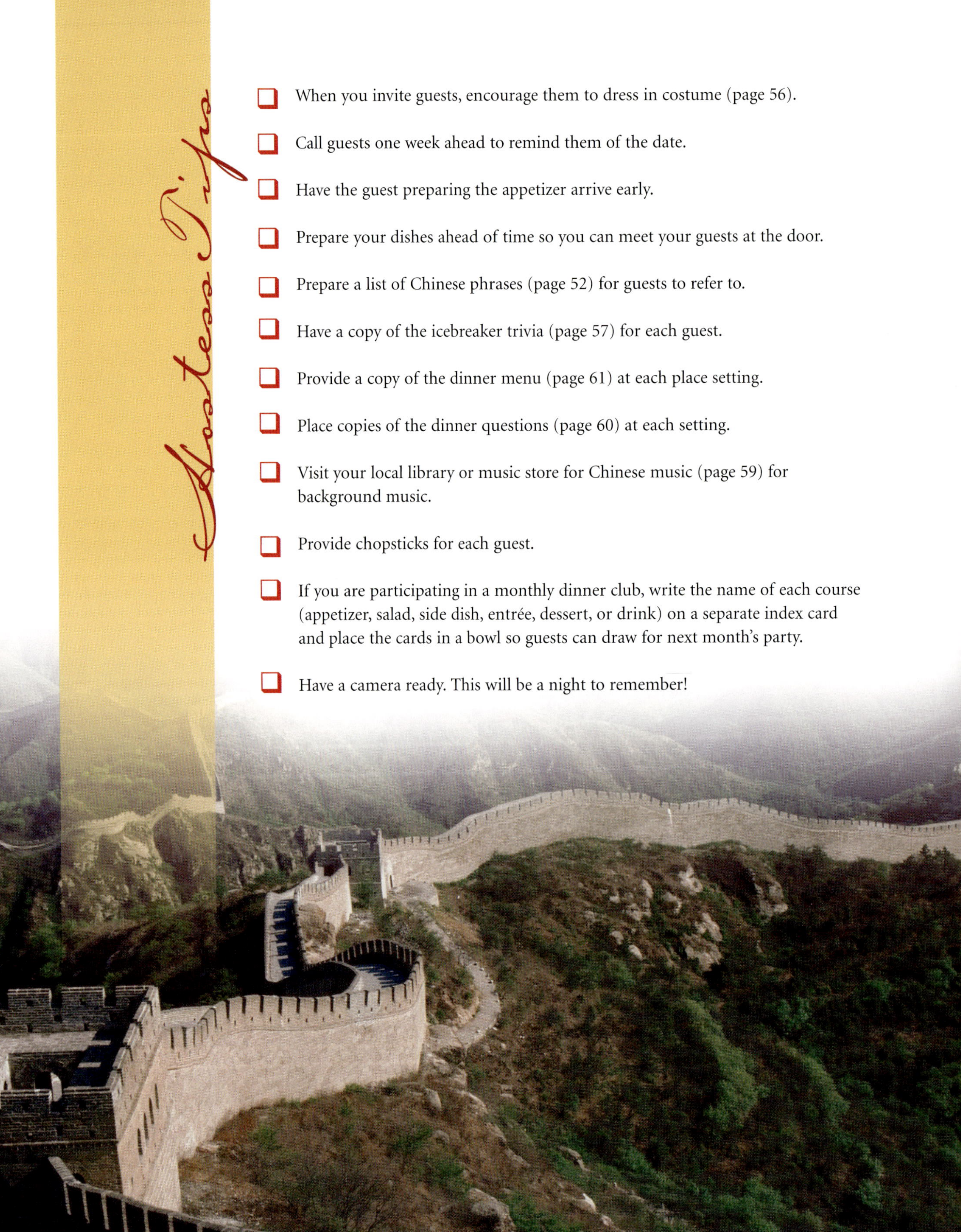

Hostess Tips

- When you invite guests, encourage them to dress in costume (page 56).
- Call guests one week ahead to remind them of the date.
- Have the guest preparing the appetizer arrive early.
- Prepare your dishes ahead of time so you can meet your guests at the door.
- Prepare a list of Chinese phrases (page 52) for guests to refer to.
- Have a copy of the icebreaker trivia (page 57) for each guest.
- Provide a copy of the dinner menu (page 61) at each place setting.
- Place copies of the dinner questions (page 60) at each setting.
- Visit your local library or music store for Chinese music (page 59) for background music.
- Provide chopsticks for each guest.
- If you are participating in a monthly dinner club, write the name of each course (appetizer, salad, side dish, entrée, dessert, or drink) on a separate index card and place the cards in a bowl so guests can draw for next month's party.
- Have a camera ready. This will be a night to remember!

Before Dinner

Set the mood for an authentic Chinese experience by greeting guests at the door with a customary bow, and the phrase *ni hao*. Ask them to remove their shoes.

Next offer tea to guests. The Chinese consider tea a mark of respect for the visitor, as well as something enjoyable to be shared. Invite guests to enjoy appetizers, music, and conversation. Encourage guests to discuss Chinese trivia (page 57).

Ask guests to review dining tips (page 53) and encourage discussion while enjoying the appetizers.

Dinner

Serve all dishes at the same time. Present the best or the finest food first to the senior members of the family or guests.

Before starting to eat dinner, the host may offer some words of greeting. Guests should not begin eating until told to do so, as a sign of respect.

Seat your guests around the dinner table and offer a toast in their honor. Lift your glass and say, "*Gampei.*" When you feel the toast is complete, lift your chopsticks and say, "*Ch'ing*" —now all are free to eat.

Invite guests to read and discuss the dinner questions. As the host or hostess, you are the discussion leader. Encourage each person to participate.

After Dinner

As guests continue discussing the dinner questions, begin to clear the table.

Serve hot tea (green, white, or black) and dessert.

Ask guests what they enjoyed most about the evening. Ask if they would like to host a dinner party, and if so, which country.

If you are participating in a monthly dinner club, invite guests to draw names of courses (appetizer, salad, side dish, entrée, dessert, or drink) from a bowl for next month's party, and decide who will host.

Greetings & Phrases

Hello	*Ni hao*
Good evening	*Wan shang hao*
Welcome	*Huan ying huan ying*
How are you?	*Ni hao ma?*
Where is the rest room?	*Ce suo zai nar*
Good–bye	*Zai jian*
Take care	*Manzou*

Food Preparation Tips

For best results cut vegetables into bite-sized pieces before cooking. Do not soak chopped vegetables in water before cooking, as this reduces the vitamin and mineral content. Rinse vegetables under running water and drain in a mesh basket before cooking.

Avoid using frozen vegetables for stir-fried dishes, because water content is higher than in fresh vegetables. This is particularly important with snow peas. If fresh ones are not available, substitute some other crunchy vegetable that is in season, such as broccoli, asparagus, or string beans.

To the Chinese, noodles are a symbol of longevity and are always served at birthdays and special occasions. Because noodles symbolize long life, it is considered unlucky to cut a strand, so do not cut or break noodles.

A traditional Chinese dinner table will not have knives—a cook would not expect guests to cut or prepare their own food once at the table. So vegetables and meat need to be in bite-sized pieces.

Strive for a balance among taste, sight, aroma, and texture in your dishes.

Table Settings

The Chinese traditional table consists of a bowl, a spoon, a small plate, and chopsticks placed on a bamboo mat. Do not place seasonings at the table. This is considered an insult to the cook who has spent hours preparing the meal.

To the Chinese anything round, such as the sun and the moon, is a symbol of perfection. Roundness also signifies harmony. Hence, the shape of round banquet tables, round cakes, and spring rolls.

An individual place setting for an everyday meal includes a bowl of rice, a pair of chopsticks, a flat-bottomed soupspoon, and a saucer. Instead of a napkin, a hot towel is often provided at the end of the meal to wipe hands and mouth.

Typically beverages and dessert are not served with a meal. People drink tea throughout the day, so at meals soup is usually the only liquid provided. At special events wine or liquor may be served. Desserts are usually reserved for special events, where they are served between courses, or for small meals at teahouses.

Place main dishes in the center of the table with supporting dishes placed evenly around them.

Dining Etiquette

In China, the meat and vegetable dishes are placed in the center of the table for people to help themselves. It is perfectly acceptable to reach across the table and serve yourself. It is normal to take a little from each plate and to continue taking small portions of food throughout the meal. Rice is served individually in small bowls.

Do not stick your chopsticks upright in your rice or on your plate. Instead, place them together uncrossed on your dish. In Chinese culture, when people die, their shrine contains a bowl of sand or rice with two sticks of incense stuck upright in it. So if you stick your chopsticks in the rice bowl, it resembles a shrine and is equivalent to wishing death upon a person at the table.

To leave even a grain of rice in your bowl is considered bad manners!

It is considered impolite to set the teapot down with the spout facing toward anyone. The spout should always be directed to where no one is sitting.

Do not tap on your bowl with your chopsticks. In China beggars tap on their bowls for charity. Also, when the food is coming too slowly in a restaurant, people will tap their bowls.

Costume Ideas

Cheongsam dress: Also called a *qipao,* banner dress, or mandarin gown. This simple one-piece long dress is the traditional dress for Chinese women. It fits snugly, with a high neck and closed collar. Sleeves may be short, medium, or long, depending on the season. It buttons on the right and slits up from the side. Accessorize with clogs and fan. You can rent this costume from your local costume shop.

Jackie Chan: Chan, who was from Hong Kong, went to live at the China Drama Academy at age six, and became one of the best-known names in kung fu and action films. Wear cotton clothing; the shirt should have cuffs you can roll back, and the pants should have a drawstring waist and cuffs. Accessorize your Kung Fu uniform with a nylon sash or belt. Wear black canvas Kung Fu shoes to complete the outfit.

Jet Li: This costume is based on the role the actor plays in the movie *Hero.* He wears a traditional Hanfu costume consisting of a knee-length tunic with narrow-cuffed sleeves, tied with a sash, and a narrow ankle-length skirt. Choose vivid primary colors.

Icebreaker: Trivia

The first emperor of China, Qin Shi Huang, built the Great Wall of China. It is the world's longest manmade structure, approximately four thousand miles long, and the only manmade object that can be seen from outer space.

China has the largest population in the world.

China has more than four hundred species of bamboo, which is used for flooring, furniture, bows and arrows, chopsticks, shoes, beds, lanterns, toys, screens, musical instruments, houses, and gardens. Before paper, bamboo was used to write on.

Bamboo shoots have long been a popular dish because of their crispness and fresh, sweet taste. They contain vitamins, sugar, fat, and protein. Bamboo makes up 99 percent of a panda's diet.

Teahouses sprang up to accommodate weary travelers journeying along the famous Silk Road.

The Chinese view tea as one of the seven necessities of life together with firewood, rice, oil, salt, sauce, and vinegar. As tea's ability to aid in digestion and cleanse the palate became known, proprietors began adding a variety of snacks, and the tradition of dim sum (a light Chinese meal served with tea) became important in teahouses.

Some of the first forms of currency in China were shells, satin, and jade.

China has fifty-five ethnic minorities and more than two hundred listed languages.

Anything that resembles gold, either phonetically or visually, is believed good for prosperity. The Cantonese word for orange has the same sound as the word for gold, so oranges are always given out during Chinese New Year.

CHINA FILM FESTIVAL

Crouching Tiger Hidden Dragon
Starring Chow Yun-Fat, Michelle Yeoh, Ziyi Zhang, Chang Chen, and Lung Sihung
Directed by Ang Lee, 2000

Farewell My Concubine
Starring Qi Lu, Leslie Cheung, Fengyi Zhang, and Gong Li
Directed by Chen Kaige, 1993

The Joy Luck Club
Starring Kieu Chinh, Tsai Chin, and France Nuyen
Directed by Wayne Wang, 1993

Mulan
Starring Lea Solonga, Pat Morita, and Eddie Murphy
Directed by Tony Bancroft and Barry Cook, 1998 (Animated)

The Wedding Banquet
Starring Ang Lee
Directed by Greg Carson, 2004

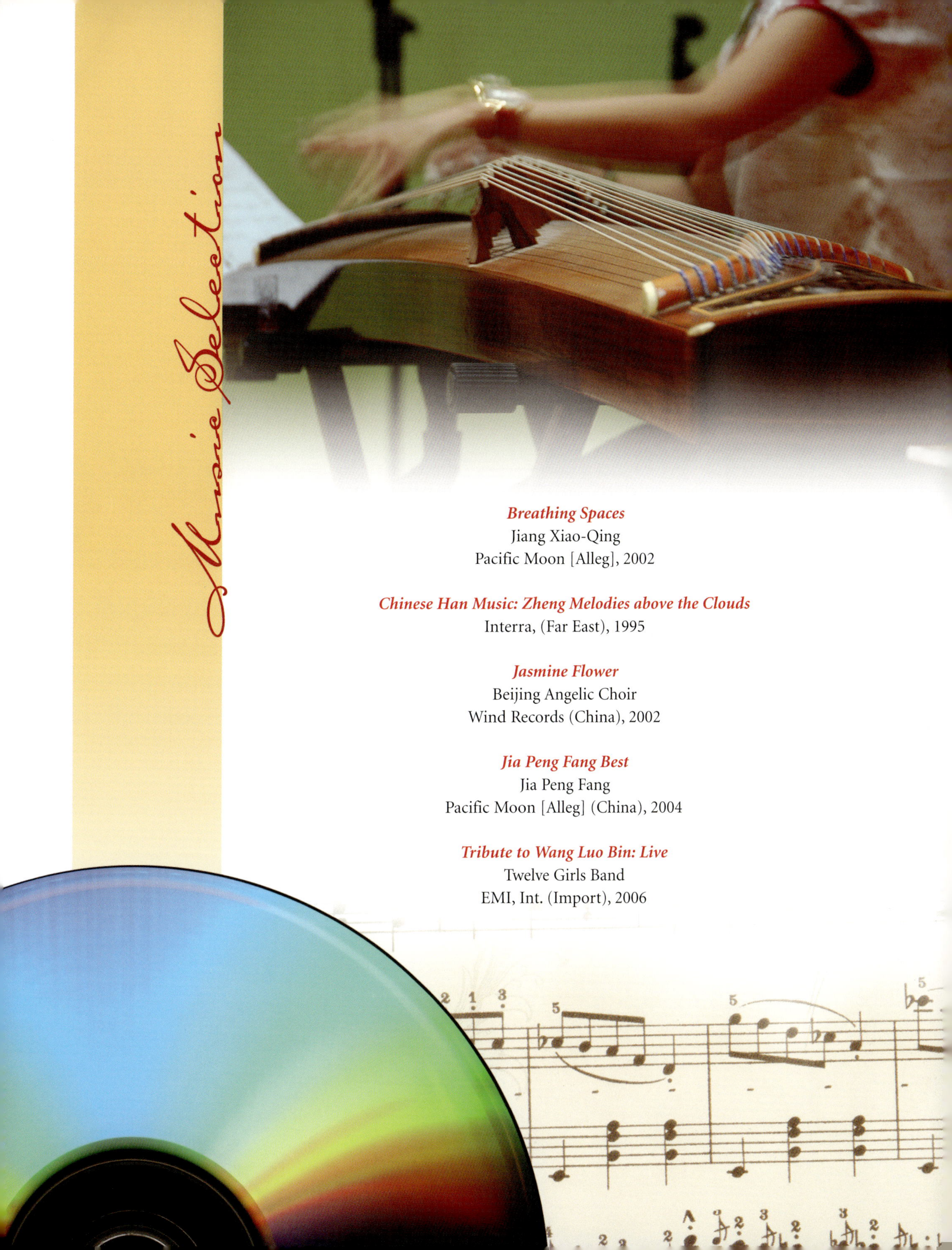

Music Selection

Breathing Spaces
Jiang Xiao-Qing
Pacific Moon [Alleg], 2002

Chinese Han Music: Zheng Melodies above the Clouds
Interra, (Far East), 1995

Jasmine Flower
Beijing Angelic Choir
Wind Records (China), 2002

Jia Peng Fang Best
Jia Peng Fang
Pacific Moon [Alleg] (China), 2004

Tribute to Wang Luo Bin: Live
Twelve Girls Band
EMI, Int. (Import), 2006

Dinner Questions

1. Acupuncture originated in China more than five thousand years ago. Have you ever tried this form of therapy? If not, would you? Why or why not?

2. There are two very important rules regarding chopsticks: don't touch your mouth with them, and don't cross the sticks when finished using them. Can you eat with chopsticks? Show us!

3. China borders many countries. How many can you name?

4. Studies suggest that ginseng may lower blood sugar and cholesterol, decrease stress, increase stamina, help fight inflammation, improve your immune system, and facilitate relaxation. What is your experience with natural or herbal medicine?

5. Silk is made from the cocoon of tiny silkworms. It takes 40,000 silkworms to produce just twelve pounds of silk. Do you own anything that is 100 percent silk? Where did you get it?

6. The Chinese believe penmanship communicates something essential about an individual's personality. What do you think your handwriting says about you? Have you ever had your handwriting analyzed?

7. Chinese women have won Olympic medals for their outstanding ability in weight lifting. What is the heaviest object you have lifted?

8. The fight scene from the film, *Crouching Tiger Hidden Dragon,* was filmed at the Bamboo Sea in Sichuan Province. Do you know any martial arts moves? Do you practice self-defense?

9. The largest U.S. Asian community can be found in New York's Chinatown, among the narrow streets of the Lower East Side. Have you ever been to New York's Chinatown? Can you name other cities that have a Chinatown?

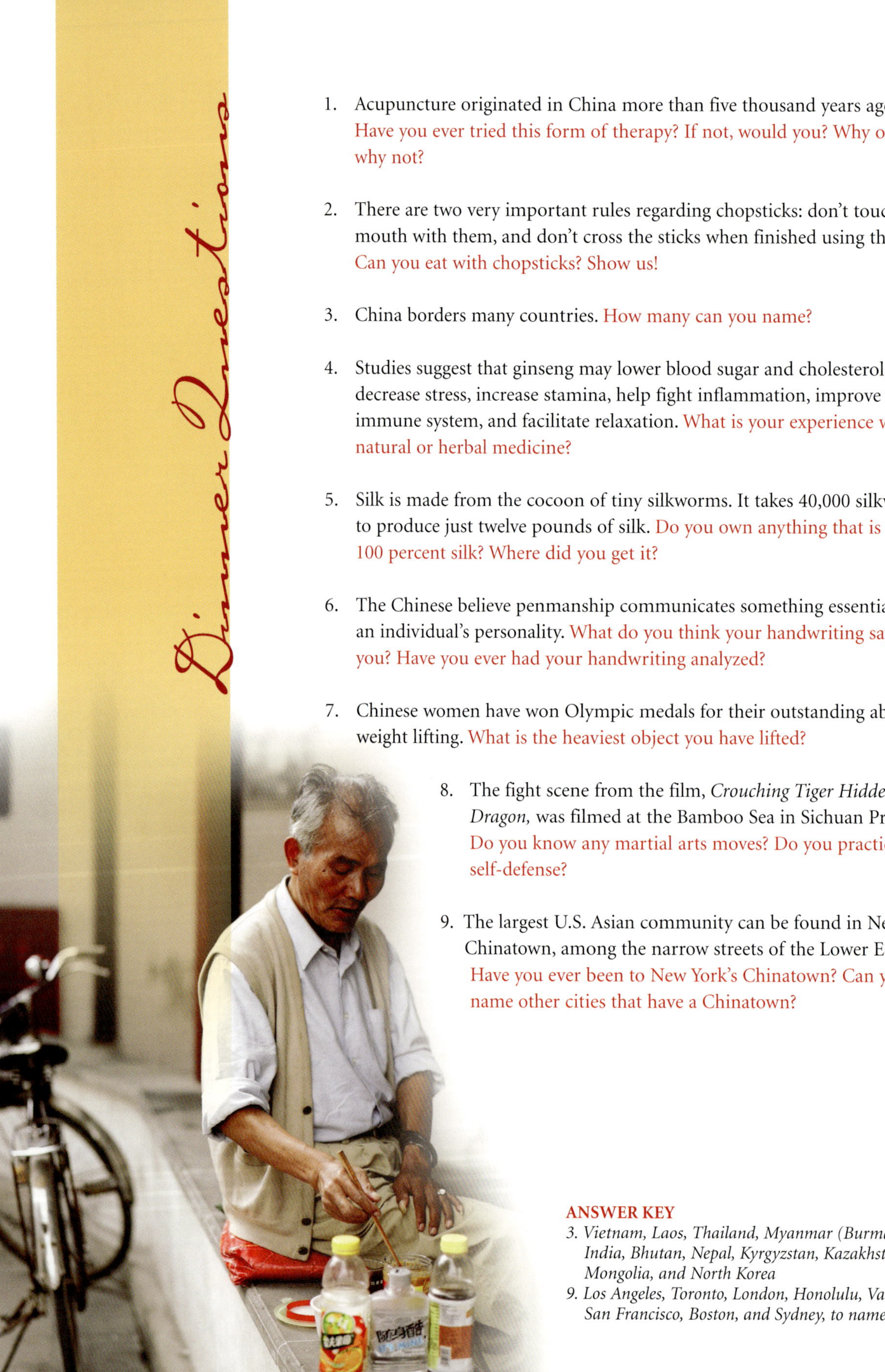

ANSWER KEY

3. Vietnam, Laos, Thailand, Myanmar (Burma), Bangladesh, India, Bhutan, Nepal, Kyrgyzstan, Kazakhstan, Russia, Mongolia, and North Korea

9. Los Angeles, Toronto, London, Honolulu, Vancouver, San Francisco, Boston, and Sydney, to name a few.

Suggested Menu

Appetizer	Won Tons
Soup	Egg-Drop Soup
Side Dishes	Chinese Broccoli, Sticky Rice
Entrée	Spicy Pepper Beef
Dessert	Almond Biscuits

Appetizer

Won Tons

❖❖❖

1 pound pork sausage, finely ground
½ cup sliced green onions
1 (8-ounce) can diced water chestnuts
½ teaspoon salt
½ teaspoon pepper
½ teaspoon garlic salt
½ pound package (30) won ton wrappers
Oil for frying

Combine the pork sausage, green onions, water chestnuts, salt, pepper, and garlic salt in a large bowl. Lay the won ton wrappers on a flat surface. Place 1 teaspoon of the mixture in the center of each skin. Dip your fingers into a cup of warm water, and moisten two edges of the wrapper, and fold it in half into a triangle shape. Moisten the two outer points of the triangle, and bring them together. Fry in oil at 350 degrees for about 3 minutes. Turn over once during cooking.

Makes 12 servings.

Egg Rolls

❖❖❖

Marinated chicken and pork:

½ cup soy sauce
¼ cup water
1 garlic clove, mashed
2 tablespoons lemon juice
1 cup ground chicken
3 cups ground pork

Egg rolls:

3 tablespoons vegetable oil
1 cup thinly sliced celery
1½ cups finely diced cabbage
3 cups finely diced onions
1 cup finely diced fresh mushrooms
1 tablespoon soy sauce
1 tablespoon salt
1 tablespoon pepper
1 pound bean sprouts, thoroughly cleaned
1 (14-ounce) package egg roll wrappers
1 egg white, lightly beaten

Dipping sauce:

½ cup soy sauce
1 teaspoon dry mustard
3 teaspoons garlic powder
1 teaspoon vinegar
1 teaspoon brown sugar

For the marinade, mix together the soy sauce, water, garlic, and lemon juice. Add the chicken and pork. Cover tightly and marinate overnight. In a large skillet over medium-high heat, brown the chicken and the pork together until cooked thoroughly.

For the egg rolls, warm the vegetable oil in a wok or deep frying pan. Over medium heat, add the celery, cabbage, onions, and mushrooms. Stir-fry until the celery and onions are tender. Add the chicken and pork. Stir until heated through. Add the soy sauce, salt, and pepper. Remove this mixture from the heat, and stir in the bean sprouts.

When working with egg roll wrappers, keep them covered with a damp cloth to prevent them from drying out. To fill each roll, mound about 2 tablespoons filling just below the center of the egg roll. Fold the bottom corner up over to cover the filling, and fold in the two outside corners. Roll to close the wrapper, sealing it shut with a bit of egg white. In a wok or deep-sided frying pan, heat the vegetable oil. The egg rolls must be completely covered in oil to fry them. Over medium-high heat, carefully add the egg rolls, one at a time. Deep-fry the egg rolls about 2 to 3 minutes, or until golden brown on both sides, turning once. Egg rolls may be kept warm in a 200-degree oven until serving time.

For the dipping sauce, combine in a small bowl the soy sauce, dry mustard, garlic powder, vinegar, and brown sugar. Stir until well dissolved.

Makes 6 servings.

Egg-Drop Soup

❖❖❖

5 cups chicken broth
4 eggs
10 spinach leaves, sliced
3 tablespoons lemon juice

Boil the chicken broth in a saucepan, and reduce to a slow simmer. Break the eggs into a cup, and beat the eggs very lightly. Hold the cup in one hand while gently swirling the fork in wide circles in the soup with the other. Slowly pour a thin stream of egg into the soup. Stop the pouring several times to form several long, filmy threads. Add the sliced spinach and lemon juice to the broth.

Makes 6 servings.

Quick Chicken Soup with Napa Cabbage

❖❖❖

- 6 cups chicken broth
- 6 garlic cloves, minced
- 1½ teaspoons ground ginger
- 2 cups sliced napa cabbage
- ½ cup sliced bamboo shoots
- 1 cup shredded chicken meat
- 1 (12.3-ounce) package semifirm tofu, cubed
- 2 tablespoons soy sauce
- 1 teaspoon dry sherry

Combine the chicken broth, garlic, and ginger in a pot. Bring to a boil, and reduce to a simmer. Add the cabbage and bamboo shoots. Simmer for another 5 minutes. Add the chicken, tofu, soy sauce, and wine.

Makes 6 servings.

Side Dish

Chinese Broccoli

1½ cups broccoli florets
½ teaspoon salt
1 teaspoon baking soda
½ teaspoon ground ginger

Sauce:
3 tablespoons chicken broth or water
2 tablespoons oyster sauce
1 tablespoon Chinese rice wine or dry sherry
½ teaspoon sugar

In a large saucepan, add enough water to cover the broccoli. Add the salt, baking soda, and ginger. Bring to a boil. Cook until the florets are tender, but crisp (3 to 4 minutes). Rinse in cold running water and drain. For the sauce, combine the chicken broth or water, oyster sauce, rice wine or dry sherry, and sugar in a small saucepan, and bring to a boil. Turn the heat down and keep warm. Pour the sauce over the broccoli. Serve immediately.

Makes 6 servings.

Sticky Rice

4 cups long grain rice
4 cups water

Pour the rice into a large bowl and rinse with cold water. Drain the rice; repeat until the drained water runs clear, and let soak for 30 minutes. Transfer the rice into a large saucepan, add 4 cups of water, and cover. Bring to a boil, and reduce to a simmer for 15 minutes. Do not uncover the rice. Let it stand for 15 minutes. Cover with a damp towel until ready to serve.

Makes 8 servings.

Pork and Bamboo Shoots

❖❖❖

¼ cup soy sauce
1 tablespoon sherry
1 teaspoon light brown sugar
1 teaspoon ground ginger
2 pounds cubed lean pork
4 cups water
4 ounces drained and shredded bamboo shoots

Mix the soy sauce, sherry, brown sugar, and ginger. Add the mixture to the pork, toss well, and leave for 10 minutes. Put the pork mixture in a large pan, add the water, and bring gently to a boil. Cover and simmer for 1 hour. Add the bamboo shoots to the pan, and simmer for 10 minutes. If desired, the liquid may be thickened with 1 tablespoon cornstarch mixed with a little cold water.

Makes 8 servings.

Almond Chicken

Marinade:
1 teaspoon salt
¼ teaspoon white pepper
1½ teaspoons cornstarch
2 tablespoons soy sauce
2 egg whites

Chicken:
2 pounds skinless, boneless chicken breasts, diced
½ cup vegetable oil
8 slices fresh ginger
6 green onions, chopped in 1-inch lengths
2 green bell peppers, chopped in 1-inch lengths
1 cup diced bamboo shoots

Seasoning sauce:
2 tablespoons rice vinegar
4 tablespoons soy sauce
2 tablespoons dry sherry
1 teaspoon salt
2 teaspoons sugar
1 teaspoon cornstarch

To complete the recipe:
1 cup slivered almonds

For the marinade, combine in a large bowl the salt, white pepper, cornstarch, soy sauce, and egg whites. Add the chicken and mix well. Let stand ½ hour. Heat the oil to medium-high in a wok, add the chicken, and stir-fry until browned. Remove the chicken and drain well. Stir-fry the ginger, green onions, green peppers, and bamboo shoots for about 1 minute, just until the vegetables are crisp-tender.

For the seasoning sauce, combine the rice vinegar, soy sauce, dry sherry, salt, sugar, and cornstarch in a small bowl. Mix well and add the sauce to the wok. Bring to a boil. Add the chicken to the boiling sauce, and stir-fry until the chicken is coated with the sauce. Add the almonds, mix well, and serve hot.

Makes 8 servings.

Spicy Pepper Beef

❖❖❖

Marinade:

1 cup soy sauce
1 teaspoon pepper

Beef:

½ pound beef sirloin, cut into stir-fry-size pieces
5½ tablespoons vegetable oil, divided
2 teaspoons minced fresh ginger
1 small green bell pepper, seeded and cut into matchstick-sized pieces
1 small red bell pepper, seeded and cut into matchstick-sized pieces
2 teaspoons sugar
1 teaspoon salt
1 teaspoon pepper
1 teaspoon ground, toasted Sichuan peppercorns (optional)
1 teaspoon sesame oil

Combine the soy sauce and pepper in a medium bowl. Add the beef and stir to coat. Set aside for about 30 minutes. Place a wok or wide frying pan over high heat until hot. Add 4 tablespoons vegetable oil, swirling to coat the sides. Add the ginger and cook, stirring, until fragrant, about 5 seconds. Add the beef and stir-fry for 2 minutes, or until barely pink. Remove the beef. Add the remaining 1½ tablespoons vegetable oil to the wok. Add the green and red peppers, and stir-fry for 1 minute, or until crisp-tender. Return the beef to the wok. Stir in the sugar, salt, pepper, peppercorns (if using), and sesame oil. Best when served over steamed white rice.

Makes 8 servings.

Garlic Chicken

- 2 egg whites
- 2 tablespoons cornstarch
- 2 tablespoons lemon juice
- 8 skinless, boneless chicken breasts
- ¼ cup vegetable oil
- 4 green onions, sliced
- 2 teaspoons finely chopped fresh ginger
- 2 tablespoons finely chopped fresh garlic

Sauce:

- 2 teaspoons chili powder
- 1 tablespoon sugar
- 2 teaspoons cornstarch
- ¼ cup lemon juice
- ¼ cup red wine vinegar
- ¼ cup soy sauce

In a medium bowl, beat the egg whites, cornstarch, and lemon juice until the cornstarch is dissolved. Add the chicken breasts, and let stand for 10 minutes. In a separate bowl, combine the chili powder, sugar, cornstarch, lemon juice, red wine vinegar, and soy sauce. Heat the vegetable oil in a large skillet; add the chicken breasts, and stir-fry until the chicken turns white. Remove the chicken. Add the green onion, ginger, and garlic, and fry lightly. Now add the chicken breasts and the sauce. Cook until the mixture becomes hot and bubbly.

Makes 8 servings.

Dessert

Almond Biscuits

❖❖❖

2 cups flour
½ teaspoon baking powder
½ teaspoon baking soda
⅛ teaspoon salt
½ cup butter
½ cup shortening
¾ cup sugar
2 eggs
2½ teaspoons almond extract
¼ pound whole, blanched almonds (one for each cookie)
1 egg, lightly beaten

Preheat the oven to 325 degrees. In a large bowl, sift the flour, baking powder, baking soda, and salt. In a medium bowl, beat the butter or margarine, shortening, and sugar together with an electric mixer. Add the eggs and almond extract, and beat until well blended. Add to the flour mixture and mix well. The dough will be dry and crumbly.

Use your fingers to form the mixture into a ball of dough, wrap the dough, and refrigerate for 2 hours. Roll into nickel-size pieces, and place on a lightly greased cookie tray, approximately 1½ inches apart. Brush each biscuit with beaten egg, and place an almond in the center of each biscuit. Bake for 15 minutes to 18 minutes, or until golden brown. Cool and store in a sealed container.

Makes 8 servings.

CUBA

ERNEST HEMINGWAY SAW CUBA AS THE BEST-KEPT SECRET OF THE CARIBBEAN ISLANDS. It was there that he introduced the Mojito, the popular rum and mint cocktail, while finishing the classic *For Whom the Bells Tolls.* Located just ninety miles off the Florida coast, Cuba boasts white sandy beaches, coral reefs, and emerald lagoons.

During the thirties, forties, and fifties, Cuba was considered the playground of the western hemisphere. Writers, actors, and scholars found their way to this luxurious island. Though the Cuba of this era evokes images of bright vintage American cars, Cuban cigars, and nightclubs where patrons danced the night away, many also remember the conflicts during the Kennedy era of the Bay of Pigs and the Cuban Missile Crisis. As you experience the history, culture, cuisine, and costumes of Cuba, keep in mind the many culinary flavors that this island has brought our way. Legend says that it was here that Columbus first tasted corn, peanuts, pineapples, sweet potatoes, pumpkins, and peppers.

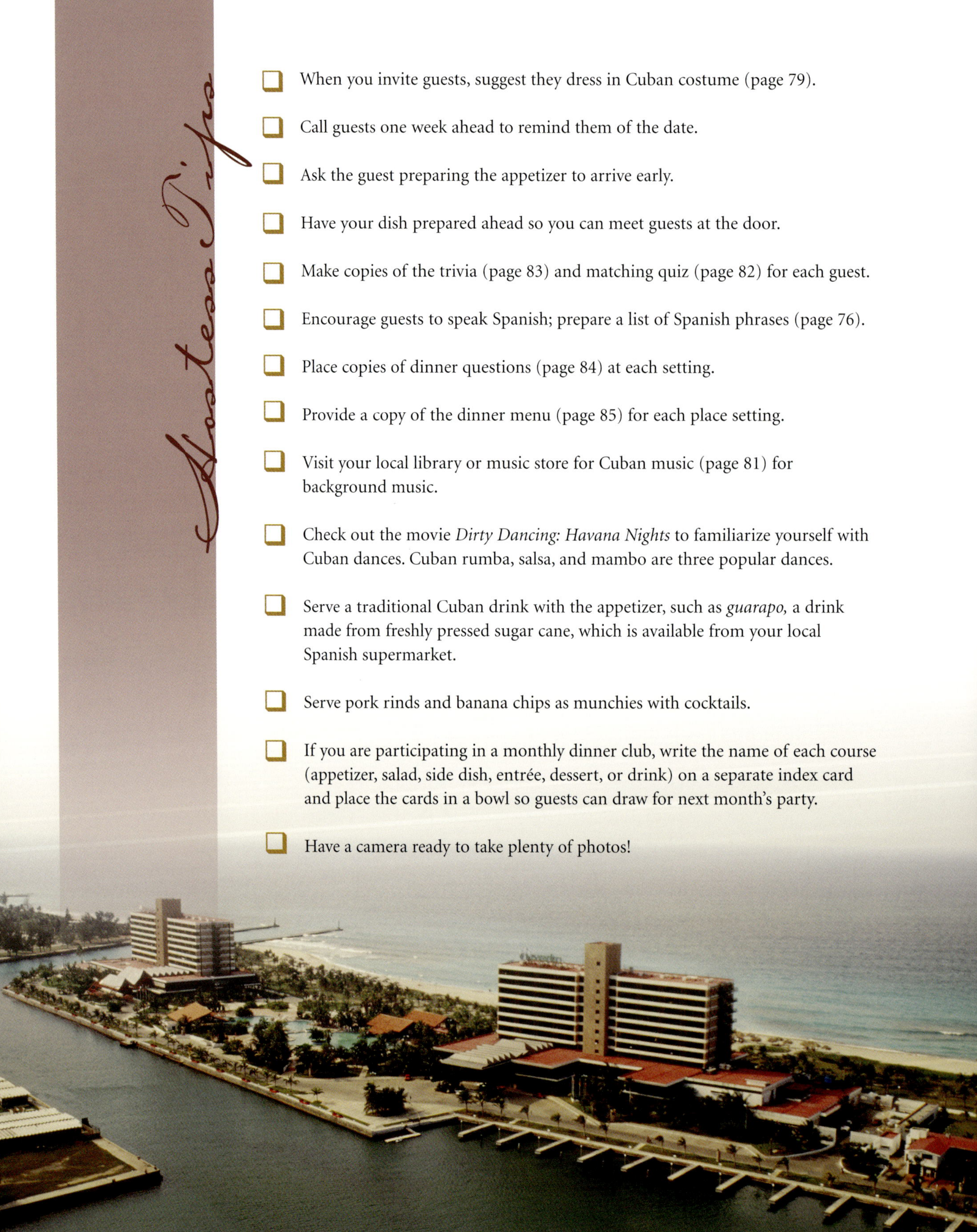

Hostess Tips

- When you invite guests, suggest they dress in Cuban costume (page 79).
- Call guests one week ahead to remind them of the date.
- Ask the guest preparing the appetizer to arrive early.
- Have your dish prepared ahead so you can meet guests at the door.
- Make copies of the trivia (page 83) and matching quiz (page 82) for each guest.
- Encourage guests to speak Spanish; prepare a list of Spanish phrases (page 76).
- Place copies of dinner questions (page 84) at each setting.
- Provide a copy of the dinner menu (page 85) for each place setting.
- Visit your local library or music store for Cuban music (page 81) for background music.
- Check out the movie *Dirty Dancing: Havana Nights* to familiarize yourself with Cuban dances. Cuban rumba, salsa, and mambo are three popular dances.
- Serve a traditional Cuban drink with the appetizer, such as *guarapo,* a drink made from freshly pressed sugar cane, which is available from your local Spanish supermarket.
- Serve pork rinds and banana chips as munchies with cocktails.
- If you are participating in a monthly dinner club, write the name of each course (appetizer, salad, side dish, entrée, dessert, or drink) on a separate index card and place the cards in a bowl so guests can draw for next month's party.
- Have a camera ready to take plenty of photos!

Before Dinner

Play Cuban music to set the mood for an authentic evening. Greet guests at the door with *hola*. Cubans speak Spanish and are very enthusiastic in their welcome.

Comment on guests' costumes. Welcome them in and invite them to enjoy the appetizer, music, and conversation. Serve specialty drinks (page 95).

Invite guests to discuss the trivia and take the matching quiz.

Suggest that guests try Cuban dancing.

After appetizer and dinner drinks, ask guests to be seated at the dinner table.

Dinner

Begin serving dinner.

Invite guests to read and discuss the dinner questions. As the host or hostess, you are the discussion leader. Encourage each person to participate.

After Dinner

After the meal is complete, begin to collect the plates and clear the table. Ask guests to continue their conversation. You may begin to serve the dessert at this time.

Serve coffee at this time. Cubans drink plenty of coffee, and they brew it strong. *Café cubano* (also called *café espresso*) is a straight shot of espresso, *café con leche* is espresso mixed with warm milk, and *café americano* is a mild "American" cup of coffee.

If you are participating in a monthly dinner club, invite guests to draw names of courses (appetizer, salad, side dish, entrée, dessert, or drink) from a bowl for next month's party, and decide who will host.

Greetings & Phrases

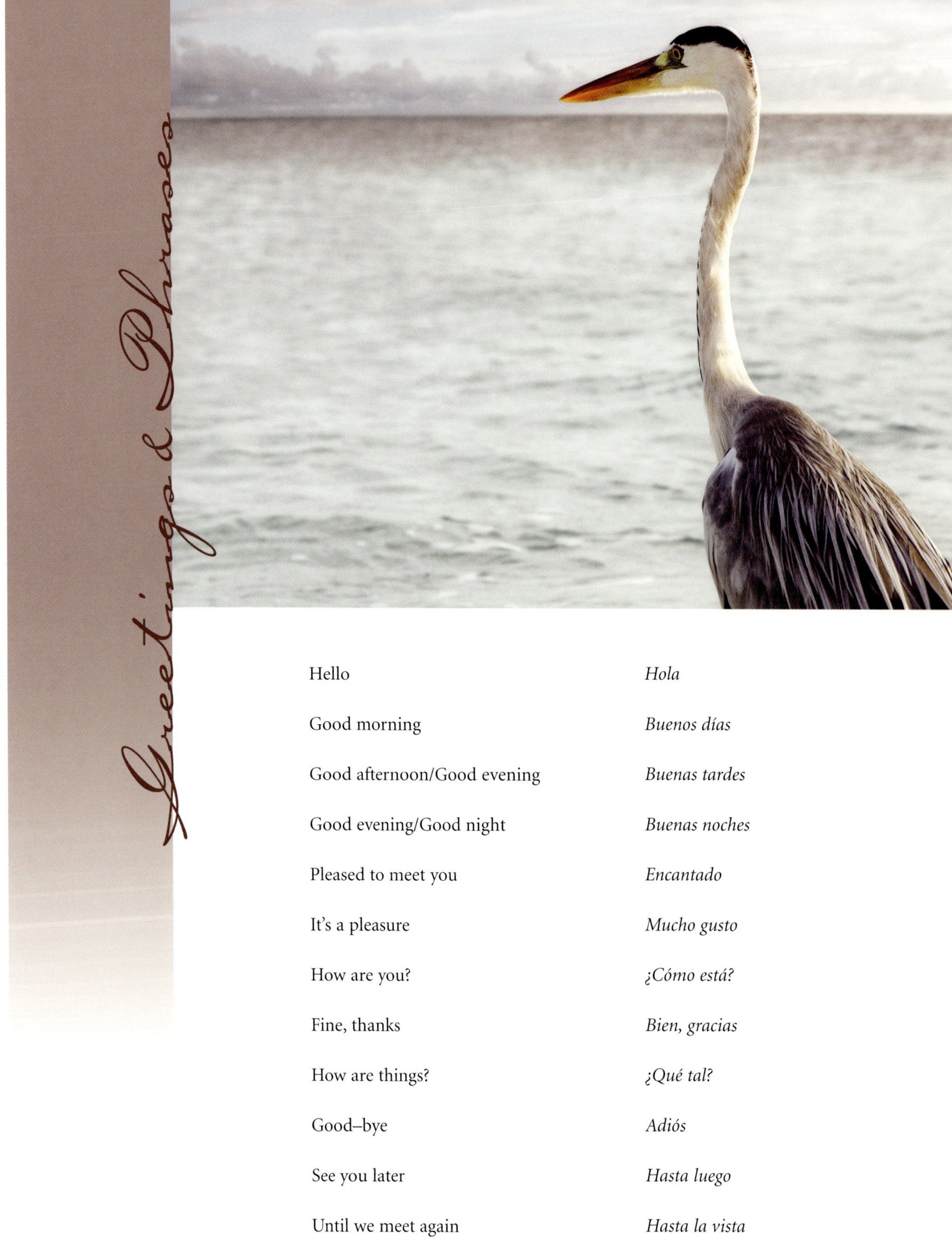

Hello	*Hola*
Good morning	*Buenos días*
Good afternoon/Good evening	*Buenas tardes*
Good evening/Good night	*Buenas noches*
Pleased to meet you	*Encantado*
It's a pleasure	*Mucho gusto*
How are you?	*¿Cómo está?*
Fine, thanks	*Bien, gracias*
How are things?	*¿Qué tal?*
Good–bye	*Adiós*
See you later	*Hasta luego*
Until we meet again	*Hasta la vista*

Table Decorations

Use a piece of burlap for your tablecloth and, if you can find them, use plastic or silk banana leaves as place mats or chargers under your plates or platters.

Items such as rum bottles, Cuban cigar boxes, loose coffee beans, and fresh fruit make great centerpieces and give an ambiance of the island. Cubans enjoy music at the table so consider providing each guest with a maraca to dance the night away.

Cuban Cuisine

Cuban cuisine has been influenced by African, French, Arabic, Chinese, Spanish, and Portuguese cultures. It does not use a lot of spice or hot peppers, but uses onions, garlic, and, green peppers fairly liberally.

The meal begins with a dish called *sofrito,* which consists of onions, green peppers, garlic, oregano, and ground pepper, sautéed in olive oil. Many dishes use a *sofrito* as their basis.

A meat, chicken, or fish entrée follows, accompanied by white rice, black beans, and sweet fried plantains. At times, a small salad of sliced tomatoes and onions or avocados might be added.

After the meal, a dessert is served, such as flan, a Cuban caramel-flavored custard, or the equally popular bread or rice puddings, followed by an additional shot of *café cubano*.

Most of the food is sautéed or slow-cooked over a low flame. Cuban cuisine has little concern with measurements, order, or timing.

Cuban cuisine has few deep-fried foods and no heavy or creamy sauces. Most Cuban cooking relies on a few basic spices, such as garlic, cumin, oregano, and bay laurel leaves. Meats and poultry are usually marinated in citrus juices, such as lime or sour orange juices, and then roasted over low heat until the meat becomes tender.

Common staples in the Cuban diet are root vegetables such as *yuca, malanga,* and *boniato,* which are found in most Latin markets. These vegetables are flavored with a marinade, called *mojo,* which consists of hot olive oil, lemon juice, sliced raw onions, garlic, cumin, and a little water.

Jose Conseco: Baseball is Cuba's national passion. Jose Conseco played for the Oakland Athletics and scored numerous home runs. Wear an Oakland A's baseball uniform. Accessorize with cleats, a baseball mitt, and a cap. Attach Conseco's name to the back of the jersey.

Ricky Ricardo: Desi Arnaz, who was from Santiago, Cuba, played a drummer and bandleader on the *I Love Lucy* show with his real-life wife, Lucille Ball. Wear a white shirt, bow tie, cummerbund, and dark pants. You can add a straw sombrero and a red neckerchief, and accessorize with a small yellow drum and drumsticks.

Traditional Cuban attire: This costume is a joyful expression of the island's culture. Cuban women wear form-fitting, brightly colored clothing; V-cut, sleeveless blouses or tube tops; shorts; skirts; and lots of stripes and polka dots. Accessorize with fuchsia, baby blue, red, purple, and orange jewelry—these are the favored colors of Cuba.

Desi Arnaz

Desi Arnaz was born in Santiago, Cuba, to an affluent family. His ancestors were of Spanish descent and among the original recipients of land grants in the eighteenth century. His father was Santiago's youngest mayor and served in the Cuban House of Representatives. During the 1933 revolution, the American-backed President Gerado Machado threw his father in jail and stripped his family of its wealth and power. Desi's father was released when U.S. officials believed him to be neutral and intervened on his behalf. The family then fled to Miami, Florida, where Desi became a band director before meeting and marrying Lucille Ball. He died in 1986.

Balseros
Documentary about Cuban Refugees
Starring Guillermo Armas and Maria Celeste Arraras
Directed by Carlos Bosch and Josep Maria Domenech, 2002

Buena Vista Social Club
Starring Luis Barzaga and Joachim Cooder
Directed by Wim Wenders, 1999

Dirty Dancing: Havana Nights
Starring Diego Luna, Romola Garai, and Sela Ward
Directed by Guy Ferland, 2004

I Am Cuba
Starring Sergio Corrieri and Jose Gallardo
Directed by Mikhail Kalatozov, 1995

I Love Lucy
Starring Lucille Ball and Desi Arnaz
Directed by Ralph Levy, 1951

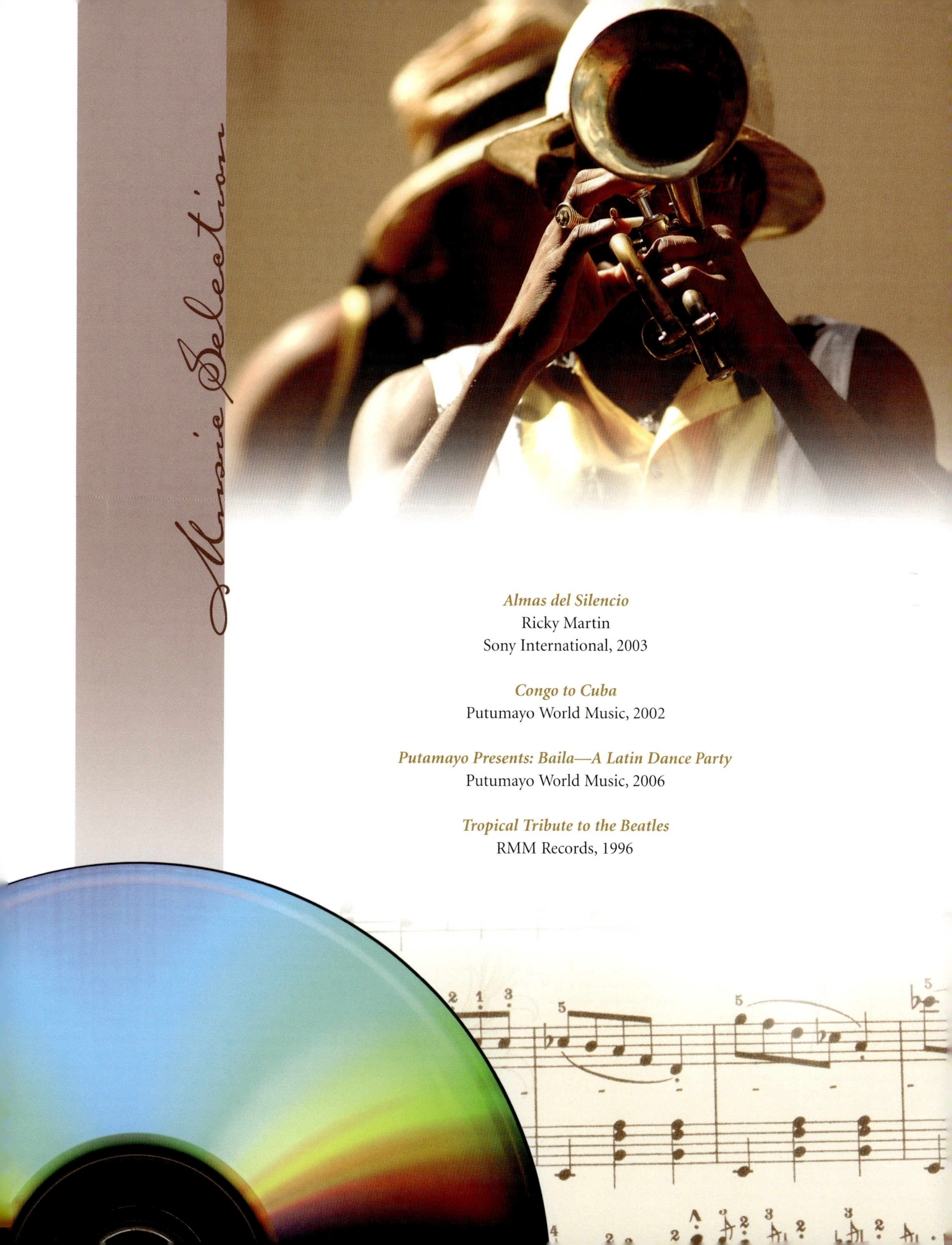

Music Selection

Almas del Silencio
Ricky Martin
Sony International, 2003

Congo to Cuba
Putumayo World Music, 2002

Putamayo Presents: Baila—A Latin Dance Party
Putumayo World Music, 2006

Tropical Tribute to the Beatles
RMM Records, 1996

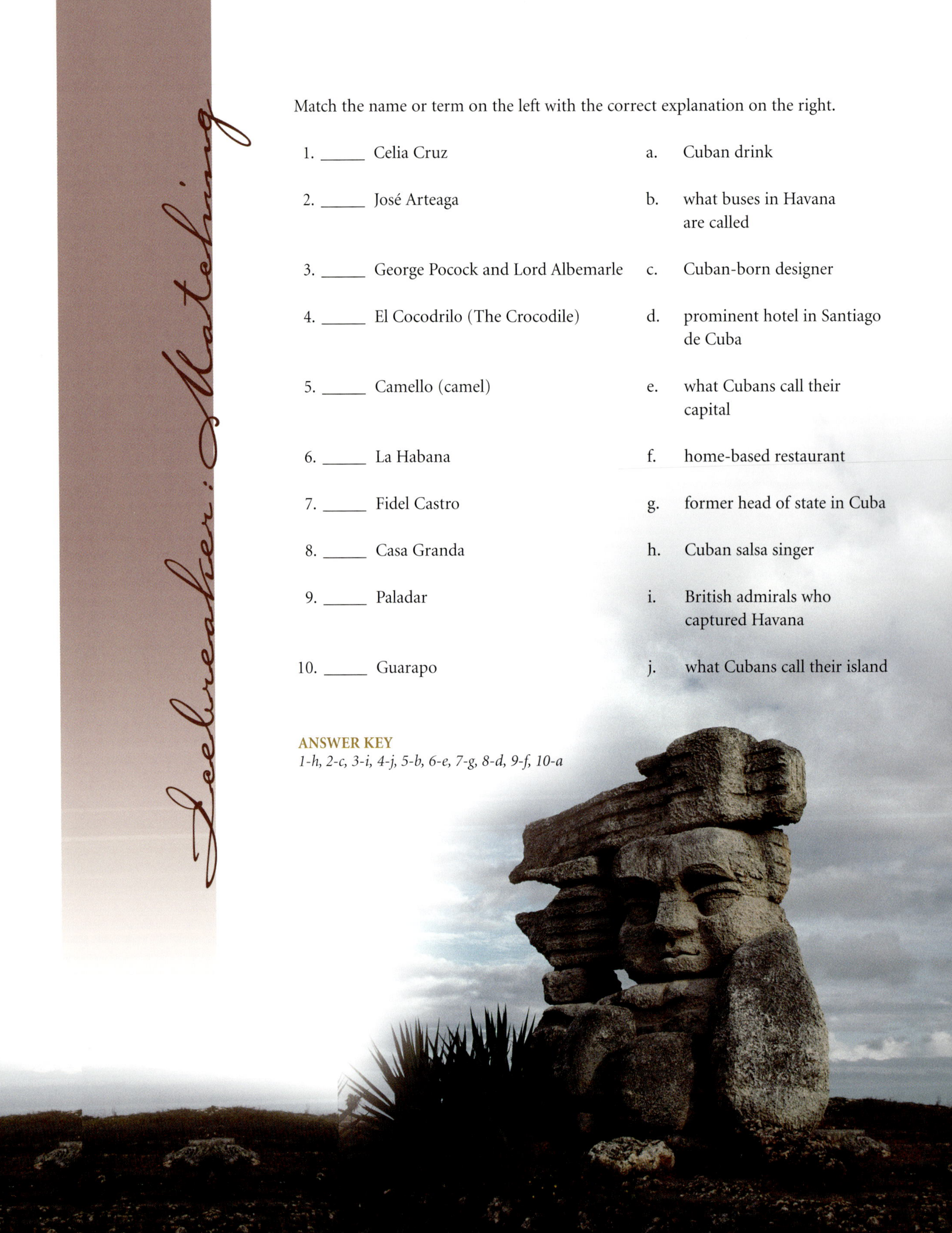

Icebreaker: Matching

Match the name or term on the left with the correct explanation on the right.

1. _____	Celia Cruz	a.	Cuban drink
2. _____	José Arteaga	b.	what buses in Havana are called
3. _____	George Pocock and Lord Albemarle	c.	Cuban-born designer
4. _____	El Cocodrilo (The Crocodile)	d.	prominent hotel in Santiago de Cuba
5. _____	Camello (camel)	e.	what Cubans call their capital
6. _____	La Habana	f.	home-based restaurant
7. _____	Fidel Castro	g.	former head of state in Cuba
8. _____	Casa Granda	h.	Cuban salsa singer
9. _____	Paladar	i.	British admirals who captured Havana
10. _____	Guarapo	j.	what Cubans call their island

ANSWER KEY
1-h, 2-c, 3-i, 4-j, 5-b, 6-e, 7-g, 8-d, 9-f, 10-a

Trivia

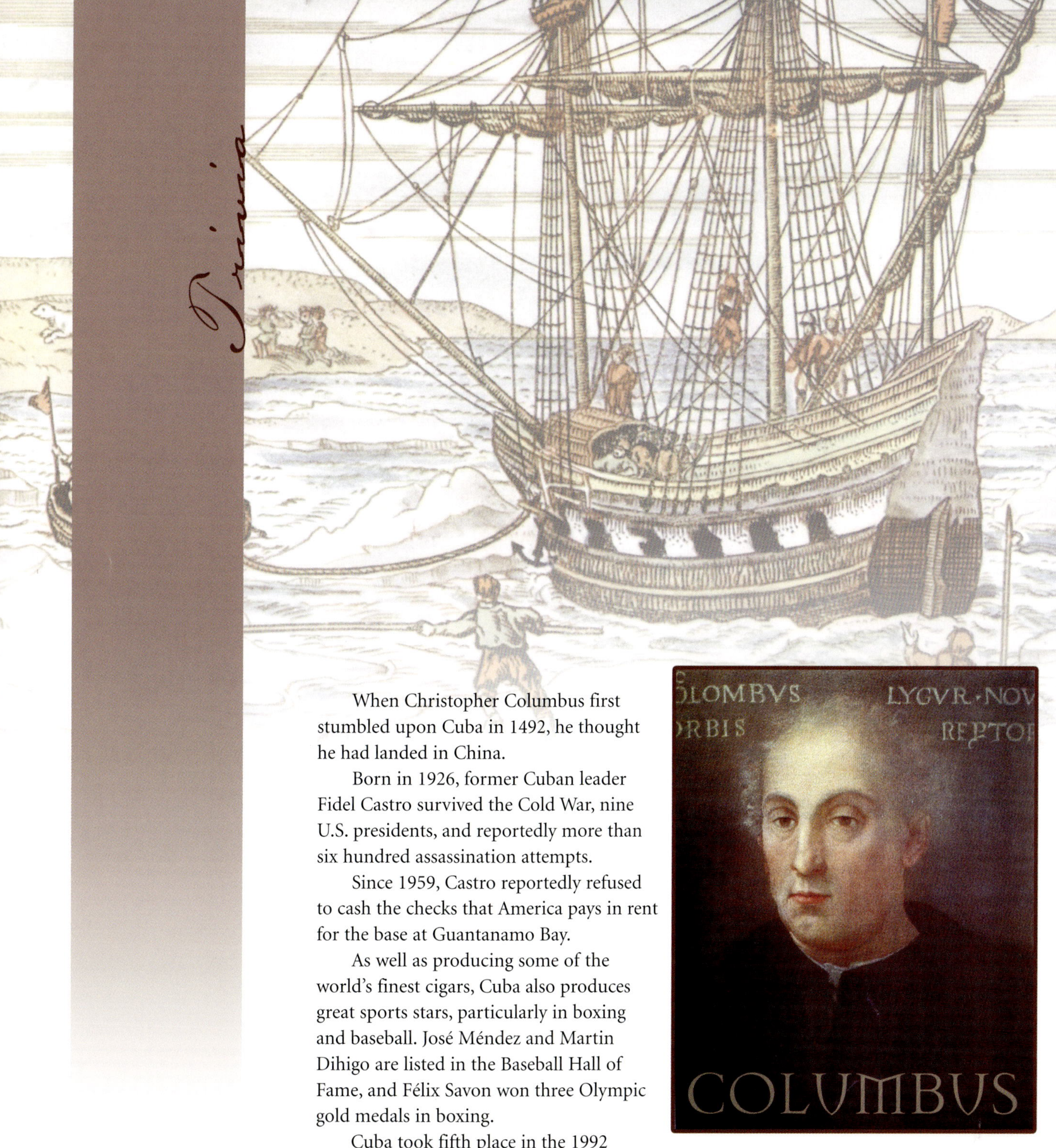

When Christopher Columbus first stumbled upon Cuba in 1492, he thought he had landed in China.

Born in 1926, former Cuban leader Fidel Castro survived the Cold War, nine U.S. presidents, and reportedly more than six hundred assassination attempts.

Since 1959, Castro reportedly refused to cash the checks that America pays in rent for the base at Guantanamo Bay.

As well as producing some of the world's finest cigars, Cuba also produces great sports stars, particularly in boxing and baseball. José Méndez and Martin Dihigo are listed in the Baseball Hall of Fame, and Félix Savon won three Olympic gold medals in boxing.

Cuba took fifth place in the 1992 Olympics at Barcelona, eighth in 1996 in Atlanta, ninth in 2000 in Sydney, and eleventh in 2004 in Athens.

Cuba is the Caribbean's largest country, slightly larger in size than England.

Ernest Hemingway, who won the Nobel Prize for literature for *The Old Man and the Sea,* lived in Cuba for twenty years.

Dinner Questions

1. Enjoying a good Cuban cigar is thought to be a source of relaxation and enjoyment. Have you ever smoked a cigar? Would you? Tell a personal smoking story. What do you do for relaxation?

2. Rumba, salsa, and mambo are a few well-known Cuban dances. When was the last time you danced? What type of dancing do you like?

3. Cuba's independence came about when the United States won the Spanish-American War in 1898 and granted Cuba independence in 1902. How did you do in high school history? What do you remember learning about Cuba?

4. U.S. baseball is making a big pitch for Cuban recruits. Who is your favorite baseball player?

5. Al–Qaeda prisoners were taken to the U.S. base in Guantanamo Bay for interrogation. What movie starring Tom Cruise and Jack Nicolson highlights Guatanamo Bay? What line from the movie is famous?

6. The Hotel Copacabana in La Habana, Cuba, is a very famous nightclub. Who sang the famous song about the Copacabana? Do you know the words? Can you sing it?

7. In 1999 six-year-old Elian Gonzalez became the center of an immigration dispute between the United States and Cuba after his mother drowned while bringing him to the United States. Elian was returned to his father in Cuba over the protests of relatives in Miami. Do you agree with this decision? Why or why not?

8. From 1523 to 1526 the rise of sugar plantations led to importing slaves from Africa. We still see slave trade in parts of our world today. What can you do to defend the helpless?

9. Fidel Castro was in power from 1959 to 2008, making him the world's longest serving political leader. Can you name three other world leaders?

10. Cuba has one of the best health care systems in the world. The average life expectancy of seventy-six years is comparable with that of the United Kingdom and the United States, and Cuban scientists have developed vaccines for hepatitis B and meningitis B. What do you think about socialized medicine? Discuss its pros and cons.

ANSWER KEY

5. A Few Good Men. "You want the truth? You want the truth? You can't handle the truth!"
6. Barry Manilow

Suggested Menu

Appetizer	Plantain Chips
Soup	Okra Chorizo Gumbo
Salad	Garbanzo Salad
Side Dish	Black Beans and Rice (Moors and Christians)
Entrée	Fried Beef
Dessert	Rice Pudding
Drinks	Cuba Libre, Rum Collins, Mojito, Guarapo

Plantain Chips

❖❖❖

6 extremely green peeled plantains
3 tablespoons lime juice
½ cup vegetable oil
2 tablespoons salt

Peel the plantains and drizzle lime juice over them. Slice the plantains into paper-thin slices. In a large, deep frying pan, heat the oil on high. When the oil is hot, place small batches of the sliced plantains in the pan. Keep the slices separated with a fork. When the slices turn golden yellow, they are ready to be placed on paper towels to soak up the excess oil. Add the salt immediately.

Makes 8 servings.

Sweet Puréed Plantain Soup

❖❖❖

1 cup chopped onions
6 tablespoons salted butter
1 teaspoon salt
2 garlic cloves, mashed
4 overripe, thinly sliced plantains (peel must be black)
5 cups beef, chicken, or vegetable broth
¾ cup canned evaporated milk
½ cup coconut milk
½ cup whole milk
¼ cup apple cider
2 tablespoons lemon juice
Dash of Tabasco sauce (optional)

In a large pot over medium heat, sauté the onion in the butter and salt until caramelized. Add the garlic, and sauté for 20 seconds. Add the sliced plantains, and sauté 2 minutes. Add the broth, and bring to a rapid boil. Immediately reduce the heat to low and simmer for 30 minutes. Pour the mixture into a blender, and blend to a smooth consistency. Pour the mixture back into the pot. Add the evaporated milk, coconut milk, whole milk, and apple cider. Simmer 5 minutes. Add the lemon juice and Tabasco, if using, and serve.

Makes 6 servings.

Okra Chorizo Gumbo

½ pound sliced Spanish chorizo
½ pound chunked ham
1½ cups chopped onions
½ cup chopped green bell pepper
2 tablespoons extra-virgin olive oil
6 garlic cloves, mashed
1 cup corn
10 green pimiento-stuffed olives, chopped
1 (8-ounce) can tomato sauce
2 ripe tomatoes, chopped
¼ teaspoon ground cumin
¼ teaspoon dried oregano
4 cups chopped okra
3 cups chicken broth
2 bay leaves
1 teaspoon salt
2 ripe plantains, peeled and chunked
½ cup lemon juice

In a large frying pan, brown the chorizo and ham. Remove the meat from the pan. Sauté the onions and peppers in the drippings and the olive oil until soft. Add the garlic and sauté for 30 seconds. Add the corn, olives, tomato sauce, tomatoes, cumin, and oregano, and stir. Add the ham and chorizo. Cook for 6 minutes. Add the okra, broth, bay leaves, and salt. Cook 20 minutes. Add the plantains. Cook 12 minutes over medium-high heat. Add the lemon juice and stir. Serve over a bed of long grain white rice.

Makes 8 servings.

Cuban Beet Salad

10 medium beets
1 cup chopped onion
1 tablespoon extra-virgin olive oil
4 garlic cloves, crushed
¾ cup lemon juice
Salt

Cook the beets with skins in salted water with the onions until the beets are soft. Refrigerate the beets and onions until completely cold. Discard onions. In a salad bowl, add the olive oil, crushed garlic, lemon juice, and salt to taste. Peel and thinly slice the beets, and chill until ready to eat. Serve with your favorite vinaigrette dressing.

Makes 8 servings.

Avocado-Pineapple-Banana Salad

4 cups chopped iceberg lettuce
2 cups chopped pineapple
2 avocados, sliced
3 bananas, sliced
1 apple, sliced
¼ cup chopped pimiento-stuffed green olives
¼ cup raisins
½ cup thinly sliced onions
¼ cup bacon bits
1 cup garlic-herbed croutons

Salad dressing:
½ cup olive oil
⅓ cup white vinegar
⅓ cup lime juice
4 garlic cloves, mashed
1 teaspoon salt

In a large salad bowl, add the lettuce, pineapple, avocados, bananas, apple, olives, raisins, and onions. Top with the bacon bits and croutons. In a small bowl, combine the olive oil, vinegar, lime juice, garlic, and salt. Whisk thoroughly and drizzle over the salad.

Makes 6 servings.

Garbanzo Salad

❖❖❖

- 2 cups garbanzo beans
- 1 cup diced green bell peppers
- 1 cup corn
- 2 cups chopped ripe tomatoes
- ½ cup chopped red onion
- ⅓ cup fresh-squeezed lime juice
- ¼ cup olive oil
- ¼ teaspoon ground cumin
- 1 teaspoon dried oregano
- 4 garlic cloves, mashed
- ½ teaspoon salt

Mix the garbanzo beans, peppers, corn, tomatoes, and onion in a bowl. In a separate bowl, whisk the lime juice, olive oil, cumin, oregano, garlic, and salt together. Pour this dressing over the garbanzo bean mixture. Refrigerate until chilled.

Makes 6 servings.

Cuban-Style Watercress Salad

❖❖❖

- 2 cups chopped watercress
- ½ cup sliced white onion
- 5 pimiento-stuffed green olives
- ½ cup raisins
- 3 tablespoons extra-virgin olive oil
- 4 tablespoons fresh lime juice
- 1 teaspoon salt

In a large salad bowl, add the watercress, onion, olives, and raisins. Drizzle with the olive oil and lime juice, and toss to mix. Sprinkle with the salt.

Makes 6 servings.

Cuban Eggplant Bake

❖❖❖

4 medium eggplants
2 onions, finely chopped
1 green bell pepper, finely chopped
¼ cup extra-virgin olive oil
8 garlic cloves, mashed
½ pound ground beef, salted
¼ pound ground chorizo
½ cup very ripe chopped tomatoes
1 cup tomato sauce
¼ teaspoon ground cumin
½ teaspoon dried oregano
2 teaspoons salt
Juice of half a lemon
3 cups savory bread stuffing
2 cups Parmesan cheese

Preheat the oven to 400 degrees. Slice the eggplants lengthwise, scoop out any seeds, and discard them. Scoop out half the eggplant meat. Sauté the eggplant meat with the olive oil, onions, and pepper until soft. Add the garlic and sauté for 30 seconds. Add the ground beef and ground chorizo. Cook and stir occasionally for 10 minutes. Add the tomatoes, tomato sauce, cumin, oregano, salt, and lemon juice. Add the bread stuffing, and stir. Remove from the heat. Fill the eggplant skins with the mixture. Bake for 24 minutes. Sprinkle the filled eggplant skins with Parmesan cheese and bake 3 more minutes.

Makes 6 servings.

Black Beans and Rice (Moors and Christians)

This blend of black beans and white rice is common on Cuban tables and is a reminder of the Spanish influence on Cuba. The popular name for this dish, *moros y cristianos* (Moors and Christians), refers to the conflict between the dark-skinned Moors and the lighter-skinned Spaniards.

8 cups water
2 teaspoons salt, divided
3 tablespoons olive oil, divided
4 cups long-grain rice
1½ cups chopped onion
1 cup chopped green bell pepper
1 cup chopped red bell pepper
3 tablespoons minced garlic cloves
4 (15-ounce) cans black beans
2 cups chicken broth
3 tablespoons red wine vinegar
1 teaspoon freshly ground pepper
½ teaspoon ground cumin
2 tablespoons chopped fresh parsley

Combine the water, 1 teaspoon salt, and 1 teaspoon olive oil in a large saucepan. Bring to a boil. Stir in the rice, cover, and reduce the heat to low. Cook for 25 minutes, or until the rice is tender. Fluff with a fork. Do not uncover until ready to serve.

In a large saucepan, heat the remaining 2 tablespoons olive oil over medium heat. Sauté the onion, green pepper, red pepper, and garlic about 5 minutes. Add the beans, chicken broth, red wine vinegar, pepper, cumin, and the remaining 1 teaspoon salt. Cover and bring to a boil. Reduce the heat to low, and let simmer for 10 minutes. Spoon the beans over the rice. Sprinkle with the parsley.

Makes 8 servings.

Tomato Chicken with Okra

❖❖❖

1 whole chicken, cut into 8 pieces
1 whole lemon, for seasoning
8 garlic cloves, mashed and divided
¼ teaspoon ground cumin
1 teaspoon salt, or more
5 tablespoons of extra-virgin olive oil, divided
1 cup chopped onion
1½ cups chopped green bell pepper
1 cup chopped okra
1½ cups chicken broth
2 extremely ripe plantains (black peels, mushy inside)
3 tomatoes, chopped and seeded
2 tablespoons tomato paste
1 (8-ounce) can tomato sauce
9 green pimiento-stuffed olives, chopped
¼ cup raisins
2 teaspoons olive juice (liquid from olive jar)

Marinate the chicken overnight with the juice of the lemon, 4 mashed garlic cloves, cumin, and a sprinkle of salt. When ready to cook, pat the chicken dry. In a large pot on medium-high heat, put 3 tablespoons of olive oil. Brown the chicken on all sides, and remove from the pot. Add the remaining 2 tablespoons of olive oil to the pot. Sauté the onion and pepper until soft. Add the okra and stir-fry for 3 minutes. Add the remaining 4 garlic cloves, and sauté for 30 seconds. Add the chicken broth, plantains, tomatoes, tomato paste, tomato sauce, olives, raisins, and olive juice; sauté 1 minute. Add water or additional chicken broth if necessary. Bring to a boil. Add the chicken. Reduce to a simmer, and cover. Let simmer on very low for 1 hour. Serve with white rice.

Makes 8 servings.

Entrée

Fried Beef

- 2 pounds flank steak
- 3 cups water
- 2 whole bay leaves
- 6 black peppercorns
- 1 teaspoon onion powder
- 2 teaspoons salt
- 4 tablespoons dry sherry
- 2 tablespoons olive oil

Seasoning rub:

- 1 teaspoon garlic powder
- ½ teaspoon pepper
- 1 teaspoon ground cumin

Garnish:

- 1 cup sliced yellow onion
- 1 cup sliced green bell pepper
- 8 lemon wedges

Place the steak in a large pot, and add just enough water to cover. Add the bay leaves and peppercorns. Cover and simmer about 1½ hours, or until tender. Allow the steak to cool, covered and in the cooking liquid. In a small bowl, combine the garlic powder, pepper, cumin, onion powder, and salt. Then add the sherry and combine with the dry ingredients. Cut the meat across the grain into serving-size pieces. Pound the meat with a meat mallet until doubled in size. Rub each piece with a bit of the dry rub and sherry mixture. Heat the olive oil in a skillet. Fry each piece of meat until it barely browns. Once the meat is done, transfer it to a serving plate. Fry the onion and pepper, and add them to the serving plate with the lemon wedges as a garnish.

Makes 6 servings.

Chicken with Okra and Plantains

- 1 teaspoon salt
- 1 teaspoon pepper
- 1 teaspoon paprika
- 1 teaspoon ground cumin
- 1 teaspoon coriander
- 6 skinless, boneless chicken breasts, diced
- 3 tablespoons vegetable oil
- ½ cup chopped onion
- 4 garlic cloves, minced
- ½ cup chopped green bell pepper
- 1½ cups water
- 2½ cups chopped ripe plantains
- 1 cup chopped okra
- 2 cups chopped tomatoes
- 2 tablespoons lime juice

In a small bowl, combine the salt, pepper, paprika, cumin, and coriander. Rub the chicken pieces with the seasoning mixture. In a heavy cast-iron skillet over medium heat, add the oil and brown the chicken pieces on all sides. Remove the chicken to a plate. In the same oil, stir-fry the onion, garlic, and green pepper for 3 minutes. In a deep stewing pot, add the chicken, onion, garlic, green pepper, water, plantains, okra, tomatoes, and lime juice. Cover and simmer until the chicken is very tender, about 15 minutes. Serve with white rice.

Makes 6 servings.

Shredded Beef with Tomatoes

❖❖❖

2 pounds dried tasajo beef (see note)
1 cup chopped onion
½ cup diced green bell pepper
2 tablespoons extra-virgin olive oil
8 garlic cloves, minced
¼ teaspoon dried oregano
¼ teaspoon ground cumin
2 bay leaves
½ cup tomato sauce
4 cups chopped ripe tomatoes
¼ cup tomato paste
Salt

Soak the beef overnight in a medium pot. Drain the water. Cover with fresh water, and boil the beef for an hour. Drain. Add more water, and boil another hour or two until the meat is tender and has released its saltiness. Drain and pound the beef into shreds. In a medium skillet, sauté the onion and pepper with the olive oil until soft. Add the garlic and sauté 30 seconds. Add the oregano, cumin, bay leaves, tomato sauce, tomatoes, and tomato paste, and stir. Add the beef, and cook until well done.

Makes 8 servings.

Note: Tasajo is Cuban cured dry beef, similar to beef jerky. You can find tasajo at a local Latin market.

Rice Pudding

❖❖❖

1½ cups medium-grain rice
4 cups water
⅔ teaspoon salt
4 tablespoons butter
1 teaspoon ground cinnamon, divided, plus extra for garnish
1 (10-ounce) can evaporated milk
⅔ cup sugar
1 teaspoon vanilla extract
Whipped cream, for garnish

Combine the rice, water, salt, butter, and ½ teaspoon cinnamon in a 2-quart saucepan. Cook over medium heat for 15 minutes. Slowly add in the evaporated milk and sugar. Reduce the heat to low, and cook the rice mixture until creamy. Remove the pan from the heat, and add the vanilla extract. Pour the rice pudding into eight individual serving cups, and chill for 1 hour before serving. Garnish with the whipped cream, and sprinkle with cinnamon.

Makes 8 servings.

Cuba Libre (Free Cuba)

3 (12-ounce) cans Coca-Cola
6 ounces lime juice
1 lime, cut into 6 wedges
12 ounces dark rum

Fill six tall glasses with ice cubes. To each glass, add 6 ounces Coca-Cola (half a can), 1 ounce lime juice, and 2 ounces dark rum. Stir. Garnish with a slice of lime on the rim.

Makes 6 servings.

Rum Collins

1 teaspoon sugar
¼ ounce lime juice
2 ounces light dry rum
4 ounces soda water
1 slice of lime

In an 8-ounce glass, dissolve the sugar in the lime juice. Add the light dry rum, and fill the glass with the soda water. Garnish with the slice of lime.

Makes 1 serving.

Mojito

4 fresh mint leaves
2 ounces lime juice
1 teaspoon powdered sugar
1 fresh mint sprig
2 ounces white rum
4 ounces club soda
Crushed ice

Place the 4 mint leaves in a glass, add the lime juice and powdered sugar, and gently grind the mint leaves. Add the sprig of mint, rum, club soda, and crushed ice, and stir.

Makes 1 serving.

Nonalcoholic Drinks

Most Cubans drink water or soft drinks, including drinks similar to Sprite and Coca-Cola, called Cachito and Tu Cola. One of the more interesting nonalcoholic drinks you're likely to run across is *guarapo,* the sweet juice of freshly pressed sugar cane. Another popular nonalcoholic drink is *malta.* Check with a local Latin market.

GLOBUS

France

OH, THE SIGHTS AND SOUNDS OF FRANCE! Laughter and hugs, smiles and kisses, pastries and lattes. You're in Paris. Gastronomy, or the art and science of good eating and drinking, has become a byword for France. Cooking is viewed as a major art form; a recipe is discussed as though it were a fine painting or celebrated piece of poetry. Charles de Gaulle reportedly said, "How can anyone be expected to govern a country that produces 265 different cheeses?"

France is a sophisticated powerhouse of architecture, art, cinema, cuisine, fashion, literature, music, and wine. Its countless attractions, enchanting culture, and pastoral countryside attract more visitors than any other country. France is one of the largest countries in Europe, and in many ways the most diverse in its cuisine, geography, and culture. The cuisine ranges from the truffles of Périgord to the apples and cream of Normandy, just as the landscape ranges from the majestic peaks of the French Alps to the coastlines of the French Riviera or of Brittany. All in all, you will find France to be a country of intellect, passion, and beauty.

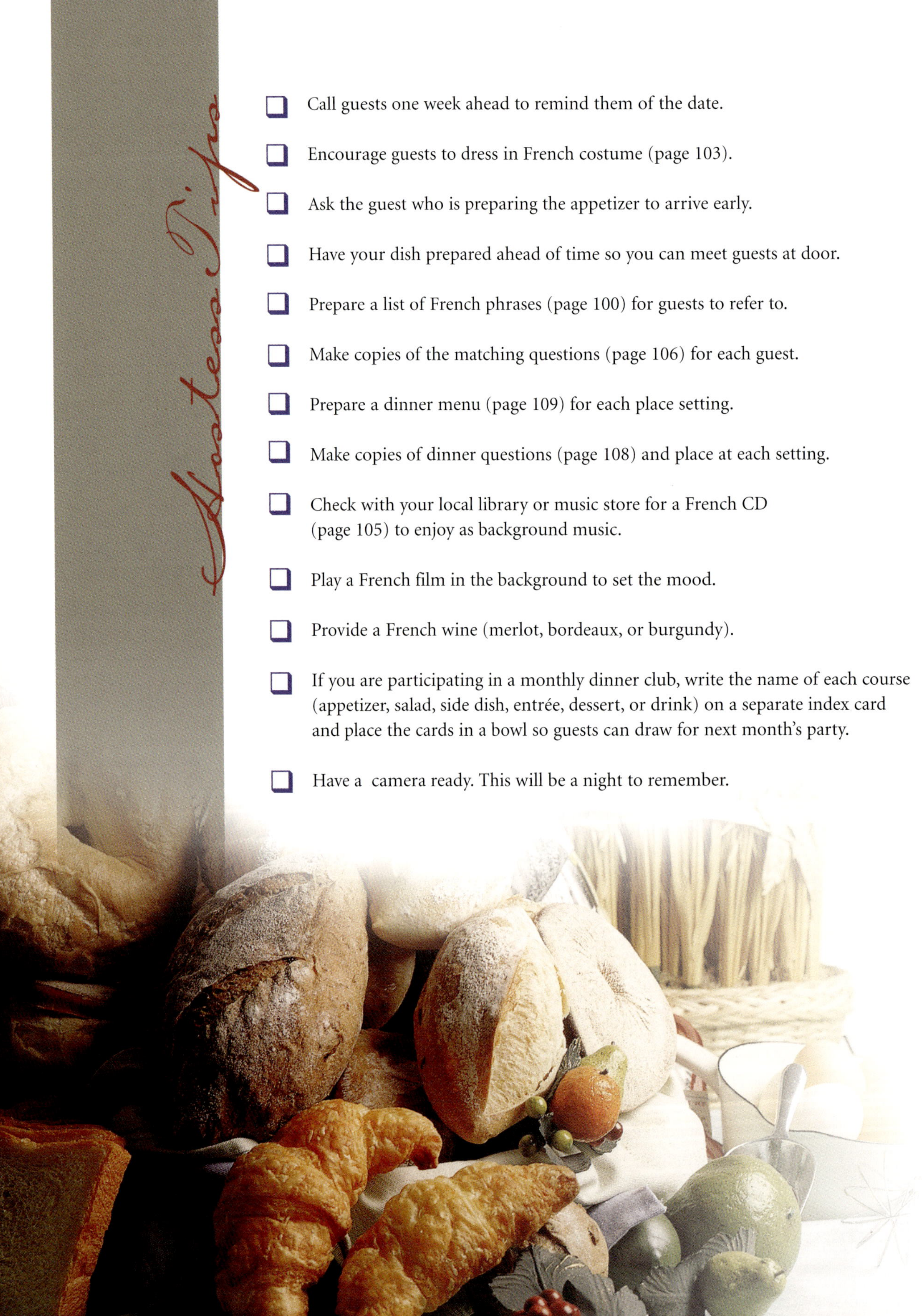

Hostess Tips

- ❑ Call guests one week ahead to remind them of the date.
- ❑ Encourage guests to dress in French costume (page 103).
- ❑ Ask the guest who is preparing the appetizer to arrive early.
- ❑ Have your dish prepared ahead of time so you can meet guests at door.
- ❑ Prepare a list of French phrases (page 100) for guests to refer to.
- ❑ Make copies of the matching questions (page 106) for each guest.
- ❑ Prepare a dinner menu (page 109) for each place setting.
- ❑ Make copies of dinner questions (page 108) and place at each setting.
- ❑ Check with your local library or music store for a French CD (page 105) to enjoy as background music.
- ❑ Play a French film in the background to set the mood.
- ❑ Provide a French wine (merlot, bordeaux, or burgundy).
- ❑ If you are participating in a monthly dinner club, write the name of each course (appetizer, salad, side dish, entrée, dessert, or drink) on a separate index card and place the cards in a bowl so guests can draw for next month's party.
- ❑ Have a camera ready. This will be a night to remember.

Before Dinner

Play French music in the background. Greet guests at the door with *bon soir*. Welcome them and take the food they have brought. Set a slow pace for a true French evening.

Invite guests to enjoy the appetizer, music, and conversation. Encourage French greetings to set the mood (page 100).

Ask guests to complete the matching section (page 106).

Offer wine or sparkling Evian with a slice of lemon.

Tell your guests about your costume or your favorite French designer. Ask if anyone has been to France. Have them share their stories.

Dinner

Seat your guests around the dinner table and begin by serving the main course.

Invite guests to read and discuss the dinner questions. As the host or hostess, you are the discussion leader. Encourage each person to participate.

After guests have completed the main course, collect the plates (remember to remove from the left side). Serve your guests their salad from the right. When salad is complete, collect plates and place cheese board on the table for all to enjoy.

Guests can use their bread plate for the cheese or you can offer them a new plate. Continue discussing dinner questions. After guests have enjoyed their cheese and wine, ask if they are ready for dessert.

After Dinner

Take coffee orders and serve before dessert. You may wish to buy or borrow a French press (a French coffee-brewing jug) for a true French experience. After coffee is served begin serving dessert.

Ask guests what they enjoyed most about the evening. Would they like to host a dinner party? If so, which country?

If you are participating in a monthly dinner club, invite guests to draw names of courses (appetizer, salad, side dish, entrée, dessert, or drink) from the bowl for next month's party, and decide who will host.

Greetings & Phrases

Hello (day)	*Bonjour*
Hello (evening)	*Bonsoir*
Hello (informal)	*Salut*
Welcome	*Bienvenu*
How are you?	*Comment ça va?*
I'm fine	*Ça va bien*
Please	*S'il vous plaît*
Thank you	*Merci*
Excuse me	*Pardon*
Yes	*Oui*
No	*Non*

Table Settings

The famous French gourmet, Anthelme Brillat-Savarin, believed that you are responsible for guests' happiness while they are in your home—and one way you can contribute to their happiness is setting a beautiful table.

The tablecloth and napkins should be white, or light in color to provide a simple background. The glasses should always be clear, to show the color of the wine. The dinner plates can be china or everyday, but should not be so ornate that they distract from the appearance of the food.

A few flowers will make your table look welcoming, but don't use large arrangements that create a barrier between your guests.

Candlelight adds to the intimacy of the evening. Use small votive candles.

Place knives on the right side of the plate, the blade turned toward the plate. Place forks on the left side with the napkin beside them. Place the soupspoon beside the fork, on the outside. Place teaspoon or dessert fork on the top, between the plate and the glasses. Glasses go on the right of the plate, in decreasing order of size.

If you are providing a bread plate, it goes to the left of the fork.

Place a breadbasket with various French breads on the table with butter.

At the end of the meal, plates are removed from the left and dessert plates are offered from the right.

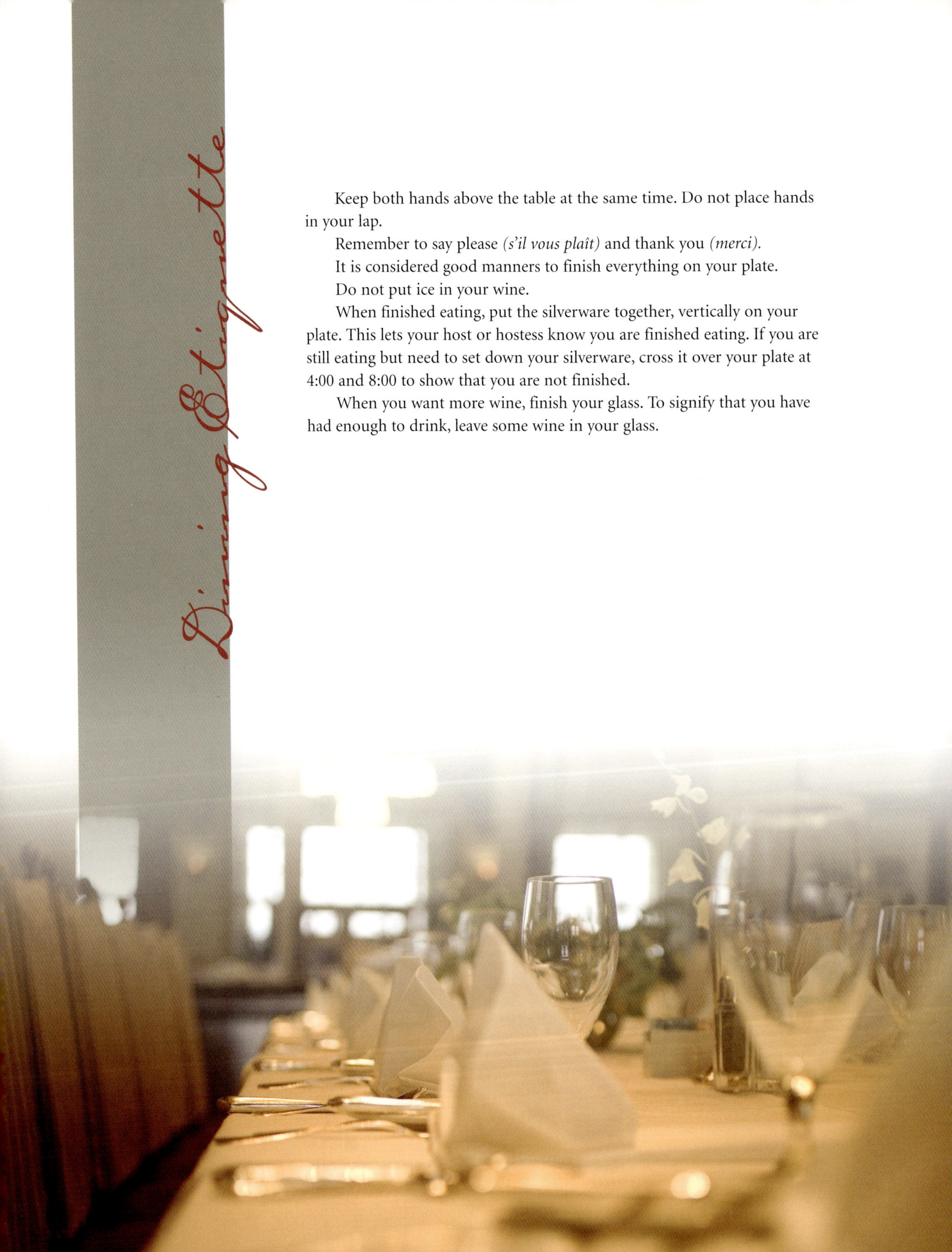

Dining Etiquette

Keep both hands above the table at the same time. Do not place hands in your lap.

Remember to say please *(s'il vous plaît)* and thank you *(merci)*.

It is considered good manners to finish everything on your plate.

Do not put ice in your wine.

When finished eating, put the silverware together, vertically on your plate. This lets your host or hostess know you are finished eating. If you are still eating but need to set down your silverware, cross it over your plate at 4:00 and 8:00 to show that you are not finished.

When you want more wine, finish your glass. To signify that you have had enough to drink, leave some wine in your glass.

Costume Ideas

Artist: (You could be Claude Monet, Pierre-Auguste Renoir, or Henri de Toulouse-Lautrec.) Wear a ruffled shirt, dress pants, and overcoat. Accessorize with a wig, cloak, beret, and painter's palette with brush.

Can-can dancer: Wear a black satin skirt with a sequined top. Accompany with a black leotard and black low heels. You can use a feather headpiece and feather shoulder wrap as accessories.

Coco Chanel: Gabrielle Chanel, better known as Coco, not only made "black" what it is today, but popularized the wardrobe staple that few women can live without—the little black dress. Wear a dress with simple lines, slightly above the knee. Accessorize with jewelry, a clutch, and heels.

French maid: This is based on the typical nineteenth-century maid's black and white afternoon uniform. The dress should have puffed shoulders, short sleeves, a white lace collar, and white lace cuffs. Accessories include a frill worn in the hair, a feather duster, and black stockings and shoes. Check with your local costume shop.

Marie Antoinette: This young French queen was executed during the French Revolution in 1793. Wear a coat-like "sack" dress, made with pleats at the back that hangs unfitted from the shoulders. Accessorize with a hoop skirt, wig, and eyeglasses. Try your local costume shop.

France Film Festival

Chocolat
Starring Johnny Depp, Juliette Binoche, and Judi Dench
Directed by Lasse Hallstrom, 2000

French Kiss
Starring Meg Ryan, Kevin Kline, and Timothy Hutton
Directed by Lawrence Kasdan, 1995

Marie Antoinette
Starring Kirsten Dunst, Jason Schwartzman, and Judy Davis
Directed by Sofia Coppola, 2006

Prêt-á-Porter
Starring Sophia Loren, Kim Basinger, Julia Roberts, and Tim Robbins
Directed by Robert Altman, 1994

Les Miserables
Starring Uma Thurman and Liam Neeson
Directed by Bille August, 1998

Moulin Rouge
Starring Nicole Kidman and Ewan McGregor.
Directed by Baz Luhrmann, 2001

La Vie en Rose
Starring Marion Cotillard, Gérard Depardieu, and Sylvie Testud
Directed by Olivier Dahan, 2007

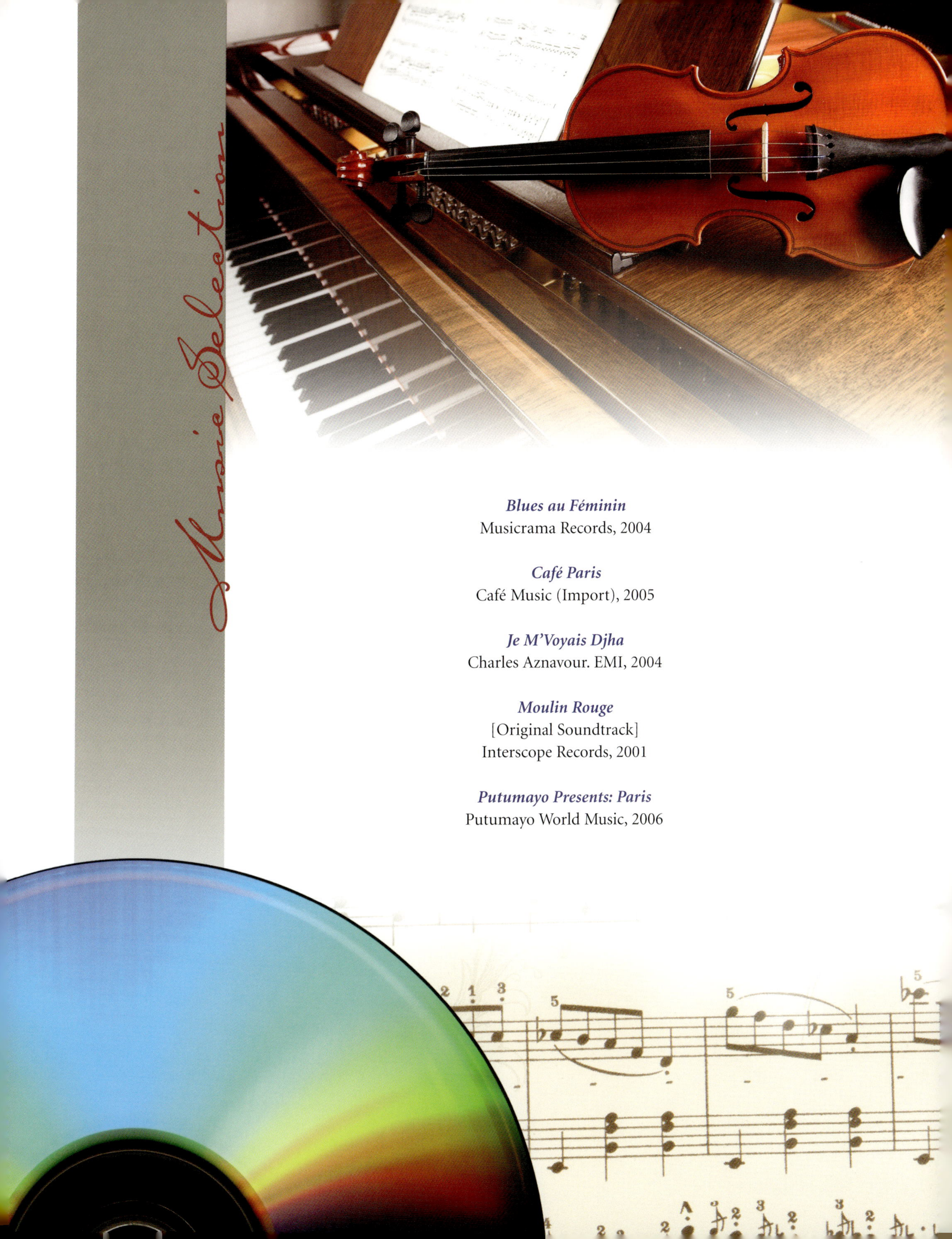

Music Selection

Blues au Féminin
Musicrama Records, 2004

Café Paris
Café Music (Import), 2005

Je M'Voyais Djha
Charles Aznavour. EMI, 2004

Moulin Rouge
[Original Soundtrack]
Interscope Records, 2001

Putumayo Presents: Paris
Putumayo World Music, 2006

Icebreaker: Matching

Match the person on the left with his or her occupation on the right.

1. _____ Napoleon Bonaparte	a. explorer
2. _____ Jean Calvin	b. military leader
3. _____ Jacque Cartier	c. emperor
4. _____ Charlemagne	d. saint
5. _____ Victor Hugo	e. writer
6. _____ Jeanne d'Arc	f. painter
7. _____ Charles de Gaulle	g. religious leader
8. _____ Pierre Auguste Renoir	h. ruler
9. _____ Brigitte Bardot	i. singer
10. _____ Jacques Cousteau	j. inventor, scientist
11. _____ Gustave Eiffel	k. actress
12. _____ Gipsy Kings	l. founder of modern Olympics
13. _____ Louis Pasteur	m. architect
14. _____ Pierre de Coubertin	n. oceanographer

ANSWER KEY

1–c; 2–g; 3–a; 4–h; 5–e; 6–d; 7–b; 8–f; 9–k; 10–n; 11–m; 12–i; 13–j; 14–l

Mirabelles are French fruits similar to plums, the size of a golf ball. They are light yellow and somewhat sour. They are very rare and grow only in the south of France and in the Alsace region. They can be harvested only during a one-month period in the summer. Because of their rarity, they are mostly used in fine patisseries and to make alcohol.

In Paris you are never more than four hundred meters from a subway station.

Avignon was once home of the Papacy.

The name France is from the Latin word *Francia,* meaning country of the Franks. The Franks were a Germanic people who conquered the area during the fifth century.

Foie gras (fat liver) is a great gastronomic delicacy in France. It is made from goose liver and marinated in cognac, often served with expensive truffles.

Truffles are edible mushrooms that grow underground on or near the roots of trees.

Dinner Questions

1. France is filled with historical sites and beautiful towns. If you could visit only one place in France, which would it be? The Eiffel Tower, the Louvre, Notre Dame, the French Riviera, Monet's Giverny, or the French countryside

2. France is known for its gourmet foods. Which is your weakness? Cheese, bread, pastries, chocolate, or wine?

3. Who do you identify with most?
   Jeanne d'Arc (visionary) Charles de Gaulle (leader)
   Claude Monet (artist) Louis Pasteur (inventor)

4. The Eiffel Tower is 984 feet high. What is the highest structure you have been to?

5. The national motto is *Liberté, Egalité, Fraternité* (Liberty, Equality, Fraternity). Which of these ideals do you think is most important? Why?

6. The French flag has the same colors as the U.S. Flag. In what order do they appear? Which way do the stripes appear? Is there an emblem on the flag?

7. Famous French directors have included Francois Truffaut *(The 400 Blows, Jules and Jim),* Louis Malle *(Vanya on 42nd Street, My Dinner with Andre),* Jean-Luc Goddard *(Breathless),* and Luc Besson *(La Femme Nikita, The Professional).* Which of their films have you seen? What did you think of these films? Who are your favorite French directors or French actors?

8. The French are known for having strong philosophical viewpoints. Read and discuss the following French quotes. Think like a philosopher.
   Judge a man by his questions rather than by his answers. —*Voltaire*
   Love is like an hourglass, with the heart filling up as the brain empties. —*Jules Renard*
   Life has taught us that love does not consist in gazing at each other, but in looking outward together in the same direction. — *Antoine de Saint-Exupery*
   Come to the edge, he said. They said: We are afraid. Come to the edge, he said. They came. He pushed them and they flew. —*Guillaume Apollinaire*

ANSWER KEY
6. Blue, white and red; vertical; no,

Appetizer	Salt and Pepper Shrimp
Soup	French Onion Soup
Salad	Endive, Radicchio, and Pecan Salad
Side Dish	Rosemary Potato Wedges
Entrée	Spicy Rib Roast
Cheese	French Cheese Board
Dessert	Baked Peaches with Almonds
Drinks	Orange-Flavored Coffee

Salt and Pepper Shrimp

2 tablespoons olive oil
1 pound (43 to 50 count) shrimp, peeled and deveined
½ teaspoon coarse sea salt
1½ tablespoons mixed cracked peppercorns

In a medium skillet, heat the oil and add the shrimp, tossing until they are fully coated with the oil. Immediately add the salt and peppercorns. Keep tossing until the shrimp turn pink and curl. Do not overcook. Place the shrimp on a plate with toothpicks, and serve immediately.

Makes 8 servings.

French Onion Soup

4 tablespoons butter
3 cups finely sliced onions
⅓ cup all-purpose flour
2 garlic cloves, finely chopped
1 cup white wine
8 cups beef broth
1 bay leaf
2 fresh thyme sprigs
6 slices stale baguette
⅔ cup finely grated Gruyère cheese

In a 3-quart heavy saucepan, melt the butter, and add the onions. Cook over low heat, stirring occasionally until the onions begin to caramelize. Add the flour and garlic to the pan, and stir continuously for 2 minutes. Gradually blend in the wine and beef broth, stirring continuously; bring to a boil. Add the bay leaf and thyme. Cover the pan and simmer for 25 minutes. Remove the bay leaf and thyme sprigs.

Preheat the grill or broiler. Toast the baguette slices on the grill or broiler. Divide the toasted baguettes among six warmed bowls, and ladle the soup over the top. Sprinkle the soup with the grated cheese, and place the bowls under the broiler until the cheese melts. Serve while hot.

Makes 6 servings.

Salad

Endive, Radicchio, and Pecan Salad

2 heads Belgian endives
1 small head radicchio
1½ cups peeled and shredded carrots
1 cup chopped pecans

Dressing:
1 tablespoon Dijon mustard
½ teaspoon salt
½ teaspoon freshly ground pepper
1 tablespoon sherry vinegar
3 tablespoons extra-virgin olive oil

Cut 1½ inches from the root end of the endive and the radicchio heads, and cut these root end pieces into ½-inch chunks. Combine the root end chunks with the shredded carrots and nuts in a large bowl. For the dressing, combine in a small bowl the mustard, salt, pepper, vinegar, and olive oil. Whisk until thoroughly combined. Add the dressing to the endive and radicchio pieces, carrots, and nuts. Toss well. Arrange the radicchio leaves attractively on the plates, and spoon the dressing mixture into the center of the leaves. arrange the endive leaf tips so they stand, pointed tips up, next to one another all around the dressed salad. Serve immediately.

Makes 6 servings.

Rosemary Potato Wedges

❖❖❖

6 medium russet potatoes, not peeled
3 tablespoons olive oil
¼ cup chopped fresh parsley
2 garlic cloves, minced
1 tablespoon chopped fresh rosemary
1 teaspoon dried oregano
1 teaspoon coarse sea salt

Preheat the oven to 425 degrees. Cut the potatoes lengthwise into 8 wedges. Combine the potatoes and oil in a large airtight bag; toss well. Using two large baking sheets, spread the wedges out in a single layer. Bake until the potatoes are a deep golden brown, turning them frequently, for 40 minutes. Transfer the potatoes to a large bowl. Toss with the parsley, garlic, rosemary, oregano, and sea salt.

Makes 6 servings.

Sautéed Green Beans and Shallots

❖❖❖

3 cups water
2 pounds haricots verts (very thin French green beans)
2 tablespoons unsalted butter
1½ tablespoons peanut oil
⅔ cup peeled and minced shallots
1 teaspoon salt
1 teaspoon freshly ground pepper

Bring the water to a boil in a large saucepan. Rinse the beans, and add them to the boiling water. Cook, covered, over high heat for 8 minutes, or until the beans are tender, but still firm to the bite. Drain the beans and let cool. When ready to serve, blend the butter and oil in a large skillet over medium heat. Add the shallots, and sauté for 15 seconds. Add the beans, salt, and pepper, and continue to sauté for about 2 minutes, or until the beans are heated through and evenly covered with the cooked shallots.

Makes 8 servings.

Tomato and Cheese Quiche

5 tablespoons extra-virgin olive oil, divided
5 large tomatoes, halved, cored, and seeded
1 tablespoon fresh thyme
2 garlic cloves, minced
1 teaspoon salt
1 teaspoon pepper
1 large pie crust, defrosted if frozen
1 cup grated provolone cheese
1 cup grated mozzarella cheese
½ cup soft goat cheese
2 tablespoons chopped fresh basil
2 large eggs
¼ cup whole cream
¼ cup freshly grated Parmesan cheese

Preheat the oven to 325 degrees. Brush a baking sheet with 1 tablespoon oil. Place the tomato halves on the baking sheet. Sprinkle the thyme and garlic over the tomatoes; drizzle the remaining olive oil over the tomatoes. Sprinkle lightly with the salt and pepper. Bake the tomatoes in the oven until they are slightly dried but still soft, about 1½ hours. When done, set the tomatoes aside to cool. Raise the oven temperature to 375 degrees, and bake the crust until the edges are golden. Remove from the oven, and cool for 10 minutes. Reduce the oven temperature to 350 degrees. In a medium bowl, mix the provolone cheese, mozzarella cheese, goat cheese, and basil. Add the eggs and cream, and stir until the mixture is well blended. Spread the cheese filling evenly into the crust. Arrange the tomato halves on the filling. Sprinkle the Parmesan cheese evenly over the top. Bake until the filling is puffed and set, about 25 minutes. When done, let cool for 5 minutes.

Makes 6 servings.

Simple Chicken Cordon Bleu

8 skinless, boneless chicken breasts
1½ teaspoons salt
1½ teaspoons pepper
4 tablespoons unsalted butter
16 spinach leaves, trimmed
8 thin slices deli ham
8 slices Gruyère cheese

Preheat the broiler. Season each breast with the salt and pepper. In a heavy skillet, heat the butter. Gently pound the chicken breasts to ¼-inch thickness. Place the chicken in the melted butter, and cook until the undersides are golden, about 2 minutes. Remove from the heat, turn the chicken over, and top each breast with 2 spinach leaves, 1 slice ham, and 1 slice cheese. Broil 3 inches from the heat until the cheese is melted, about 2 minutes.

Makes 8 servings.

Spicy Rib Roast

❖❖❖

Rub:

4 large garlic cloves, minced
3 tablespoons minced fresh ginger
2 teaspoons sugar
2 tablespoons soy sauce
½ teaspoon cayenne pepper
1 teaspoon dry mustard
½ teaspoon paprika

Roast:

1 (3-rib) standing rib beef roast (about 7 pounds)
½ cup water

Preheat the oven to 400 degrees. Combine the garlic, ginger, sugar, soy sauce, cayenne pepper, dry mustard, and paprika in a blender, and blend until smooth. Rub the mixture on the top and sides of the roast. In a small roasting pan, place the roast meat side up, and cook for 30 minutes. Turn the meat, bones side up, and cook for another 30 minutes. Remove the roast from the oven. Place the roast on a platter, discarding the fat that has accumulated in the roasting pan. Add ½ cup water to the drippings, and mix well. Place the roast back in the roasting pan and in the oven for at least 20 to 30 minutes before carving.

Makes 6 to 8 servings.

Filet Mignon in Brandy Cream Sauce

❖❖❖

8 (2-inch thick) beef tenderloin steaks
Freshly ground pepper
4 tablespoons unsalted butter, divided
2 tablespoons olive oil
Salt
4 medium shallots, minced
4 tablespoons brandy
1 cup whipping cream
2 teaspoons Dijon mustard
Fresh parsley and chives

Sprinkle the steaks generously with the pepper over both sides. Melt 2 tablespoons butter and the 2 tablespoons oil in a large skillet over medium-high heat. Salt the steaks on one side, and add to the skillet salted side down. Sear the steaks for 2 minutes. Salt the tops, turn, and sear the second side for 2 minutes. Lower the heat to medium-low, and cook to desired doneness, turning occasionally (cook 8 to 10 minutes for medium rare). Remove from the skillet.

Discard the drippings from the skillet. Add the remaining 2 tablespoons butter, and melt over medium heat. Add the shallots, and cook for 2 to 3 minutes, stirring. Remove from the heat, and add the brandy. Return to the heat, and bring to a boil. Boil until the liquid is almost gone, scraping the bottom of the skillet. Add the cream, and boil until the sauce thickens, about 3 to 5 minutes. Add the mustard and any juices exuded from the steaks. Season to taste, and spoon the juices over the steaks. Garnish with the parsley and chives.

Makes 8 servings.
Recipe by Staff Fieldhouse

French Cheese Board

❖❖❖

Beaufort
Brie
Camembert
Fourme d'Ambert
Munster
Roquefort

Arrange the cheeses, or a selection of your favorites, on a serving board with a knife.

Easy Banana Foster

6 tablespoons butter
1½ cups light brown sugar, firmly packed
2 tablespoons dark rum flavor
1 teaspoon ground cinnamon
½ teaspoon ground cloves
6 ripe medium bananas, peeled, sliced in half lengthwise and crosswise
Vanilla ice cream, as desired
½ cup chopped pecans, divided, optional

In a large skillet over medium heat, melt the butter, and add the brown sugar; stir until the sugar completely dissolves. Add the rum flavor, cinnamon, and cloves while stirring. Add the bananas to the skillet, spooning the sauce over the bananas. Simmer for 4 minutes. Spoon the sauce and banana pieces over individual servings of vanilla ice cream, and top each serving with the pecans, if desired.

Makes 6 servings.

Baked Peaches with Almonds

6 firm, ripe peaches, cut in half and pitted
2 cups water
½ cup maple syrup
1½ tablespoons brown sugar
1 tablespoon unsalted butter, broken into pieces
⅔ cup whole almonds, not blanched
Ice cream, optional

Preheat the oven to 350 degrees. In a baking dish, arrange the peaches cut side down in one layer. Add the water, maple syrup, brown sugar, butter, and almonds. Place the baking dish on a cookie tray, and place the tray in the oven for 40 minutes. Turn the peach halves so they are skin side down, and cook for another 15 minutes. The juice around the peaches should look syrupy. Turn the peaches carefully in the syrup so they are skin side up again, and cool them to room temperature. Serve two peach halves per person with some of the syrup. Top with ice cream if desired.

Makes 6 servings.

Orange-Flavored Coffee

8 scoops ground Italian roast coffee
3 tablespoons grated orange zest
6 cups boiling water
4 tablespoons brown sugar
1¼ cups prepared whipped cream
1 cup dark chocolate-covered espresso beans
½ teaspoon ground cinnamon

Place the coffee and orange zest in a French press or a filtered coffee maker. Pour the boiling water over the coffee, and let stand for 4 minutes if using a French coffee press. Pour the coffee into six cups. Add a little of the brown sugar to the coffee if desired. Top the coffee with the whipped cream, several espresso beans, and a sprinkle of cinnamon.

Makes 6 servings.

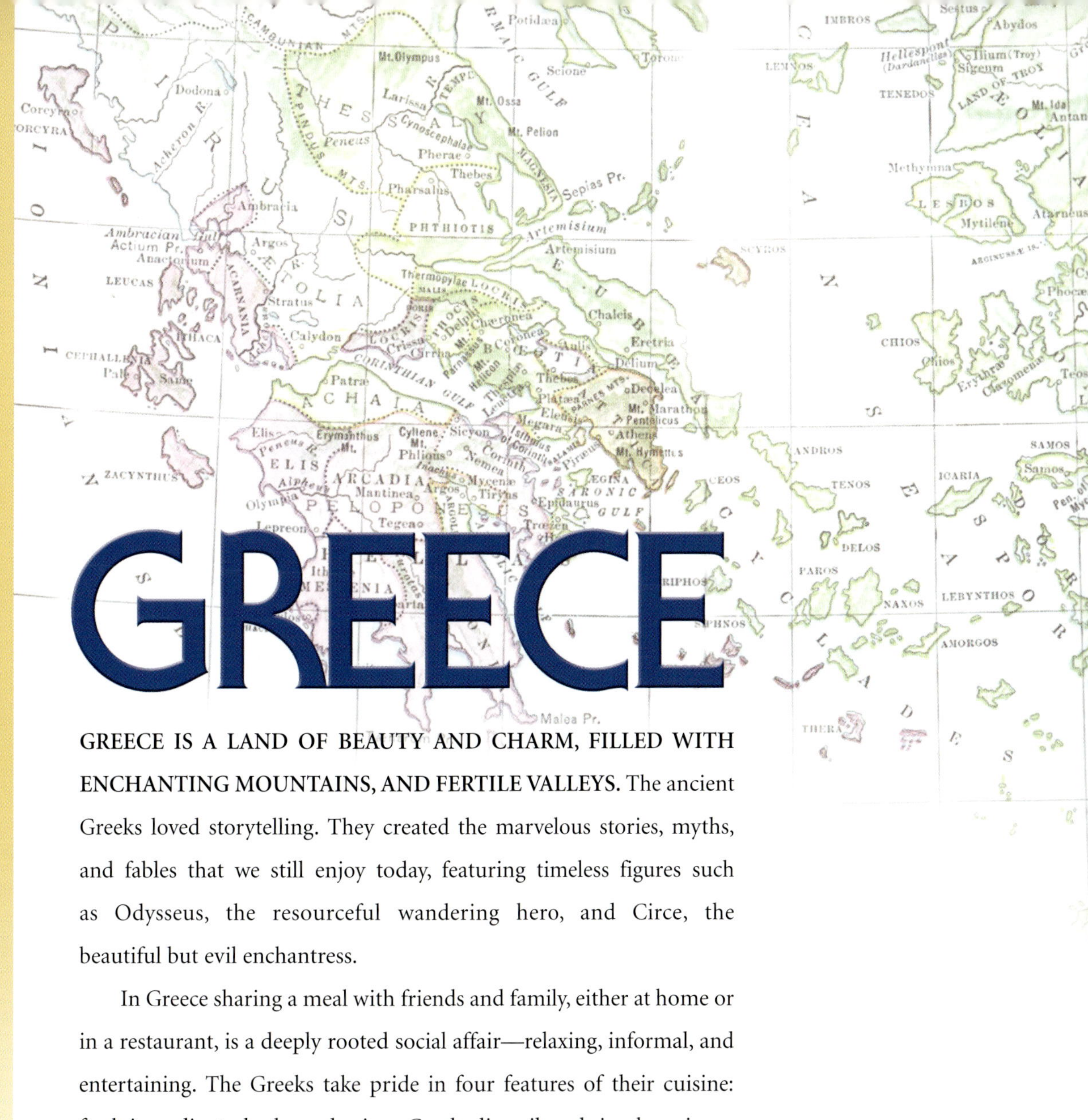

GREECE

GREECE IS A LAND OF BEAUTY AND CHARM, FILLED WITH ENCHANTING MOUNTAINS, AND FERTILE VALLEYS. The ancient Greeks loved storytelling. They created the marvelous stories, myths, and fables that we still enjoy today, featuring timeless figures such as Odysseus, the resourceful wandering hero, and Circe, the beautiful but evil enchantress.

In Greece sharing a meal with friends and family, either at home or in a restaurant, is a deeply rooted social affair—relaxing, informal, and entertaining. The Greeks take pride in four features of their cuisine: fresh ingredients, herbs and spices, Greek olive oil, and simple recipes.

Greece and its sun-kissed isles offer a tantalizing cuisine that is fresh and fragrant, served with warmth and vitality. The Greeks' zest for the good life and love of simple, well-seasoned foods is reflected at the table. It is an unpretentious cuisine that makes the most of its surroundings. It is a cuisine entrenched in history and punctuated by the cultures of its neighbors: Turkey, Macedonia, Albania, and Cyprus.

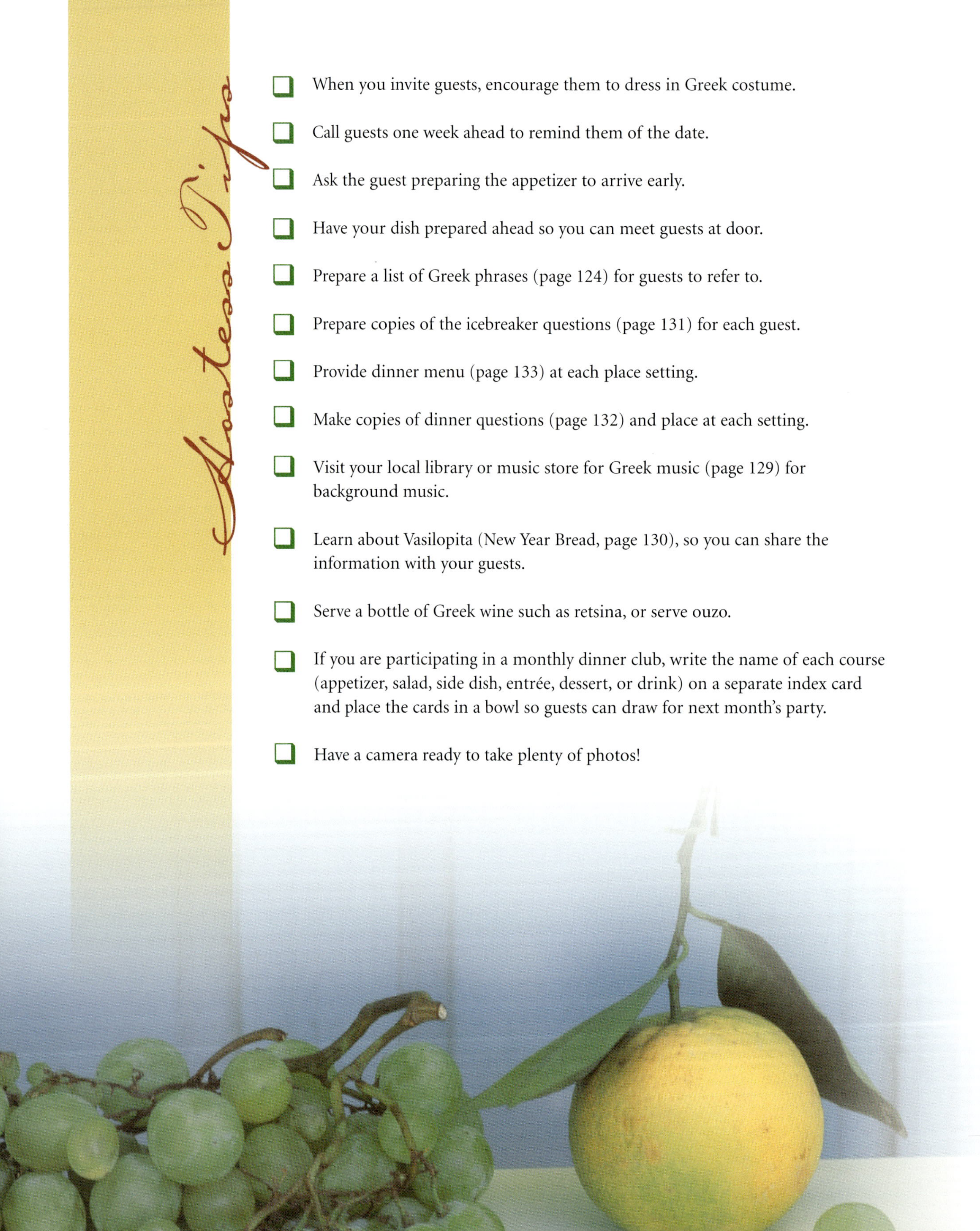

Hostess Tips

- When you invite guests, encourage them to dress in Greek costume.
- Call guests one week ahead to remind them of the date.
- Ask the guest preparing the appetizer to arrive early.
- Have your dish prepared ahead so you can meet guests at door.
- Prepare a list of Greek phrases (page 124) for guests to refer to.
- Prepare copies of the icebreaker questions (page 131) for each guest.
- Provide dinner menu (page 133) at each place setting.
- Make copies of dinner questions (page 132) and place at each setting.
- Visit your local library or music store for Greek music (page 129) for background music.
- Learn about Vasilopita (New Year Bread, page 130), so you can share the information with your guests.
- Serve a bottle of Greek wine such as retsina, or serve ouzo.
- If you are participating in a monthly dinner club, write the name of each course (appetizer, salad, side dish, entrée, dessert, or drink) on a separate index card and place the cards in a bowl so guests can draw for next month's party.
- Have a camera ready to take plenty of photos!

Before Dinner

Greet your guests at the door with *yassou* and a double cheek kiss.

Have Greek music playing in the background.

Welcome guests and invite them to enjoy appetizers, music, and conversation. Place appetizers on the center of the table to be shared by everyone. Provide bread or pita if serving dips. Greek appetizers are often salty and very tart, so accompany them with ouzo and other drinks.

Participate in icebreaker questions, and share the story of the Vasilopita bread. Discuss costume selection with the guests.

Dinner

Ask guests to remain standing until each guest has been invited to have a seat. Serve all courses at the same time.

Invite guests to read and discuss the dinner questions. As the host or hostess, you are the discussion leader. Encourage each person to participate.

After Dinner

Dessert can be fresh fruit or baklava, the popular syrup-drenched pastry. Greeks enjoy a cup of Turkish coffee with their dessert.

Ask guests what they enjoyed most about the evening. Would they like to host a dinner party? If so, what country?

If you are participating in a monthly dinner club, invite guests to draw names of courses (appetizer, salad, side dish, entrée, dessert, or drink) from a bowl for next month's party, and decide who will host.

Greetings & Phrases

Hello	*Yassou*
Good morning	*Kalimera*
Good evening	*Kalispera*
How are you?	*Ti kanete?*
Please	*Parakalo*
Thank you	*Efcharisto*
Excuse me	*Signomi*
Yes	*Nai*
No	*Ochi*
Good-bye	*Andio*

Dining Etiquette

It is the responsibility of the host or hostess to introduce each guest to one another.

Hospitality goes hand in hand with self-esteem. The Greek hostess may be insulted if you only take one helping of what is offered.

Using fingers instead of forks and knives is very common. Eating meat with a fork and knife is considered to be missing out on the most enjoyable part of the dining experience. It is up to you whether to use utensils for this meal.

When pouring wine, do not fill the glass to the brim: one-half to three-quarters is acceptable.

The oldest person and guest of honor are generally served first.

If using utensils, the fork is held in the left hand and the knife in the right while eating.

Platters are all placed on the table at the same time. Pass dishes with your right hand only. Expect to be offered second and even third helpings. It is polite to finish everything on your plate.

If you are using utensils with your meal and would like more to eat, simply cross your knife over your fork. To indicate you have finished eating, lay your knife and fork parallel across the right side of your plate.

Say good-bye to each person individually when leaving.

Greek Meal

Appetizers play an important role on the Greek table. The most common Greek appetizers are dips or spreads such as *taramasalata* (fish roe salad), *melitzanosalata* (eggplant salad), or *tzatziki* (a yogurt, cucumber, and garlic dip), all of which are served with pita or white bread. *Dolmades* (stuffed grape leaves) are also popular appetizers. Main courses can be lamb, stuffed tomatoes, *souvlaki* (huge chunks of meat on a skewer with vegetables and served with rice), or *moussaka* (the Greek version of lasagna). Greek salads are perfect appetizers. They consist of cucumbers, tomatoes, black olives, feta cheese, and lots of olive oil.

Greek Gods and Goddesses

Apollo:	God of music, healing, light, and truth.
Aphrodite:	Goddess of love and beauty.
Artemis:	Goddess of the moon, hunting, and archery, and the twin sister of Apollo.
Athena:	Goddess of wisdom, crafts, and defensive warfare, and the patron of Athens.
Demeter:	Goddess of agriculture, grain, harvest, and earth.
Hephaestus:	God of fire and the forge; god of smiths and weavers.
Hera:	Goddess of marriage, family, and motherhood, and queen of the gods. She is Zeus's jealous wife.
Hermes:	God of thieves and commerce, guide for the dead to go to underworld, and Zeus's messenger. Wears winged sandals and hat, and carries a magic wand.
Zeus:	King of the gods; husband of Hera.

Costume Ideas

Chiton: This garment was worn by both male and female. It's made from a rectangular piece of fabric six to nine feet long and three to four feet wide, and can vary from mid-thigh to full length. It is tubular and fastened at the shoulders with the extra material pulled up over the belt, producing a blouse-like effect. It is fastened at the top with pins on either side of the neck opening, giving the appearance of sleeves. Accessorize with a garland crown, a scepter, and sandals.

Himation: This garment can be worn draped around the body in a variety of ways. Start with a rectangular piece of fabric twelve to fifteen feet in length, or you can use a sheet. Run it from the right shoulder across the chest and under the left arm, then up over the back to the right shoulder again. The remainder of the fabric hangs loosely on the ground. Use a gold cord as belt and crisscross it several times around, starting below the chest and tying it at the waist. Accessorize with sandals, a garland crown, and a scepter. These items can be found at your local costume shop.

Toga: The draped fashion of the tunic was known as the toga. It was usually white and worn for special occasions; you may have seen drawings of Socrates, Plato, or Aristotle wearing togas. You will need four yards of fabric. Begin by placing one end over the left shoulder so that it flows in front of you. Next, wrap the fabric around your body and back under your right arm. Drape the remaining fabric over your shoulder. Women may wish to wear a tube top underneath. Accessorize with sandals and a garland crown.

Tunic: The male gods wore this garment. Sew two large T-shaped pieces of fabric together. The tunic should be a bit longer in the front than the back. Drape at waist with leather belt or gold cord. Accessorize with sandals, a garland crown, and a cape.

Peplos: This garment, worn by female goddesses, features an overfold or drape. Each garment is sewn to fit the size of the individual; it should be as long as your height from shoulder to ankle plus twelve to fifteen inches for draping. It is belted at your natural waist to give a narrow silhouette. Accessorize with a belt (called a girdle), which could be an elaborate woven cord or even gold embossed leather. Wear a garland crown and sandals.

Eleni
Starring Kate Nelligan and John Malkovich
Directed by Peter Yates, 1985

The Greek Tycoon
Starring Anthony Quinn and Jacqueline Bisset
Directed by J. Lee Thomson, 1978

My Big Fat Greek Wedding
Starring Nia Vardalos, Michael Constantine,
and John Corbett
Directed by Joel Zwick, 2002

Never on Sunday
Starring Melina Mercouri, Jules Dassin, and Giorgos Foundas
Directed by Jules Dassin, 1960

Shirley Valentine
Starring Pauline Collins, Tom Conti, and Julia McKenzie
Directed by Lewis Gilbert, 1989

Zorba the Greek
Starring Anthony Quinn, Alan Bates, and Irene Papas
Directed by Mihalis Kakogiannis, 1964

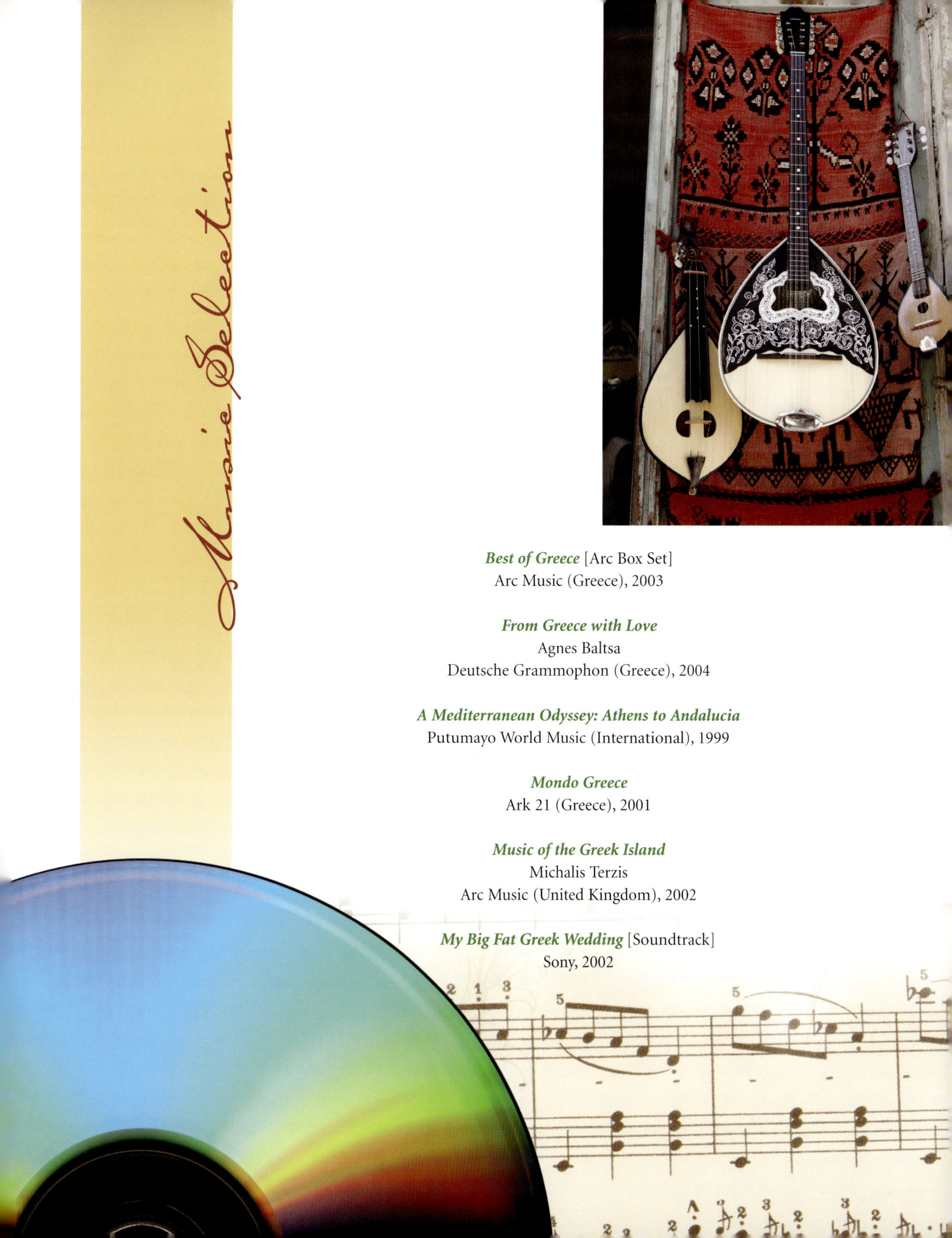

Music Selection

Best of Greece [Arc Box Set]
Arc Music (Greece), 2003

From Greece with Love
Agnes Baltsa
Deutsche Grammophon (Greece), 2004

A Mediterranean Odyssey: Athens to Andalucia
Putumayo World Music (International), 1999

Mondo Greece
Ark 21 (Greece), 2001

Music of the Greek Island
Michalis Terzis
Arc Music (United Kingdom), 2002

My Big Fat Greek Wedding [Soundtrack]
Sony, 2002

Traditional Food and Drink

New Year's Bread

Vasilopita, or New Year's Bread, is made to honor the good acts of St. Basil. To guarantee that the needy would be provided for, he asked the ladies of the church to bake bread and place a coin in each loaf. The tradition is to cut the bread at midnight on New Year's Eve. The person who finds the coin will have luck in the new year. Often the coin is mixed in with the dough and baked with the bread. But many believe that it is undesirable to bake a coin in the bread because of the nickel content found in coins today. Instead, you can make a small slice at the base of the loaf after baking and insert the coin, or wrap it in foil as described in the recipe in this chapter.

What Is Ouzo?

Ouzo is an anise-flavored liqueur that is an integral part of the Greek culture—its consumption is as much a philosophy and an art form as enjoyment. Ouzo is made from a combination of pressed grapes, herbs, and berries mixed with various ingredients, including mint, wintergreen, hazelnut, and fennel. Hundreds of varieties of ouzo are available.

The anise oil dissolves and becomes invisible when combined with alcohol so that ouzo is completely clear. The anise oil causes a bold licorice flavor.

Ouzo should not be consumed straight but mixed with water or ice cubes, which lowers the percentage of alcohol and causes the anise oils to slowly transform into white crystals. Ouzo is to be taken slowly and can be served with nuts, olives, or appetizers such as calamari, fried cheeses, or blackened octopus. These items can be found in some grocery stores or ethnic markets.

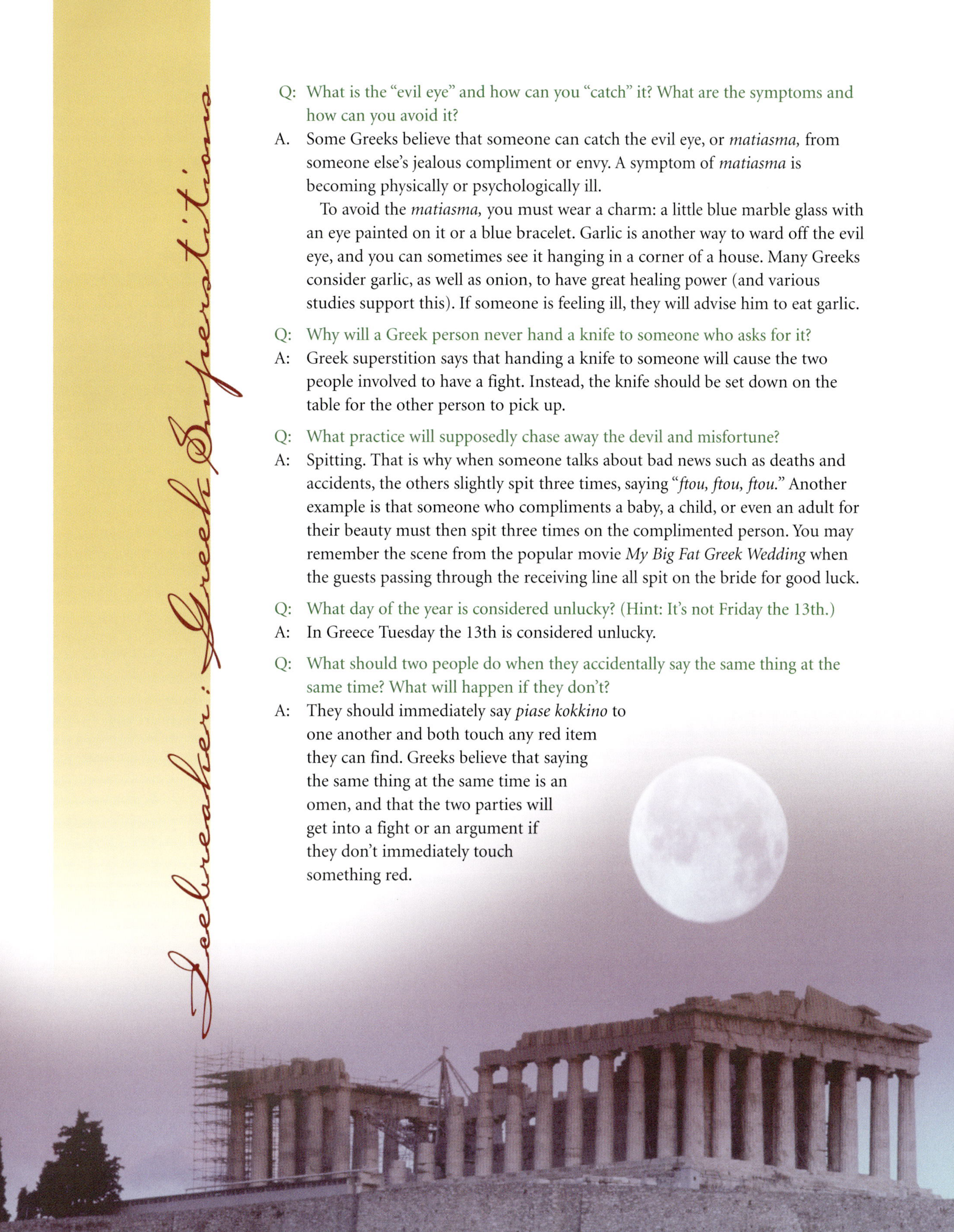

Icebreaker: Greek Superstitions

Q: What is the "evil eye" and how can you "catch" it? What are the symptoms and how can you avoid it?

A. Some Greeks believe that someone can catch the evil eye, or *matiasma,* from someone else's jealous compliment or envy. A symptom of *matiasma* is becoming physically or psychologically ill.

To avoid the *matiasma,* you must wear a charm: a little blue marble glass with an eye painted on it or a blue bracelet. Garlic is another way to ward off the evil eye, and you can sometimes see it hanging in a corner of a house. Many Greeks consider garlic, as well as onion, to have great healing power (and various studies support this). If someone is feeling ill, they will advise him to eat garlic.

Q: Why will a Greek person never hand a knife to someone who asks for it?

A: Greek superstition says that handing a knife to someone will cause the two people involved to have a fight. Instead, the knife should be set down on the table for the other person to pick up.

Q: What practice will supposedly chase away the devil and misfortune?

A: Spitting. That is why when someone talks about bad news such as deaths and accidents, the others slightly spit three times, saying "*ftou, ftou, ftou.*" Another example is that someone who compliments a baby, a child, or even an adult for their beauty must then spit three times on the complimented person. You may remember the scene from the popular movie *My Big Fat Greek Wedding* when the guests passing through the receiving line all spit on the bride for good luck.

Q: What day of the year is considered unlucky? (Hint: It's not Friday the 13th.)

A: In Greece Tuesday the 13th is considered unlucky.

Q: What should two people do when they accidentally say the same thing at the same time? What will happen if they don't?

A: They should immediately say *piase kokkino* to one another and both touch any red item they can find. Greeks believe that saying the same thing at the same time is an omen, and that the two parties will get into a fight or an argument if they don't immediately touch something red.

1. The hit 2002 movie *My Big Fat Greek Wedding,* written by and starring Nia Vardalos apparently was based on her Greek family. Which character do you most identify with?
    - Mother (protective)
    - Father (controlling)
    - Sister (predictable)
    - Brother (stuck in tradition)
    - Cousin (wild and crazy)

2. Greeks celebrate the birthday of the saint they were named after. Who were you named after?

3. The Phoenicians were traders from Lebanon who had set up colonies throughout the Mediterranean, including Cyprus. They were the first people to have a phonetic alphabet. The Greeks learned and used the alphabet. Can you say the Greek alphabet?

4. Four countries surround Greece. Can you name three of them? Which would you like to visit? Why?

5. The Trojan War was a long, hard battle fought between the Trojans and the Greeks that lasted ten years with no end in sight. According to legend, Odysseus hollowed out a giant wooden horse and filled it with Greek soldiers; when the Trojans pulled the horse inside the city, the soldiers emerged and seized the city. What war heroes or military figures are you familiar with?

6. In Greece most restaurants have a cover charge that includes the table setting and a small basket of bread. Would you tip less if you had to pay a cover charge?

7. Most dining establishments in Greece do not open for dinner until 9:00 pm. What is your favorite time to eat dinner? What time did you eat dinner growing up?

ANSWER KEY

3. alpha, beta, gamma, delta, epsilon, zeta, eta, theta, iota, kappa, lambda, mu, nu, xi, omicron, pi, rho, sigma, tau, upsilon, chi, psi, omega
4. Albania, Italy, Macedonia, and Turkey

Suggested Menu

Appetizer	Tzatziki
Salad	Greek Salad
Side Dish	Potato Pudding
Bread	Vasilopita (New Year's Bread)
Entrée	Moussaka
Dessert	Baklava
Drink	Turkish Coffee

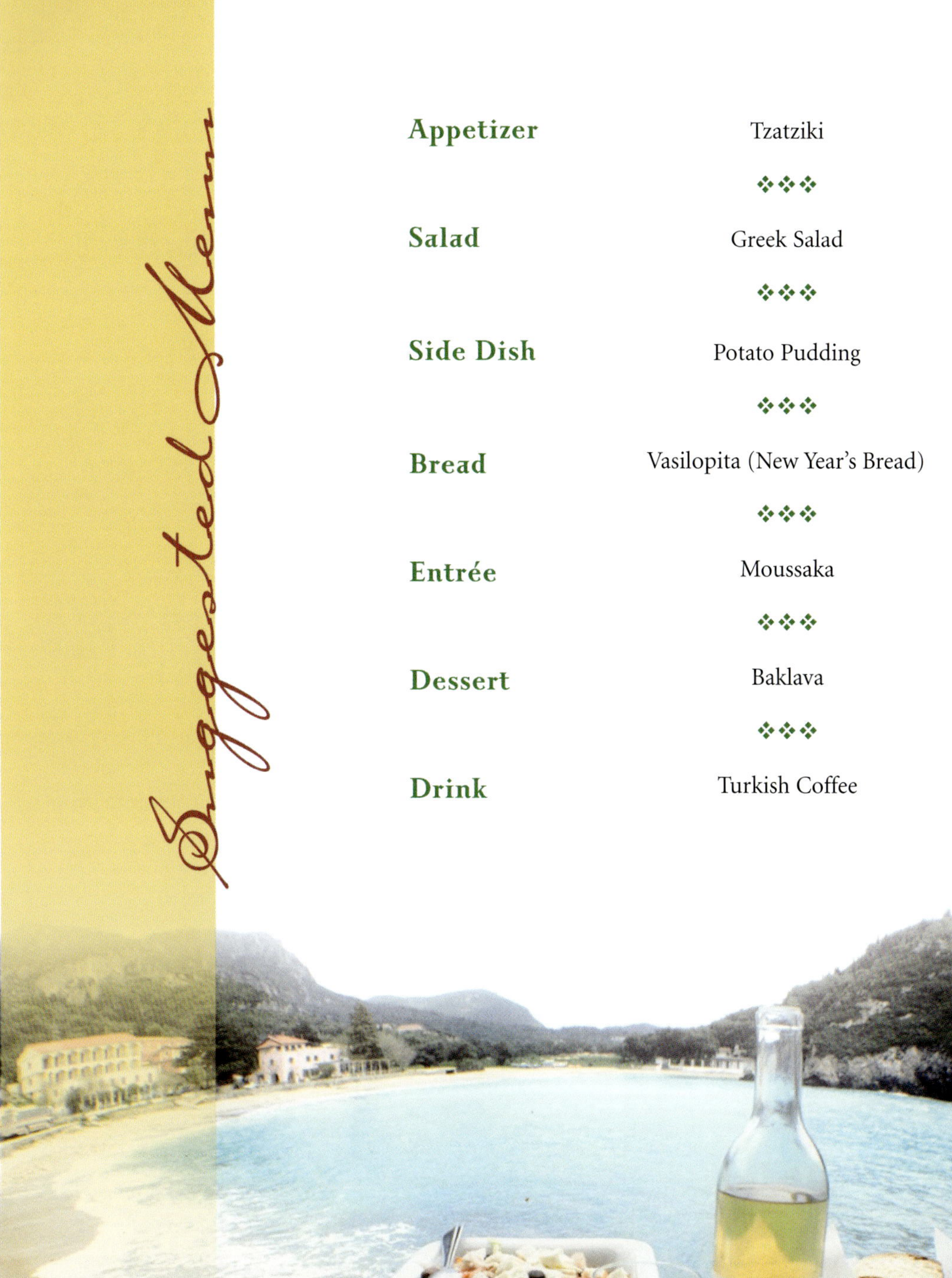

Tzatziki (Yogurt and Cucumber Dip)

❖❖❖

- 2 tablespoons olive oil
- 2 teaspoons white vinegar
- 3 garlic cloves, chopped
- 2¼ cups plain yogurt
- 2 cups peeled and diced cucumber
- 2 tablespoons chopped fresh mint leaves
- 1 teaspoon salt
- 1 teaspoon pepper
- 4 pitas

Whisk the olive oil, vinegar, garlic, and yogurt in a medium bowl. Gently fold the cucumber into the yogurt mixture. Sprinkle with the mint, salt, and pepper. Refrigerate until chilled. Toast the pitas, and cut each into 8 slices.

Makes 8 servings.

Dolmades (Stuffed Grape Leaves)

❖❖❖

- ⅔ cup olive oil, divided
- 1 cup minced onion
- 1½ teaspoons grated lemon zest
- ½ cup toasted pine nuts
- 1½ cups rice
- 1½ cups chicken broth, divided
- 2 tablespoons finely chopped dill
- ¼ cup finely chopped fresh parsley
- 1 teaspoon salt
- 1 teaspoon freshly ground pepper
- 5 cups water
- 1 (8-ounce) jar grape leaves, rinsed and drained
- 1 cup lemon juice

For the filling, put ¼ cup olive oil in a large sauté pan over medium heat. Add the onion and lemon zest, and sauté for 10 minutes. Add the pine nuts and rice, and sauté for 2 minutes. Pour in ½ cup chicken broth, and lower the heat. Simmer for 10 minutes. Transfer the rice mixture to a medium bowl, and stir in the dill, parsley, salt, and pepper. Let cool. Bring the water to a simmer. Blanch the grape leaves in the hot water for 5 minutes, or until pliable. Drain and trim the stems and any hard veins from the leaves. Gently pat the leaves dry with paper towels.

To assemble the dolmades, place a grape leaf on a work surface shiny side down. Spoon 2 tablespoons rice filling near the stem part of the leaf. Fold the stem part over the filling, fold both sides toward the middle, and roll up the leaf, but not too tightly because the rice will swell once it is fully cooked. Squeeze the roll lightly in the palm of your hand. Repeat with the remaining grape leaves and filling.

Place the rolled dolmades in a large deep skillet, seam-side down in a single layer. Pour the remaining chicken broth, olive oil, and lemon juice over them. The liquid should reach halfway up the rolls, so add water if necessary. Cover the pan, and simmer over low heat for 35 minutes, or until the dolmades are tender when pierced with a fork.

Makes 8 servings.

Fidelini Soup

❖❖❖

6 cups chicken broth
1½ cups diced and seeded tomatoes
1 teaspoon salt
6 rolls broken fidelini (see note)
1 cup grated kefalotyri cheese (see note)

In a medium saucepan, combine the chicken broth and tomatoes. Cover and boil gently for 10 minutes. Add the salt and fidelini and continue boiling gently, uncovered, for 10 minutes. Sprinkle with the cheese.

Makes 6 servings.

Note: Fidelini is a noodle product that resembles very fine spaghetti. It is also known as *fideos,* or as "noodles in nests." Kefalotyri cheese is an unpasteurized sheep's milk cheese and is produced in various regions of Greece. Similar to Parmesan and Romano, it is firm yet dry, with a slightly sharp taste. If kefalotyri cheese is unavailable, you can use Parmesan or Romano.

Greek Salad

4 cups shredded iceberg lettuce
1 cucumber, thinly sliced
1 cup sliced radishes
4 green onions, cut in 1/2-inch pieces
3 firm red tomatoes, each cut in 6 wedges
12 kalamata olives
⅓ cup olive oil
¼ cup red wine vinegar
½ teaspoon salt
1 teaspoon dried oregano
6 slices feta cheese
6 anchovy fillets

Combine the lettuce, cucumber, radishes, green onions, tomatoes, and olives in a large bowl. In a small bowl, combine and whisk together the olive oil, vinegar, salt, and oregano. Pour this over the vegetables and toss to mix. Divide into individual bowls, and place a slice of cheese and an anchovy fillet on top of each.

Makes 6 servings.

Side Dish

Baked Orzo and Cheese

2 (14½-ounce) cans unsalted chicken broth
4 teaspoons salt, divided
2 pounds orzo pasta
1 cup whipping cream
⅓ cup olive oil
⅔ pound crumbled feta cheese
2 tablespoons chopped fresh dill
2 teaspoons dried oregano
2 teaspoons pepper
1 cup grated Romano cheese

Pour the chicken broth into a 2-quart pot. Add water to the broth to almost fill the pot, about 2 cups. Add 1 teaspoon salt and bring to a boil. Stir in the orzo and boil until just tender, but still firm to bite, stirring occasionally. Drain well. Return to the pot. Mix the cream, oil, feta, dill, oregano, pepper, and the remaining salt in a bowl. Transfer the orzo to a 1½-quart baking dish. Preheat the oven to 350 degrees. Sprinkle the orzo with the cheese. Bake until heated through, about 40 minutes.

Makes 8 servings.

Pancetta Lima Beans

⅓ cup olive oil
1 cup chopped onion
1 fresh fennel bulb, trimmed and sliced
3 cups baby lima beans
1 teaspoon coarsely ground fennel seeds
1⅓ cups canned chicken broth, divided
4 tablespoons chopped fresh dill, divided
½ cup chopped pancetta (see note)
½ teaspoon ground thyme
2 tablespoons fresh lemon juice
1 teaspoon salt
1 teaspoon pepper

Heat the oil in a large skillet. Add the onion and fennel bulb; sauté for 5 minutes. Add the lima beans and fennel seeds; sauté for 3 minutes. Add 1 cup broth and 2 tablespoons dill; bring to a boil. Reduce the heat; simmer 10 minutes to blend the flavors. Stir in the pancetta and thyme, adding the remaining ⅓ cup broth if the mixture is dry. Simmer for 5 minutes. Mix in the lemon juice, the remaining 2 tablespoons dill, and the salt and pepper. Cover and chill. Bring to room temperature before serving.

Makes 6 servings.

Note: Pancetta is a type of bacon that has been cured in salt and is available at many supermarkets and some specialty foods stores.

Seafood Pasta

❖❖❖

2 cups orzo (rice-shaped pasta)
8 tablespoons olive oil, divided
2 cups crumbled feta cheese, divided
1 cup freshly grated Parmesan cheese
1 cup chopped fresh basil, divided
1½ pounds uncooked medium shrimp, peeled, deveined
5 garlic cloves, chopped
1 (14-ounce) can diced tomatoes
1 cup dry white wine
1 tablespoon dried oregano
1 teaspoon crushed red pepper flakes
2 teaspoons salt
2 teaspoons freshly ground black pepper

Preheat oven to 400 degrees. Brush an 11 x 7-inch glass baking dish with oil. Cook the orzo according to package directions. Drain well and return the orzo to the same pot. Add 4 tablespoons olive oil, 1 cup feta cheese, the Parmesan cheese, ½ cup basil, and blend. Place the orzo mixture in the prepared dish. In a large skillet, heat 2 tablespoons oil. Add the shrimp and sauté until slightly pink, about 2 minutes (shrimp will not be cooked through). Place the shrimp on top of the orzo. Add the remaining 2 tablespoons oil, and heat in the same skillet. Add the garlic and sauté over medium-high heat, stirring, about 30 seconds. Add the tomatoes with juice, and cook 1 minute. Stir in the wine, oregano, crushed red pepper, and the remaining ½ cup basil. Simmer, uncovered, until reduced to a thick sauce consistency, stirring occasionally, about 2 minutes. Add salt and pepper. Bake the orzo until heated through, about 10 minutes. Sprinkle with the remaining 1 cup feta cheese.

Makes 8 servings.

Potato Pudding

❖❖❖

2¼ cups peeled and diced white potatoes
2 tablespoons all-purpose flour
3 eggs
½ teaspoon salt
¼ teaspoon nutmeg
1¼ cups warm milk
2 tablespoons butter
¼ cup grated kefalotyri cheese (see note, page 135)

In a large pot, boil the potatoes until cooked through. Cool the potatoes, and mash them in a bowl. Add the flour, eggs, salt, nutmeg, and milk. Beat with an electric mixer on medium speed until smooth. Spread the mixture onto a buttered, 8 x 8 x 2-inch casserole baking dish. Sprinkle the kefalotyri cheese on top. Bake at 350 degrees uncovered for 20 minutes.

Makes 6 servings.

Vasilopita (New Year's Bread)

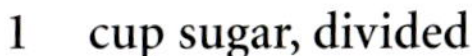

- 1 cup sugar, divided
- ½ teaspoon salt
- 11 tablespoons melted, unsalted butter, divided
- ½ cup scalded milk
- ½ cup lukewarm water
- 3 packages active dry yeast (1/4 ounce each)
- 3 medium eggs, well beaten
- 6 cups sifted all-purpose flour, divided
- 1 tablespoon ground mahlepi (see note)
- ¼ cup whole blanched almonds
- 1 small egg, beaten
- 1 cup sesame seeds
- 1 large silver coin

Combine ¾ cup sugar, the salt, 10 tablespoons melted butter, and the scalded milk in a large bowl. Allow to cool. Pour the lukewarm water into a large mixing bowl. Add the remaining ¼ cup sugar, and sprinkle in the yeast. Cover with a clean towel, and set aside for 15 minutes. Add the milk mixture and the well-beaten eggs to the yeast mixture and stir. Slowly add 3 cups flour and the mahlepi, and stir until smooth. Work the remaining 3 cups flour in very slowly until the dough starts to leave the side of the bowl. If you have added all the flour and the dough is still sticky, add a bit more, a little at a time, until the dough leaves the sides of the bowl. Put the dough on a lightly floured board, and knead it for 15 minutes, or until smooth. Then put the dough in a lightly greased bowl, and brush the top with the remaining 1 tablespoon melted butter. Place in a warm area, and cover with a clean dish towel. Allow 2 hours for rising.

When the dough has doubled in bulk, punch it down, and knead lightly for 2 minutes in a bowl or on a clean board. Form into one round cake, and place in a 13-inch shallow cake pan. (Always make cakes 1 inch smaller than the baking pan to allow for the last rising expansion.) Wrap a clean silver coin in foil, and push it up into the dough from the bottom of the cake. Lightly cover the cake with a clean dish towel, wrap a bath towel around the pan, and let the cake rise in a warm area until the dough has doubled (about 2 hours). When the cake has risen, decorate with the almonds. Place the almonds very low on the sides, since they will rise with the cake. Brush the cake with the beaten egg. Preheat the oven to 350 degrees, and sprinkle the cake with the sesame seeds. Bake for 45 minutes. Remove from the oven, and allow to cool completely before removing from the pan. For perfect texture, always allow at least 6 hours before cutting.

Makes 1 cake, 8 servings.

Note: Mahlepi is an unusual Greek spice with a distinctive, fruity taste. The finely ground mahlepi powder is made from the inner kernels of the fruit pits of a native cherry tree. For many Greeks, the sweet smell of mahlepi is a reminder of the Easter holiday. Mahlepi can be found at some supermarkets or Greek grocery shops. If mahlepi is unavailable, you can substitute a pinch of crushed aniseed and a pinch of cinnamon.

Moussaka

❖❖❖

4 large eggplants, sliced 1/4-inch thick
1 cup flour
½ cup vegetable oil

Meat sauce:

2 tablespoons unsalted butter
½ cup finely chopped onion
1½ pounds ground chuck beef
½ pound lean ground pork
½ tablespoon salt
½ teaspoon pepper
¼ teaspoon nutmeg
2 tablespoons chopped fresh parsley
3 tablespoons canned tomato sauce
1 cup dry red wine
½ cup boiling water
2 eggs
1 cup grated kefalotyri cheese, divided (or Parmesan or Romano)
2 slices dry toast, grated, divided

Cream sauce:

¼ cup unsalted butter
2 tablespoons flour
¼ cup cold milk
2¾ cups warm milk
1 cup half-and-half
3 eggs plus 3 egg yolks
½ teaspoon salt
½ teaspoon nutmeg
⅓ cup grated kefalotyri cheese (see note, page 135)

Topping:

⅓ cup grated kefalotyri cheese, divided

Coat the eggplant slices with the flour. In a large, heavy skillet over medium-high heat, pour ½ cup vegetable oil, and fry the eggplant until golden brown. Remove from the skillet, and drain on paper towels. In the same skillet, add the butter and sauté the onion in the butter until translucent. Add the ground beef and pork, and brown. Add the salt, pepper, nutmeg, parsley, tomato sauce, wine, and boiling water. Cover and cook until the sauce thickens. Beat the eggs and add to the skillet. Add ¾ cup cheese and half of the grated toast; blend well. Grease a 12 x 10 x 3-inch baking pan. Spread the remaining half of the grated toast over the bottom of the pan. Top with half the eggplant. Cover with the meat sauce, and sprinkle with the remaining ¼ cup cheese. Cover with the remaining eggplant.

For the cream sauce, melt the butter in a saucepan. In a separate bowl, make a paste of the flour and cold milk. Add the flour paste, warm milk, and half-and-half to the saucepan. Blend until smooth and simmer for 15 minutes. In a small bowl, beat the eggs and egg yolks; add the beaten eggs to the saucepan while stirring the sauce vigorously. Stir in the salt, nutmeg, and ⅓ cup cheese. Pour over the eggplant dish. Sprinkle the top with the remaining ⅓ cup cheese. Bake at 375 degrees for 45 minutes. Let stand for 20 minutes.

Makes 8 servings.

Dessert

Baklava

3½ cups chopped walnuts
1 cup finely chopped blanched almonds
½ cup sugar
2 teaspoons ground cinnamon
1½ pounds butter, melted
1 pound phyllo dough

Basic syrup:
2 cups sugar
1½ cups water
¼ cup finely grated lemon zest
5 whole cloves
2 cinnamon sticks
1 cup honey
4 tablespoons lemon juice
2 tablespoons rum or brandy
½ tablespoon rum flavoring

Combine the walnuts, almonds, sugar, and ground cinnamon in a medium bowl. Divide this mixture in four equal parts. Using a 13 x 9 x 2-inch baking pan, line the bottom with 10 layers of phyllo dough, brushing each sheet with butter before applying the next. Sprinkle one-fourth of the nut mixture over the entire layer. Add six more layers of phyllo, brushing each layer with butter, and cover with a second one-fourth of the nut mixture. Repeat twice more, and then top with 10 layers of phyllo. Before baking, cut the baklava in 2-inch, diamond-shape pieces, being sure to cut through to the bottom of the pan. Pour the remaining melted butter over the top. Bake at 325 degrees for 1 hour, covering with foil the last 20 minutes.

While the baklava are baking, prepare the basic syrup. Combine the sugar, water, lemon zest, clove, and cinnamon sticks in a saucepan. Bring to a boil, and cook the syrup until it thickens slightly. Remove from the heat, and add the honey, lemon juice, liquor, and flavoring. Store in a cool place. (Do not refrigerate or it will crystallize.)

When the baklava are done, remove from the oven and slowly pour 2 cups basic syrup over them. Store the baklava in the same pan and in a cool place (do not refrigerate). They are best served the following day, but will keep for 10 days or more if properly stored.

Makes 8 servings.

Note: Phyllo dough consists of paper-thin sheets of raw, unleavened flour dough. Phyllo can be found at most supermarkets or specialty shops.

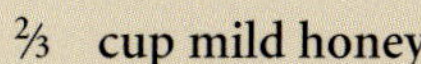

Greek Cookies

- ⅔ cup mild honey
- 3 tablespoons anise-flavored liqueur, divided
- 2 tablespoons fresh lemon juice
- 4 tablespoons butter
- 4¼ cups all-purpose flour
- 1½ teaspoons salt
- 1 teaspoon baking powder
- 1 cup (2 sticks) unsalted butter, room temperature
- 1 cup sugar
- 3 large eggs
- 2 tablespoons aniseed
- 2 teaspoons finely grated lemon zest
- Sesame seeds

In a small bowl, mix the honey, 2 tablespoons liqueur, and the lemon juice. Set the glaze aside to cool. Preheat the oven to 350 degrees. Lightly butter the baking sheets. In a medium bowl, combine the flour, salt, and baking powder. In a large bowl, beat the butter and sugar using an electric mixer; add this mix to the flour mixture. Add the eggs, one at a time, beating well after each addition. Beat in the remaining 1 tablespoon liqueur, the aniseed, and lemon zest, and add to the flour mixture. Working with 1 tablespoon-size dough at a time, roll the dough between your palms and the work surface into 6-inch ropes. Form into bow ties or twists. Place on prepared baking sheets, spacing evenly. Brush the glaze over the cookies. Sprinkle with the sesame seeds. Bake the cookies until pale golden, about 15 minutes. Transfer the cookies to racks, and lightly brush them again with the glaze. Let cool.

Makes 40 cookies.

Turkish Coffee

Turkish coffee is brewed in a *dzezva* (pronounced jezva). You'll want to grind beans on the finest possible setting. You can purchase a Turkish coffee pot online or at a kitchenware shop. Another option is to brew very strong coffee and serve it sweetened.

- 4 cups water
- 2 teaspoons sugar
- 4 teaspoons finely ground coffee

Place the water into the *dzezva*. Add the sugar. Bring to a boil on the stovetop. After the sugar water comes to a boil, remove from the stovetop and add the ground coffee. Place the pot back onto the stove. Do not leave the pot unattended, as the coffee will boil over. Allow the coffee to boil as a layer of foam appears. Remove from the heat, and allow the coffee to sit for up to 2 minutes. Serve with additional sugar. Remind guests that coffee grinds may appear in bottom of cups.

Makes 4 servings.

INDIA

INDIA IS A LAND OF DENSE FORESTS, ARID DESERTS, FERTILE PLAINS, AND TROPICAL COASTS, AND IS HOME TO ONE BILLION PEOPLE. Hindi is the national language, although there are fourteen major languages and more than a thousand different dialects. Geography and climate play a major role in Indian cuisine. While the dry northern region produces large quantities of wheat, providing the main ingredient in the staples *chapati* and *puri* (wheat breads), the humid southern part of the country produces the much needed and revered rice crop.

Holidays and festivals also play a major role in Indian culture and cuisine. Whether they commemorate a historical event, honor a religious leader, or express gratitude for a much awaited harvest, they are all celebrated with enthusiasm. One of the most anticipated holidays is Diwali, the festival of lights, observed in October or November. The rituals of this festival symbolize the defeat of spiritual darkness in India. Families whitewash their homes and adorn them with colorful designs, oil lamps, and candles. Indians travel throughout the streets with garlands of lights and offer sweet treats to friends and neighbors. There are many wonderful treats shared during the celebration of Diwali—sweet carrots, sweet rice, and almond cookies, to name a few.

Of course, Indian cuisine features delicious food not only on holidays but throughout the year. Savory dishes with exotic spices are an integral part of the culture, so preparing and eating Indian cuisine is a wonderful way to become acquainted with this fascinating country.

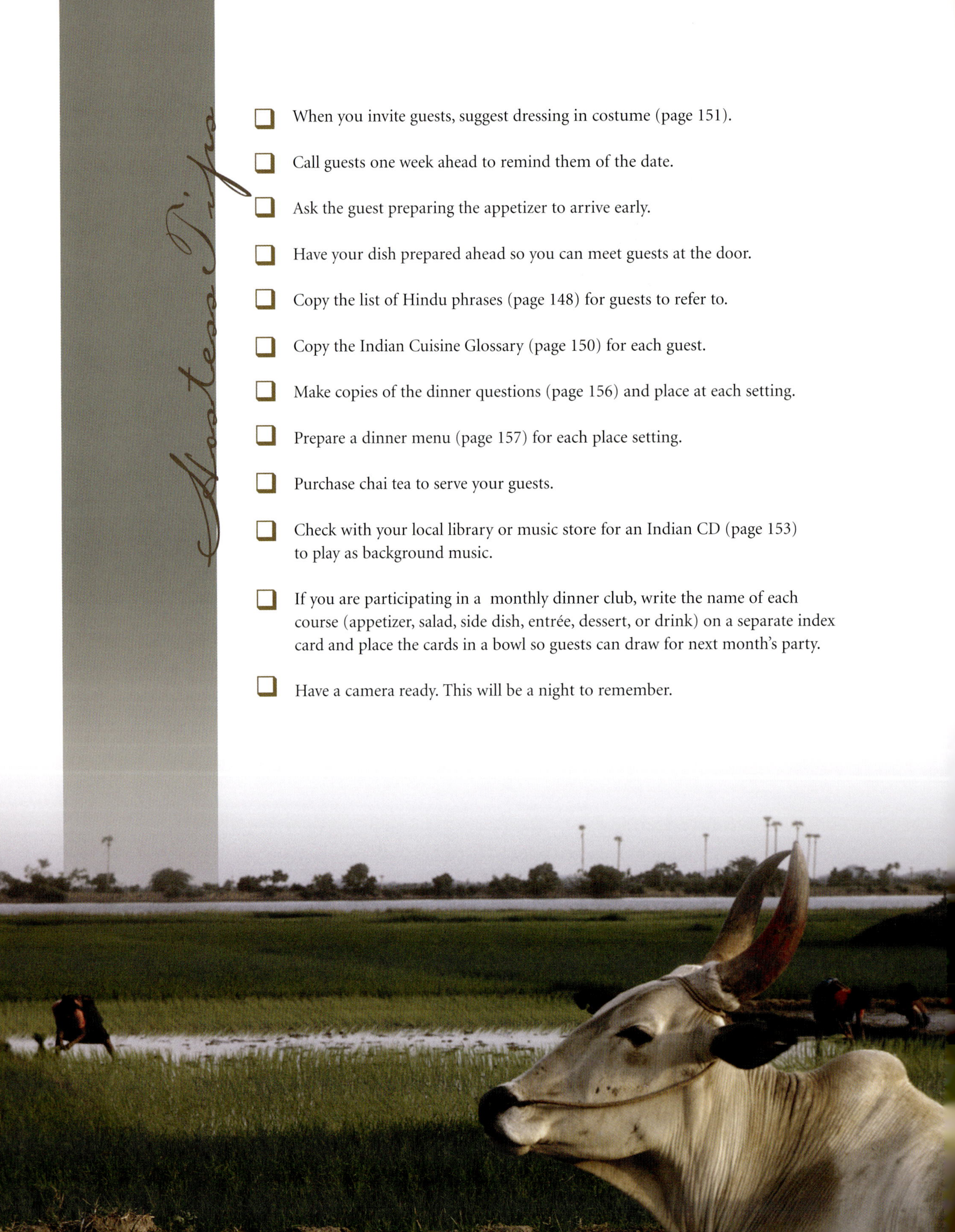

Hostess Tips

- ☐ When you invite guests, suggest dressing in costume (page 151).
- ☐ Call guests one week ahead to remind them of the date.
- ☐ Ask the guest preparing the appetizer to arrive early.
- ☐ Have your dish prepared ahead so you can meet guests at the door.
- ☐ Copy the list of Hindu phrases (page 148) for guests to refer to.
- ☐ Copy the Indian Cuisine Glossary (page 150) for each guest.
- ☐ Make copies of the dinner questions (page 156) and place at each setting.
- ☐ Prepare a dinner menu (page 157) for each place setting.
- ☐ Purchase chai tea to serve your guests.
- ☐ Check with your local library or music store for an Indian CD (page 153) to play as background music.
- ☐ If you are participating in a monthly dinner club, write the name of each course (appetizer, salad, side dish, entrée, dessert, or drink) on a separate index card and place the cards in a bowl so guests can draw for next month's party.
- ☐ Have a camera ready. This will be a night to remember.

Before Dinner

Set the mood for an authentic Indian experience by greeting guests at the door with *namaste.*

If practicing the traditional style of entertaining, ask guests to remove their shoes at the door. (Footwear is not typically worn in Indian homes as it is considered unhygienic.)

Welcome guests and invite them to enjoy the appetizer, music, and conversation. Have Indian music playing in the background. Encourage guests to discuss Customs and Traditions (page 154).

Ask guests to look over the Indian Cuisine Glossary for terms they may not know. Discuss your costume selection with the guests.

Dinner

Seat your guests around the table and begin serving the meal. Serve all dishes together. Place flatbread, pitas, or pappadams in basket on table.

Invite guests to read and discuss the dinner questions. As the host or hostess, you are the discussion leader. Encourage each person to participate.

After Dinner

Serve hot chai tea. After tea has been served begin to serve dessert.

Ask guests what they enjoyed most about the evening. If they would like to host a dinner party, which country?

If you are participating in a monthly dinner club, invite guests to draw names of courses (appetizer, salad, side dish, entrée, dessert, or drink) from a bowl for next month's party, and decide who will host.

Indian Beverages

Chai tea is a staple beverage throughout India; the finest varieties are grown in Darjeeling and Assam. It is prepared with a mixture of spices boiled in milk. Other beverages include *nimbu pani* (lemonade) and *lassi,* which is sweetened diluted buttermilk.

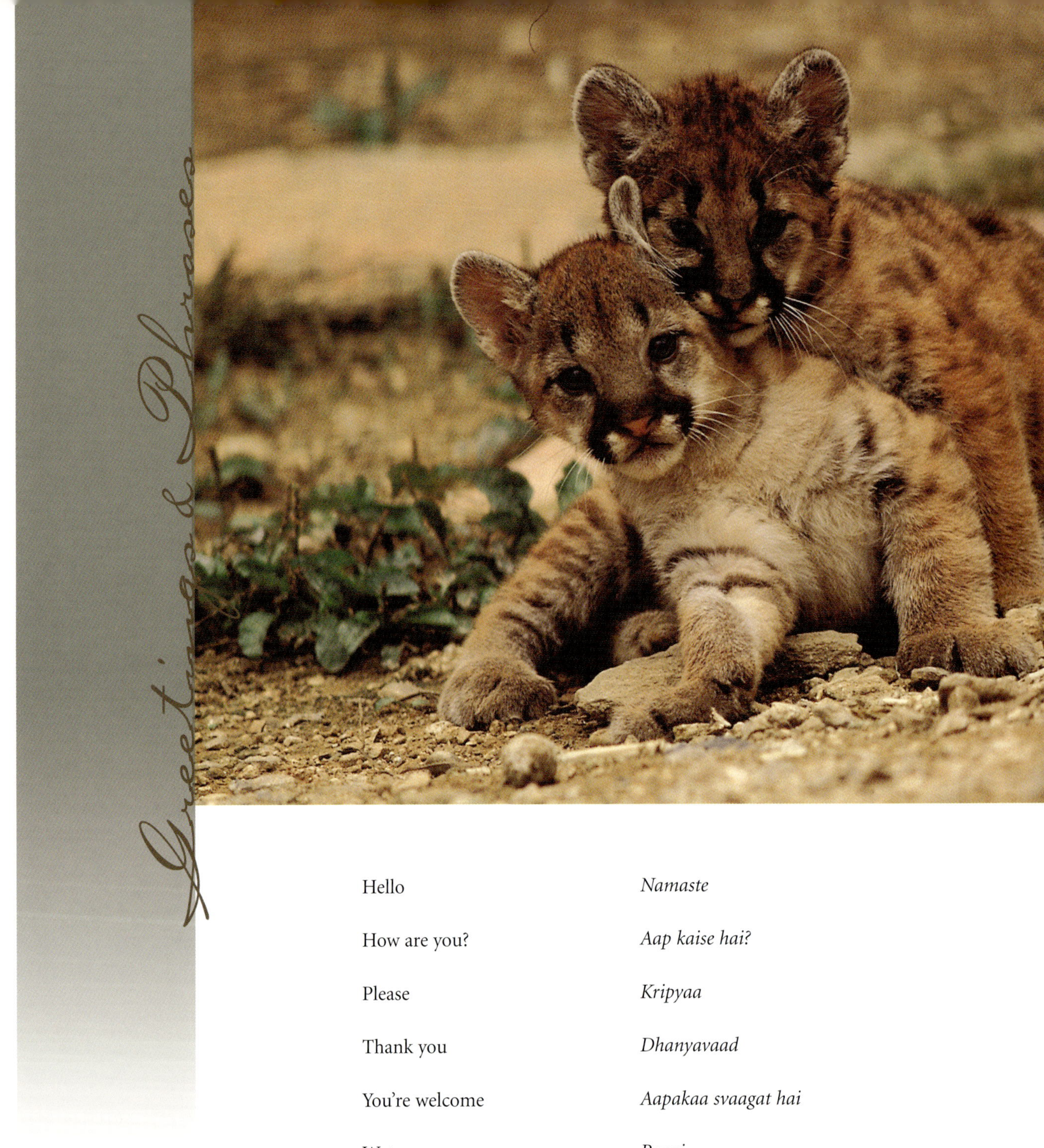

Greetings & Phrases

Hello	*Namaste*
How are you?	*Aap kaise hai?*
Please	*Kripyaa*
Thank you	*Dhanyavaad*
You're welcome	*Aapakaa svaagat hai*
Water	*Paani*
Tea	*Chai*
Coffee	*Coffee*
Good–bye	*Alavidha*

Traditionally, meals are eaten while seated either on the floor or on very low stools or cushions.

Many foods such as Indian breads and curry are eaten with the fingers.

Each guest is given an individual tray or large banana leaf to be used as a placemat.

When flatbreads such as *chapati, roti,* or *naan* are served with the meal, it is acceptable and expected to use pieces of them to gather food and soak up gravies and curries.

The cardinal rule of dining is to always use the right hand when eating or receiving food, never the left (which is considered unclean). It is considered unorthodox to use your spoon or fingers to taste food from someone else's plate once you have begun eating. It is not necessary to taste every dish, but you should finish everything on your plate to be respectful to the host or hostess.

The hostess is expected to serve and monitor guests for second helpings. Traditionally the men and children of the house are served first, then the women have their meals.

Spicing Up Indian Meals

Most of the spices used in Indian cooking were chosen originally for their medicinal qualities rather than for flavor. Many of them, such as turmeric, cloves, and cardamom are used in treating ailments from stomach cramps to throat infections. Others, like ginger, are good for digestion.

Curry powder consists of several pungent ground spices (such as cayenne pepper, fenugreek, and turmeric) used as a spice or seasoning in poultry, meat, vegetables, or fish, prepared as a stew-like dish. A dish containing curry powder is often referred to as a "curry," and an authentic Indian curry combines onion, garlic, ginger, and tomatoes. All curries are made using a wide variety of spices, and few cooks use the same quantity or variety as another. Therefore, no two curries taste the same.

Side dishes and condiments such as chutneys, curries, and Indian pickles contribute to the flavor and texture of a meal. You can find these relishes at your local Indian market.

Icebreaker: Cuisine Glossary

Aloo: the Hindi word for potato.

Asafetida: the dried gum resin of an Indian plant, with a very strong flavor and odor, not to be eaten raw.

Atta: finely ground whole-wheat flour used in many Indian breads.

Basmati: flavorful long-grain rice that cooks up dry, fluffy, and tender. It smells like popcorn while it's cooking.

Biriani: a dish made of rice baked with a vegetable- or meat-based filling.

Chutney: a blend of fruits and spices cooked into a thick sauce. Can be sweet or savory; most common type is made of mango.

Elaichi: cardamom, a spice common in curry blends and garam masala.

Fenugreek: small flat seeds that are used in curries for slightly bitter flavor.

Garam masala: literally, warm spices; a blend of spices used to flavor dishes. The combination varies not only from region to region, but from cook to cook.

Ghee: clarified butter, made by slowly melting butter, skimming off the foam, and saving the golden liquid, leaving the white butter solids behind. This butter can be heated to a higher temperature without burning than ordinary butter.

Halwa: a congealed, translucent sweet dish made of fruits and syrups.

Jaggery: dried, concentrated sugarcane juice; a common sweetener in India.

Korma: a sauce made with yogurt and ground nuts or seeds, especially poppy seeds.

Masala: the Hindi word for spice.

Paratha: unleavened fried bread made with whole-wheat flour, sometimes filled with meat and vegetables.

Pappadams: spicy wafers made from lentils or legumes.

Raita: a cooling salad made from vegetables and yogurt served as an accompaniment to hot and spicy dishes.

Roti: the Hindi word for bread.

Samosas: a crisp pastry, filled with vegetables or meat and deep-fried, served as an appetizer.

Tandoor: a large, deep oven made from clay that cooks food at very high temperatures.

Tandoori: any recipe cooked in the tandoor.

Vindaloo: a very spicy dish made with garam masala, meat, and vinegar, a specialty of the Indian province of Goa.

Mahatma Gandhi: He was the most popular as well as the most influential political and spiritual leader of India. Wear a white T-shirt under a white cotton robe. Accessorize with reading glasses and book.

Sari: A sari is the traditional garment worn by many Indian women. It is a strip of unstitched cloth ranging from thirteen to thirty feet long, which can be draped in various styles, most commonly around the waist, then draped over the shoulder and leaving the midriff bare. The sari is usually worn over a petticoat, with a blouse known as a *choli* on top. The *choli* has short sleeves with a low neck and is usually cropped to bare the midriff. Cover your head with a length of fine cotton fabric (this scarf is known as an *orhni* or a *dupatta*). Accessorize with a belt to emphasize the hip area. You can find a sari at your local costume shop.

Traditional Indian male/female attire: Wear a *salwar,* pajama-like trousers drawn tightly at the waist and the ankles. Over the *salwar,* wear a long, loose tunic known as a *kameez*. Instead of the *salwar*, you might choose to wear a *churidar*, which is tighter fitting at the hips, thighs, and ankles. Over this, you could wear a collarless or mandarin collar tunic called a *kurta*. You can find these items at your local costume shop.

INDIA FILM FESTIVAL

Bride and Prejudice
Starring Aishwarya Rai and Martin Henderson
Directed by Gurinder Chadha, 2005

Calcutta
Starring Louis Malle
Directed by Louis Malle, 1971

Gandhi
Starring Ben Kingsley and Candice Bergen
Directed by Richard Attenborough, 1982

Lagaan: Once Upon a Time in India
Starring Amhir Khan, Gracy Singh, Rachel Shelley, and Paul Blackthorne
Directed by Ashutosh Gowariker, 2001

Monsoon Wedding
Starring Naseeruddin Shah and Lillete Dubey
Directed by Mira Nair, 2001

Mother Teresa: In the Name of God's Poor
Starring Geraldine Chaplin and Keene Curtis
Directed by Kevin Connor, 1997

Mystic India
Starring Peter O'Toole and Latesh Patel
Directed by Keith Melton, 2005

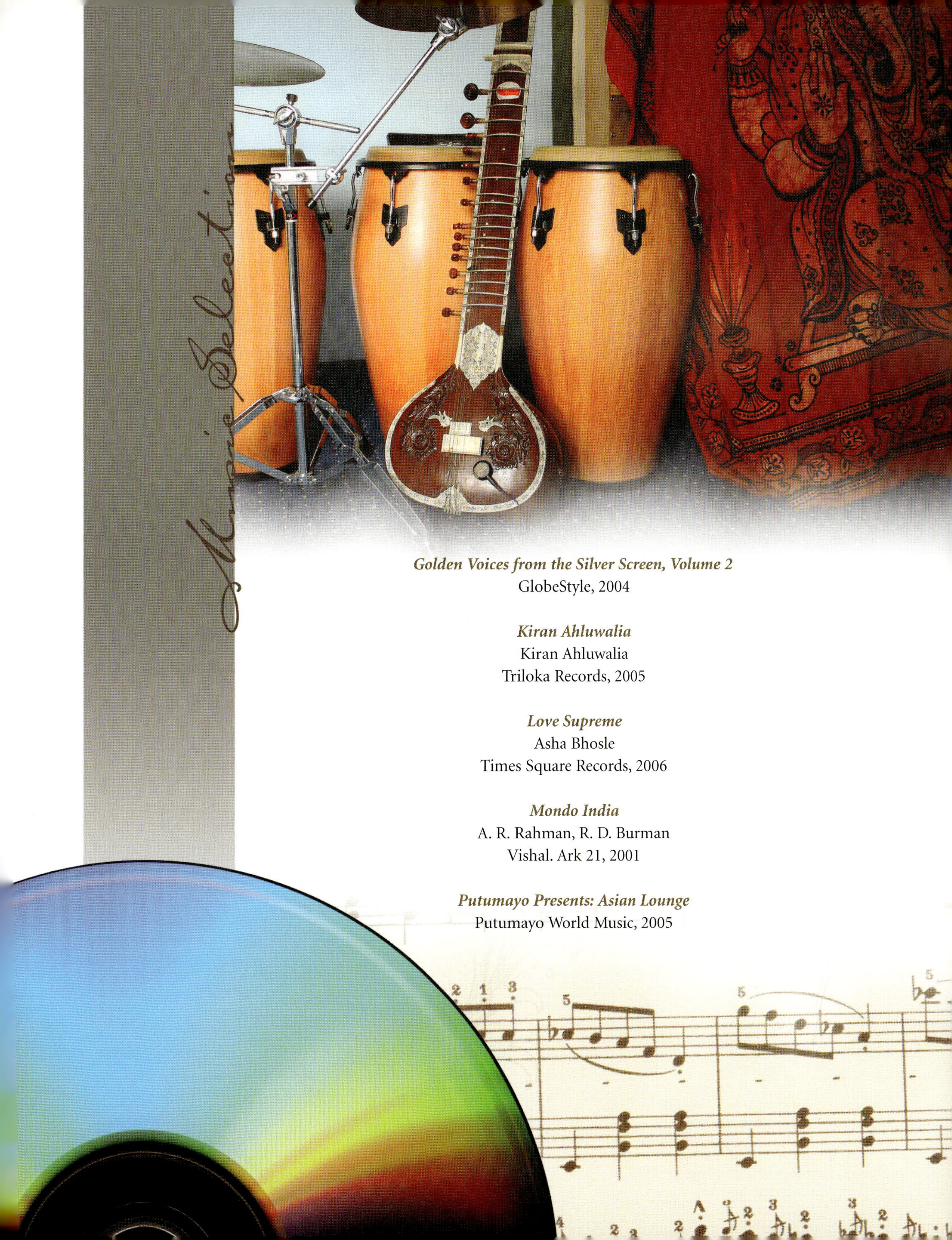

Music Selection

Golden Voices from the Silver Screen, Volume 2
GlobeStyle, 2004

Kiran Ahluwalia
Kiran Ahluwalia
Triloka Records, 2005

Love Supreme
Asha Bhosle
Times Square Records, 2006

Mondo India
A. R. Rahman, R. D. Burman
Vishal. Ark 21, 2001

Putumayo Presents: Asian Lounge
Putumayo World Music, 2005

Namaste is the most popular form of greeting in India, in which both the palms are placed together and raised to just below the face with a slight bow of the head to greet a person. It is a general salutation that is used to welcome somebody and also for bidding farewell.

Flower garlands are given as a mark of respect and honor. They are also offered as a welcome to visitors or guests. The garlands are generally made with white jasmine and orange marigold flowers; rose garlands are also common.

A *bindi* is a mark worn by young girls and women. *Bindi* is derived from *bindu,* the Sanskrit word for dot. It is usually a red dot made with vermilion powder, worn between the eyebrows on their forehead. A *bindi* is traditionally a symbol of marriage, but in recent years has become decorative and is worn by unmarried girls as well as women. Many Indian women wear a studded nose pin. This is a symbol of purity and marriage, although many unmarried girls wear them as well.

A *mangalsutra* is a necklace made of black beads, usually with a gold pendant, worn by married women. It is the Indian equivalent of the Western wedding ring. At the ceremony the groom ties the *mangalsutra* around the bride's neck. The black beads are believed to act as protection against evil. Some *mangalsutras* are dipped in turmeric paste, which is believed to ward off evil spirits.

Cooking Utensils

A *handi* is a deep, narrow-mouthed cooking vessel used in Indian cooking. *Handis* resemble American soup pots and are used similarly.

A *karahi* is a thick, circular, deep vessel similar in shape to a wok, useful for shallow or deep frying.

A *kadai* is a dish used to cook in a *karahi.* Dishes in India are often presented "*kadai* fresh," such as Kadai Chicken and Kadai Paneer, where the dish is served with a miniature *kadai* and hot coals underneath.

A *tava* or *twah* is a flat or slightly concave disc-shaped griddle made from cast iron, steel, or aluminum. It is used to prepare *roti* or breads, including *partha, chaap,* and *chaat.*

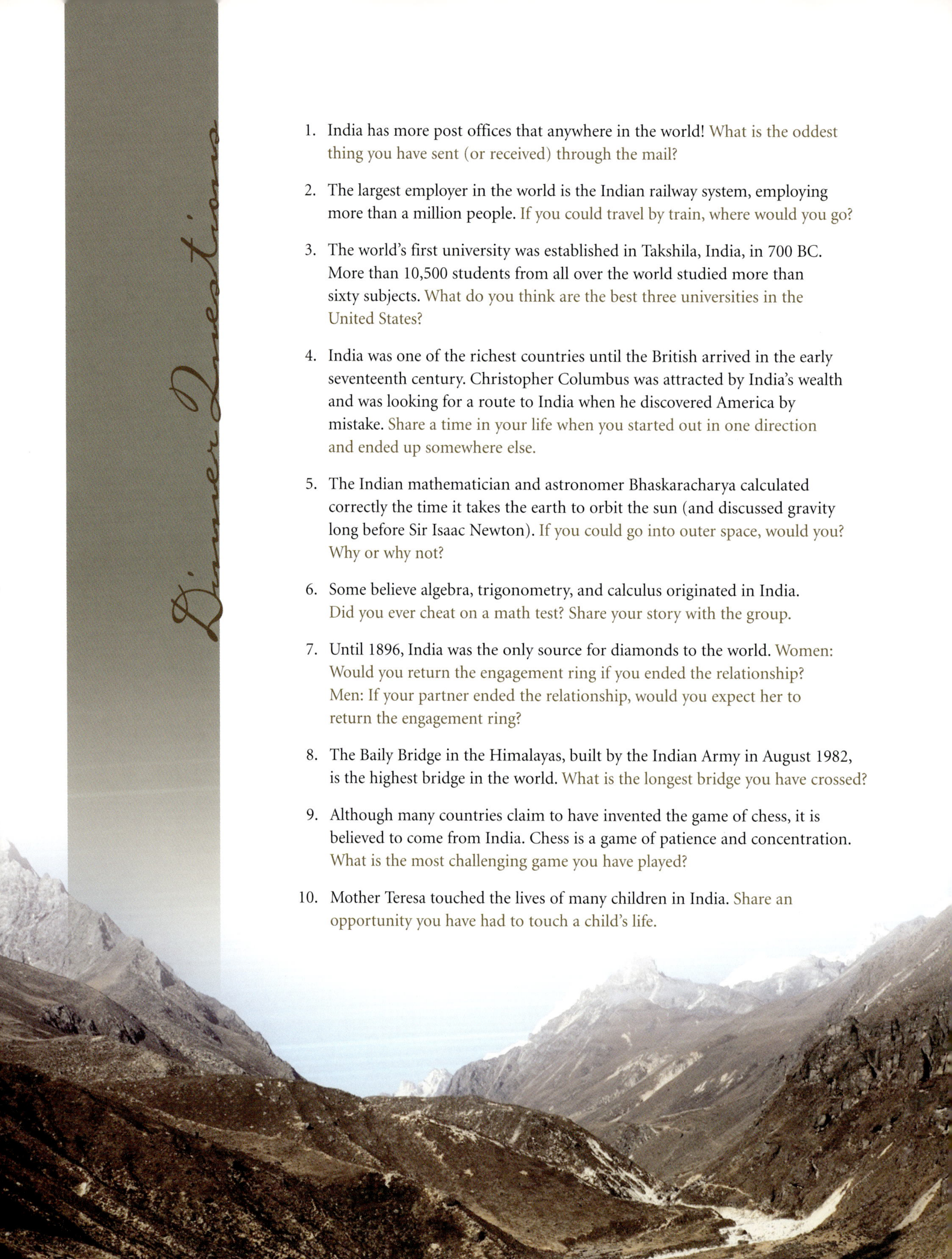

Dinner Questions

1. India has more post offices that anywhere in the world! What is the oddest thing you have sent (or received) through the mail?

2. The largest employer in the world is the Indian railway system, employing more than a million people. If you could travel by train, where would you go?

3. The world's first university was established in Takshila, India, in 700 BC. More than 10,500 students from all over the world studied more than sixty subjects. What do you think are the best three universities in the United States?

4. India was one of the richest countries until the British arrived in the early seventeenth century. Christopher Columbus was attracted by India's wealth and was looking for a route to India when he discovered America by mistake. Share a time in your life when you started out in one direction and ended up somewhere else.

5. The Indian mathematician and astronomer Bhaskaracharya calculated correctly the time it takes the earth to orbit the sun (and discussed gravity long before Sir Isaac Newton). If you could go into outer space, would you? Why or why not?

6. Some believe algebra, trigonometry, and calculus originated in India. Did you ever cheat on a math test? Share your story with the group.

7. Until 1896, India was the only source for diamonds to the world. Women: Would you return the engagement ring if you ended the relationship? Men: If your partner ended the relationship, would you expect her to return the engagement ring?

8. The Baily Bridge in the Himalayas, built by the Indian Army in August 1982, is the highest bridge in the world. What is the longest bridge you have crossed?

9. Although many countries claim to have invented the game of chess, it is believed to come from India. Chess is a game of patience and concentration. What is the most challenging game you have played?

10. Mother Teresa touched the lives of many children in India. Share an opportunity you have had to touch a child's life.

Suggested Menu

Appetizer	Okra Crisp
	❖❖❖
Salad	Beet Salad
	❖❖❖
Side Dish	Indian Vegetables
	❖❖❖
Bread	Naan Bread
	❖❖❖
Entrée	Chicken Tikka
	❖❖❖
Dessert	Sweet Treats and/or Melon Pudding
	❖❖❖
Beverage	Chai Tea

Appetizer

Okra Crisp

½ cup thinly sliced red onion
1 cup seeded and roughly diced tomatoes
¼ cup chopped fresh cilantro
7½ cups vegetable oil for frying
1 pound fresh okra, trimmed and cut lengthwise into thin strips
4½ teaspoons fresh lemon juice
½ teaspoon salt
1½ teaspoons chaat masala (see note)

Blend together the onion, tomatoes, and cilantro in a small mixing bowl. Refrigerate until ready to use. In a wide, 4-inch-deep, heavy pot, heat 1½ to 2 inches of oil until a deep-fat thermometer registers 350 degrees. Fry the okra in batches (returning the oil to 350 degrees between batches) until golden brown, about 5 to 7 minutes. Transfer the fried okra to paper towels to drain. In a large mixing bowl, combine the okra, onion-tomato mixture, lemon juice, salt, and chaat masala. Toss gently and serve immediately.

Makes 8 servings.

Note: Chaat masala is a blend of spices used most often in Indian street food. It is available at Indian markets or online at www.kalustyans.com.

Pappadams with Chutney

4 cups vegetable oil
1 (7-ounce) package mini pappadams (see note)

Chutney:
1½ cups fresh cilantro
3 seeded and coarsely chopped jalapeño chiles
3 tablespoons water
3 teaspoons packed light brown sugar
3 teaspoons fresh lime juice
1 teaspoon salt
4 tablespoons plain yogurt

Heat the oil over medium heat in a 2-quart saucepan. Fry the pappadams in batches until puffed and lightly browned, for about 1 minute. Transfer them with a slotted spoon or tongs to paper towels to drain. For the chutney, purée the cilantro in a blender with the jalapeño, water, brown sugar, lime juice, and salt. Transfer to a bowl, and stir in the yogurt. Serve the pappadams with chutney and pickles for dipping.

Makes 6 servings.

Note: Pappadams, spicy wafers made from lentils or legumes, are available at East Indian markets and some specialty shops.

Salad

Beet Salad

❖❖❖

1 small beet
1 bag mixed salad greens
1 large tomato, seeded and chopped
Salt
Freshly ground pepper
1 bunch green onions, chopped
1 small head green cabbage, chopped
1 cup chopped celery
1 large onion, diced
1 large cucumber, grated
1 large carrot, grated
3 tablespoons fresh lemon juice

Steam and peel the beet, and slice it into thin rounds. Rinse a large glass bowl with cold water. Stick the beet slices around the inner wall of the bowl evenly. Spread the mixed salad greens over the beet slices and then the tomatoes at the bottom of the bowl. Sprinkle with the salt and pepper. Top the tomatoes with the green onion, cabbage, celery, onion, cucumber, and carrot. Season each layer with salt and pepper. Sprinkle with the lemon juice.

Makes 6 servings.

Indian Vegetables

2¼ cups water, divided
2 cups peeled and diced baby carrots
½ cup green peas
1 cup peeled and diced beets
1 cup peeled and diced potato
2 cups diced tomatoes
2 tablespoons vegetable oil
1 cup diced onion
2 teaspoons desiccated coconut powder
4 whole green cardamon pods
2 teaspoons ground ginger
¼ teaspoon ground cloves
½ teaspoon ground cinnamon
2 bay leaves
Salt

Steam 2 cups water, the carrots, green peas, beets, and potato in a large skillet until they are tender. Add the tomatoes, and put the mixture in a bowl. Add the vegetable oil to the skillet and heat. When the oil is hot, add the diced onions and fry until they are lightly browned. In a blender, put the coconut powder, cardamom, ginger, cloves, cinnamon, bay leaves, and salt. Add the remaining ¼ cup water and grind the ingredients into a thick paste. Add the mixture to the skillet and fry with the onions for 2 minutes. Add the steamed vegetables and mix well. Cook slowly over low heat until the mixture is thick, about 8 minutes.

Makes 8 servings.

Side Dish

Potatoes with Cauliflower

❖❖❖

- 2 tablespoons olive oil
- 3 garlic cloves, minced
- 2 teaspoons peeled and minced fresh ginger
- ¼ teaspoon turmeric
- ¼ teaspoon ground coriander
- ¼ teaspoon paprika
- 1 pound russet potatoes, peeled and cubed
- 4 cups cauliflower florets, cut into bite-size pieces
- 1⅓ cups canned, low-salt chicken broth
- 1 teaspoon salt
- 1 teaspoon pepper
- 1 tablespoon fresh lemon juice
- 1 cup chopped fresh cilantro

Heat the oil in a large nonstick skillet over medium heat. Add the garlic, ginger, turmeric, coriander, and paprika, and sauté for 1 minute. Mix in the potatoes and cauliflower, and add the chicken broth. Cover and cook for 5 minutes. Uncover, increase the heat to medium-high, and cook, stirring gently, until the potatoes are tender and the liquid is reduced to a glaze, about 9 minutes. Season with the salt and pepper. Drizzle the potatoes with lemon juice, and sprinkle with the chopped cilantro.

Makes 8 servings.

Naan Bread

❖❖❖

¾ cup warm water
1 teaspoon active dry yeast
1 teaspoon sugar
2½ cups sifted all-purpose flour
1 teaspoon salt
¼ cup ghee, divided (see note, page 166)
2 tablespoons plain yogurt
2 teaspoons kalonji (see note)

Whisk the warm water with the yeast and sugar until the yeast is dissolved. Cover and let stand in a warm place for 10 minutes. In a large bowl, combine the yeast mixture, 2 cups sifted flour, and the salt. Add half the ghee and the yogurt. Mix into a soft dough, and knead with the remaining ½ cup flour on a surface for about 5 minutes, or until the dough is smooth and elastic. Place the dough in a large, greased bowl. Cover and let stand in a warm place for 1½ hours, or until the dough is doubled in size. Punch down the dough, and knead it for 5 minutes. Divide the dough into six pieces. Roll each piece out into an 8-inch-round naan. Cover an oven tray with foil, and grease the foil. Brush the naan bread with a little of the remaining ghee, and sprinkle with some of the kalonji. Cook the naan rounds one at a time under a very hot grill for about 2 minutes on each side, or until puffed and just browned.

Makes 6 servings.

Note: Kalonji is onion seed. You can substitute coriander or fennel seeds.

Chicken Tikka

3 pounds skinless, boneless chicken breasts
1 cup yogurt
1 tablespoon minced garlic
1 tablespoon ground ginger
2 tablespoons lemon juice
2 tablespoons chili powder
1 teaspoon salt
1 teaspoon pepper
2 tablespoons olive oil

Cut the chicken breasts into long, 2-inch-thick strips. In a large bowl, combine the yogurt, garlic, ginger, lemon juice, chili powder, salt, and pepper, and mix well. Add the chicken strips to the bowl, and marinate for 2 hours in the refrigerator. Thread the chicken strips onto skewers. Brush the strips with olive oil, and cook on a grill for 5 minutes on each side until fully cooked.

Makes 8 servings.

Chicken Curry

- 3 tablespoons tomato paste
- 4 tablespoons plain yogurt
- 1½ cups water, divided
- 1½ teaspoons ground ginger
- 4 tablespoons garlic powder
- 6 skinless, boneless chicken breasts, cubed
- 3 tablespoons vegetable oil
- 2 bay leaves
- 1¼ teaspoons ground cinnamon
- 5 cardamom pods
- 5 whole cloves
- 2 teaspoons crushed red pepper flakes
- 2 teaspoons turmeric
- 2 teaspoons salt
- 1 teaspoon pepper
- 2 tablespoons lemon juice

Mix the tomato paste, yogurt, and 1 cup water. In a separate small bowl, blend the ginger, garlic, and the remaining ½ cup water until smooth. Brown the chicken pieces in the oil, remove the chicken from the skillet, and lower the heat. Add the bay leaves, cinnamon, cardamom pods, cloves, and crushed red pepper. Stir for 30 seconds. Add the ginger and garlic mixture, and turmeric. Stir for 1 minute. Add the tomato mixture, salt, pepper, and lemon juice, and stir. Add the chicken, cover, and simmer for 30 minutes.

Makes 6 servings.

Sweet Treats

1 cup raw cashew nuts
2 cups boiling water
1 cup sugar
2 teaspoons milk
2 teaspoons ghee (see note)
1 tablespoon vanilla

Soak the cashew nuts in boiling water for 1 hour. Drain the cashews, and blot with a paper towel. Combine the cashews, sugar, and milk in a food processor to create a smooth paste. Heat the ghee in a large pan, add the cashew nut paste, and cook over medium heat, stirring constantly until the mixture becomes thick. Add the vanilla, and mix thoroughly. Spread the mixture onto a greased tray, and spread evenly. Let it cool. After it is cooled, cut into diamond-shaped pieces.

Makes 6 servings.

Note: Ghee is clarified butter and is made by simmering unsalted butter in a large pot until all water has boiled off and the protein has settled to the bottom. It is then spooned off to avoid disturbing the milk solids on the bottom of the pan. Ghee can be stored for extended periods without refrigeration, provided it is kept in an airtight container.

Melon Pudding

4 cups diced fresh mango
1 tablespoon water
1 teaspoon ground nutmeg
1 teaspoon ground cinnamon
1 teaspoon ground ginger
1½ teaspoons confectioners' sugar
2 cups seedless watermelon balls
Fresh mint sprigs, for garnish

In a food processor, purée the mango, adding 1 tablespoon water if necessary to achieve a pudding-like consistency. Add the nutmeg, cinnamon, and ginger, and blend thoroughly. Add the confectioners' sugar. Cover and chill 3 to 4 hours. Pour the purée into shallow bowls, and arrange the watermelon balls on top. Garnish with the mint sprigs.

Makes 6 servings.

Mini Chai Bundt Cakes with Spiced Syrup

2½ cups all-purpose flour
1½ cups (packed) light brown sugar
2 teaspoons baking soda
½ teaspoon salt
1¾ cups hot water
1 cup instant chai tea powder (see note)
½ cup honey
½ cup (1 stick) unsalted butter, melted
½ cup room temperature buttermilk
2 large eggs
1 large egg yolk
Vanilla ice cream
Spiced Syrup (recipe follows)

Preheat the oven to 350 degrees. Grease and flour 2 nonstick mini-Bundt pans (6 cakes per pan). Sift the flour, brown sugar, baking soda, and salt into a large bowl. Whisk 1¾ cups hot water and the chai tea powder in another large bowl to blend. Whisk the honey, melted butter, buttermilk, eggs, and egg yolk into the chai mixture to blend. Stir the chai mixture into the flour mixture until just blended. Divide the batter between the prepared Bundt pans. Bake the cakes for 25 minutes, or until a toothpick inserted near the center comes out clean. Invert immediately onto a cooling rack. Cool 10 minutes. Serve warm with a scoop of vanilla ice cream drizzled with Spiced Syrup.

Makes 12 servings.

Note: Chai tea powder can be found in the coffee and tea section of most supermarkets.

Spiced Syrup

2 cups (packed) light brown sugar
2 cups water
¾ cup dark corn syrup
1½ tablespoons fresh lemon juice
1¼ teaspoons ground cinnamon
½ teaspoon vanilla extract

In a large deep saucepan, add the brown sugar, water, corn syrup, lemon juice, cinnamon, and vanilla extract. Cook over medium-low heat until the sugar dissolves. Attach a candy thermometer to one side of the pan. Increase the heat to high. Boil, without stirring, until a candy thermometer registers 220 degrees, occasionally swirling the pan and brushing down the sides with a wet pastry brush for about 12 minutes. Carefully strain the syrup into a medium bowl. Cool to room temperature.

Makes 12 servings.

BIO CHANG WECHS
Change
Wechsel

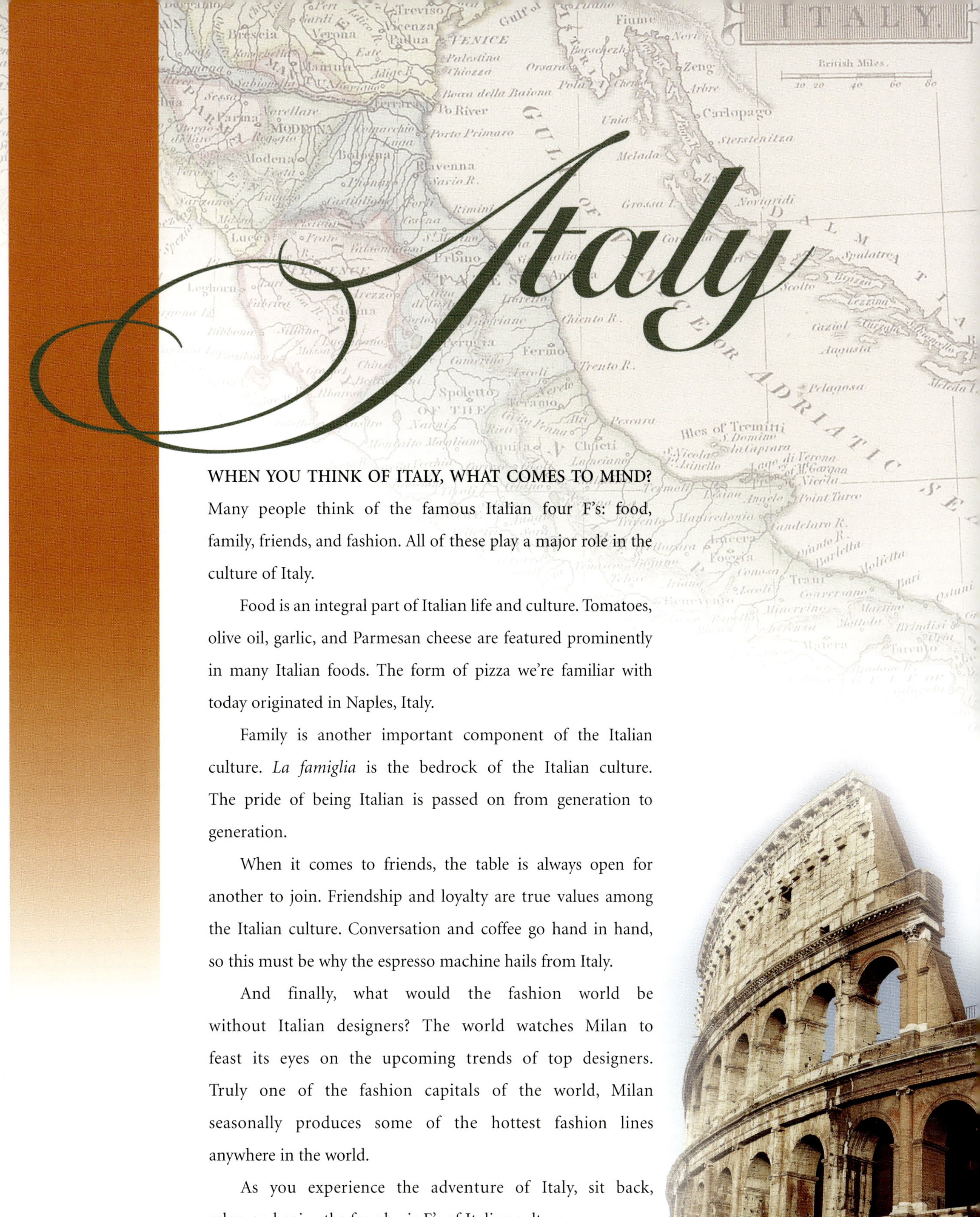

Italy

WHEN YOU THINK OF ITALY, WHAT COMES TO MIND? Many people think of the famous Italian four F's: food, family, friends, and fashion. All of these play a major role in the culture of Italy.

Food is an integral part of Italian life and culture. Tomatoes, olive oil, garlic, and Parmesan cheese are featured prominently in many Italian foods. The form of pizza we're familiar with today originated in Naples, Italy.

Family is another important component of the Italian culture. *La famiglia* is the bedrock of the Italian culture. The pride of being Italian is passed on from generation to generation.

When it comes to friends, the table is always open for another to join. Friendship and loyalty are true values among the Italian culture. Conversation and coffee go hand in hand, so this must be why the espresso machine hails from Italy.

And finally, what would the fashion world be without Italian designers? The world watches Milan to feast its eyes on the upcoming trends of top designers. Truly one of the fashion capitals of the world, Milan seasonally produces some of the hottest fashion lines anywhere in the world.

As you experience the adventure of Italy, sit back, relax, and enjoy the four basic F's of Italian culture.

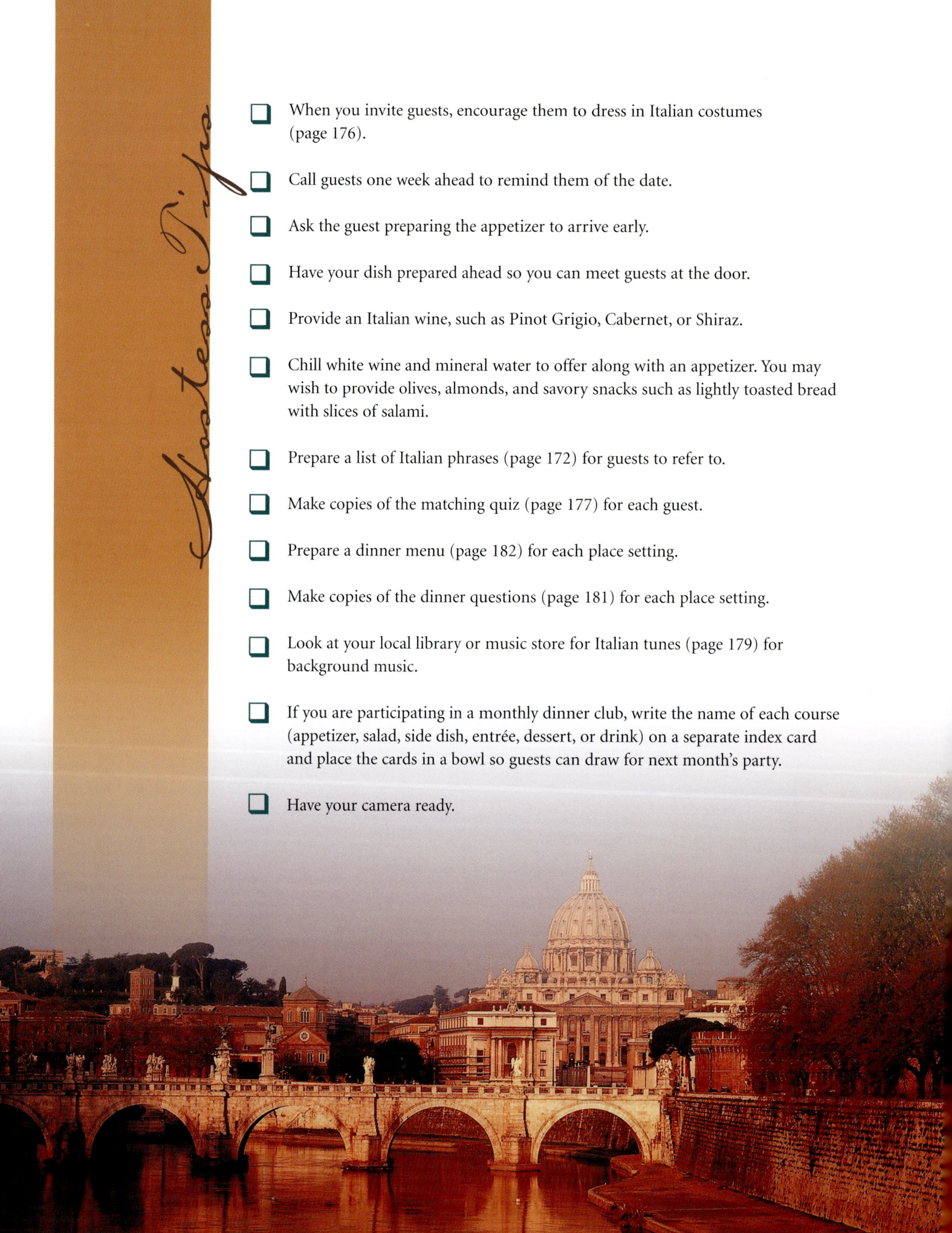

Hostess Tips

- [ ] When you invite guests, encourage them to dress in Italian costumes (page 176).
- [ ] Call guests one week ahead to remind them of the date.
- [ ] Ask the guest preparing the appetizer to arrive early.
- [ ] Have your dish prepared ahead so you can meet guests at the door.
- [ ] Provide an Italian wine, such as Pinot Grigio, Cabernet, or Shiraz.
- [ ] Chill white wine and mineral water to offer along with an appetizer. You may wish to provide olives, almonds, and savory snacks such as lightly toasted bread with slices of salami.
- [ ] Prepare a list of Italian phrases (page 172) for guests to refer to.
- [ ] Make copies of the matching quiz (page 177) for each guest.
- [ ] Prepare a dinner menu (page 182) for each place setting.
- [ ] Make copies of the dinner questions (page 181) for each place setting.
- [ ] Look at your local library or music store for Italian tunes (page 179) for background music.
- [ ] If you are participating in a monthly dinner club, write the name of each course (appetizer, salad, side dish, entrée, dessert, or drink) on a separate index card and place the cards in a bowl so guests can draw for next month's party.
- [ ] Have your camera ready.

Before Dinner

Greet guests with the typical Italian greeting *salve* or *buona sera,* and air kissing on both cheeks, starting with the left side. Encourage guests to try Italian greetings. Have Italian music playing in the background.

Welcome your guests and begin to serve the appetizers. Offer a chilled white wine and mineral water with lemon, along with olives, almonds, and savory snacks such as lightly toasted bread with slices of salami. Offer a breadbasket of rolls or Italian bread and olive oil.

Comment on guests' costumes. As you enjoy the appetizers, invite your guests to try the matching questions.

Dinner

Seat your guests around the dinner table and begin serving the meal.

Invite guests to read and discuss the dinner questions. As the host or hostess, you are the discussion leader. Encourage each person to participate.

After Dinner

After your guests have eaten and you have removed the dinner plates, serve the dessert and coffee. Consider using a coffee press and demitasse cups for an authentic Italian experience.

If you are participating in a monthly dinner club, invite guests to draw names of courses (appetizer, salad, side dish, entrée, dessert, or drink) from a bowl for next month's party, and decide who will host.

Hello	*Salve*
Good evening	*Buona sera*
Good night	*Buona notte*
Please	*Per favore*
Thank you	*Grazie*
Excuse me	*Mi scusi*
May I . . .	*Posso . . .*
Good-bye	*Arrivederci*
See you soon	*A presto*

Table Settings

In Italy you "lay the table" not set the table. For guests at dinner, hosts typically use a cotton or linen tablecloth. They may choose to use place mats only, which is referred to as *all Americana*, although this is not normal for the evening meal. Most often the centerpiece is a flower arrangement, a soup tureen, or some type of silver object.

The knife and soupspoon are placed to the right. The fork for the pasta and the main course are the same size and placed on the left side. The main course knife should always have the blade side pointing toward the plate.

Water and wine glasses are placed to the upper right. The large plate for the entrée is placed below the smaller plate for antipasto.

When the smaller plate is removed, a bowl for soup or pasta replaces it.

Water should be served in a glass pitcher or decanters for a dinner party. This holds true both for flat or carbonated water. The wine can either be put in a decanter or served in its own bottle. Place water and wine on both sides of the table for easy pouring.

Salt and pepper are placed on the table in individual shakers, or shakers are passed from one guest to another.

Salad is often brought to the table dressed, but olive oil and vinegar may be placed on the table so that guests may dress their own salads.

Italians always eat bread with their meal, without butter, so don't place butter on the table. Serve bread either in rolls or cut into thick slices; do not put a bread-cutting knife on the table. Bring the bread to the table in a breadbasket and invite guests to place rolls or slices on individual bread plates.

The napkin is placed on the left side, folded either square or in a triangle. At the end of the dinner party, guests should leave the napkin unfolded, to the right of their plates.

Dining Etiquette

Table manners are Continental; the fork is to be held in the left hand and the knife in the right hand while eating.

Follow the lead of the hostess regarding when to sit, when to begin eating, and when to be dismissed. The host or hostess gives the first toast.

Always take a small amount so you can accept a second serving.

Keep elbows close to the body so as not to disturb those seated on either side of you. Italians keep their arms on the table throughout the meal, but never their elbows.

It is acceptable to leave a small amount of food on your plate.

Pick up cheese with your knife rather than with your fingers.

If you do not want more wine, leave a little wine in your glass.

At the end of each course, leave your knife and fork parallel on the plate with the sharp side of the knife blade facing inward, and fork prongs down to the left of the knife.

Pasta is never served directly onto the plates but is passed after guests have been seated. Pasta is served on a large serving plate or in a pasta bowl. Always offer seconds.

Whenever possible, eat fruit with a fork and a knife.

Serving Tips

Fish is served whole and divided at the table.

Roasts are served already cut and divided into serving-size pieces. Do not carve a roast or fowl at the table.

Cheese is served at room temperature. Remove the cheese from the refrigerator at least one hour before it is served.

Before dessert is served the bread must be removed from the table. Sweets are to be served immediately after the cheese and before the fruit. Cakes are presented whole and then cut into pieces at the table. Pastries are served on a tray with dessert wines and coffee.

Clean plates and food are served from the left and plates are removed from the right.

Water is to be on the table in decanters when the guests are seated. The water glasses are to be filled half full. The wine glass is filled only half full. Water and wine are served from the right.

If different wines are served, the glasses must be changed. Wine should be served in the following order:

1. Light white wine 2. Light red wine 3. Heavy red wine

Red wine should be opened ahead of time; dessert wine is served at the table. Coffee and liqueurs are typically served in the living room.

Gianni Versace and Donatella Versace: These are famous Italian fashion designers. Gianni's costume could be a white T-shirt with a long-sleeved black designer V-neck sweater, black designer jeans, and black designer shoes. Donatella's costume would be an elegant evening dress of gold or yellow. Wear straight blond hair or a blond wig, designer high-heeled red shoes, and designer diamond jewelry.

Gondola driver: The gondola was used as a private means of transport for the rich, but thanks to its great maneuverability, it became the most important means of transporting people. Wear a striped shirt, a straw hat with red ribbon, a red neckerchief, a red sash, and black pants.

Leonardo da Vinci: The artist was renowned for, among other works of art, the *Mona Lisa* and *The Last Supper.* The costume should reflect the Renaissance period, with a long white tunic shirt with billowy sleeves and an open neck with crossover front (no buttons), and black knee breeches (knickers). Accessorize with a leather belt, a white beard, a wig of long flowing white hair, and a painter's palette with a paintbrush. You can find these items at your local costume shop.

Michelangelo: This sixteenth-century artist and sculptor is perhaps most famous for the statue of *David* and the ceiling of the Sistine Chapel. Wear a long black tunic shirt with billowy sleeves and an open neck, and black knee breeches. Accessorize with a short black hair wig, a black mustache, a black beard, and a painter's palette with a paintbrush.

Pulcinella, Arlecchino, Columbina: These characters are from *Commedia dell'arte* (Comedy of Art), a popular form of humorous improvisational theater that began in Italy in the fifteenth century. For Pulcinella, a male character known in English as Punch or Punchinello, wear a black mask and long white coat. For Arlecchino, another male character, wear patched, ragged clothing with a mask. For Columbina, his female counterpart, wear a patched dress and mask.

Icebreaker: Matching

This boot-shaped country has a lot to offer, from pizza to *The Last Supper,* so you are sure to find something that suits your taste. Match the city on the left with the correct description on the right.

1. _____ Venice	a. home of da Vinci's *The Last Supper*
2. _____ Naples	b. known for its leaning tower
3. _____ Milan	c. setting of Shakepeare's *Romeo and Juliet*
4. _____ Sicily	d. known for vaporetti and gondolas
5. _____ Genoa	e. home of Michelangelo's sculpture *David*
6. _____ Siena	f. home of the Pantheon and Colosseum
7. _____ Lake Como	g. birthplace of Christopher Columbus
8. _____ Florence	h. birthplace of Sophia Loren and pizza
9. _____ Pisa	i. an independent country
10. _____ Rome	j. house of Saint Catherine
11. _____ Vatican City	k. site of George Clooney's summer home
12. _____ Verona	l. where *The Godfather: Part III* was filmed

ANSWER KEY

1-d, 2-h, 3-a, 4-l, 5-g, 6-j, 7-k, 8-e, 9-b, 10-f, 11-i, 12-c

ITALY FILM FESTIVAL

The English Patient
Starring Ralph Fiennes, Juliette Binoche, and Willem Dafoe
Directed by Anthony Minghella, 1996

The Godfather
Starring Marlon Brando, Al Pacino, and James Caan
Directed by Francis Ford Coppola, 1972

Life Is Beautiful
Starring Roberto Benigni, Nicoletta Braschi, and Giorgio Cantarini
Directed by Roberto Benigni, 1998

Roman Holiday
Starring Gregory Peck and Audrey Hepburn
Directed by William Wyler, 1953

A Room with a View
Starring Maggie Smith and Helena Bonham Carter
Directed by James Ivory, 1986

Tea with Mussolini
Starring Cher, Judi Dench, and Lily Tomlin
Directed by Franco Zeffirelli, 1999

Under the Tuscan Sun
Starring Diane Lane
Directed by Audrey Wells, 2003

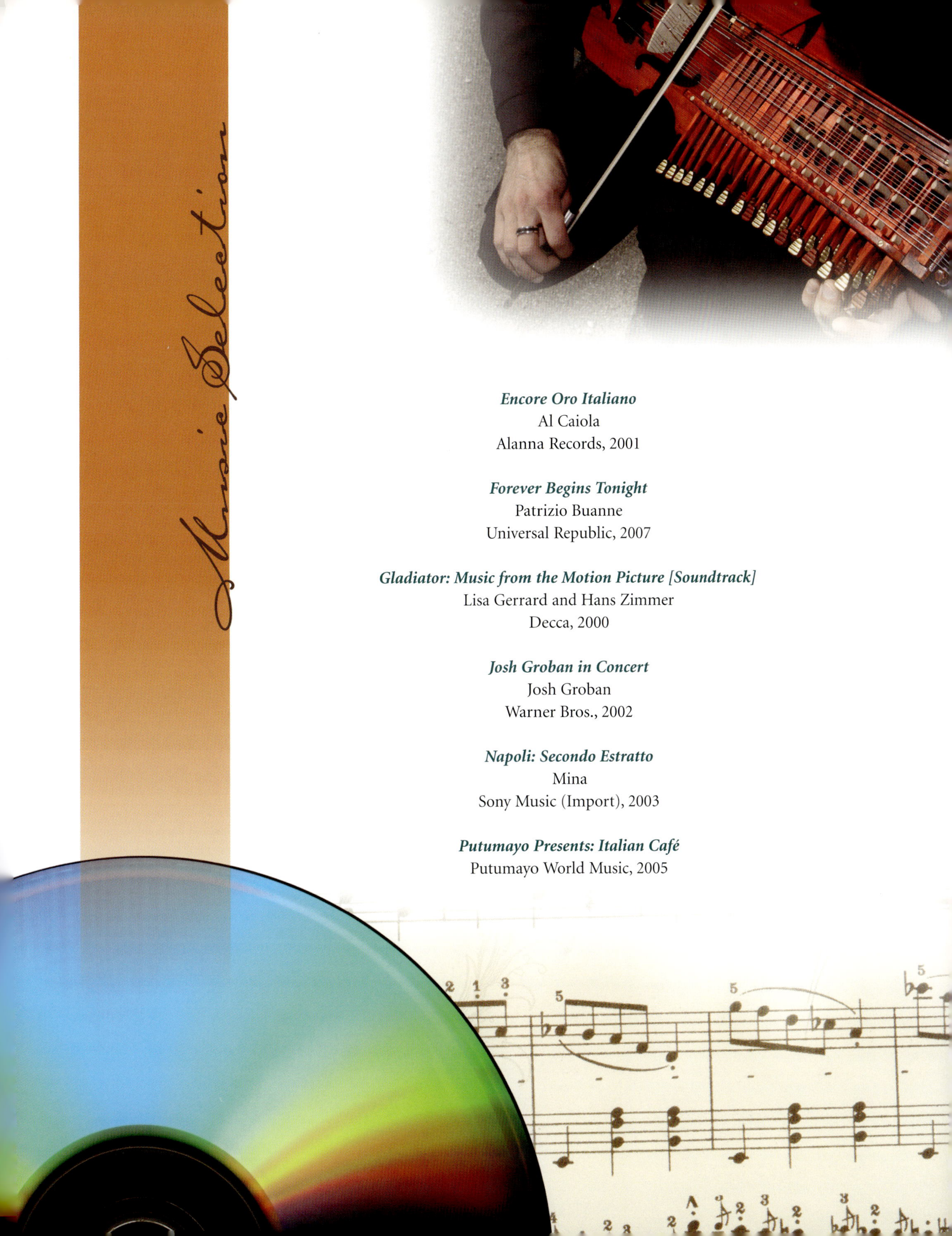

Music Selection

Encore Oro Italiano
Al Caiola
Alanna Records, 2001

Forever Begins Tonight
Patrizio Buanne
Universal Republic, 2007

Gladiator: Music from the Motion Picture [Soundtrack]
Lisa Gerrard and Hans Zimmer
Decca, 2000

Josh Groban in Concert
Josh Groban
Warner Bros., 2002

Napoli: Secondo Estratto
Mina
Sony Music (Import), 2003

Putumayo Presents: Italian Café
Putumayo World Music, 2005

Trivia

Sicily is the largest island in the Mediterranean.

Legend says that Greek philosopher and mathematician Archimedes discovered the concept of buoyancy force while taking a bath in Sicily—shouting *Eureka!* (I have found it).

Leonardo Da Vinci wasn't born in Florence or the nearby town of Vinci, as some believe. He was born a few kilometers away in the small town of Anchiano.

The movie *The Passion of the Christ* was filmed in the Basilicata province of Italy, not in Jerusalem as many think.

Christopher Columbus set sail to discover the new world from Spain, but he was originally from the northern Italian port city of Genoa.

Over two-thirds of the city of Siena's population was wiped out when the plague struck in 1348. Siena was the worst hit of all the towns in Tuscany.

The Italian flag was designed by Napoleon in 1796. He changed the blue stripe in the French flag to a green strip for the Italian flag.

Italy is the birthplace of Leonardo da Vinci, Michelangelo, Dante, Petrarch, Boccaccio, Nicolo Machavelli, Pierre Cardin, Sophia Loren, Rudolph Valentino, Gianni Versace, and Frank Capra.

Dinner Questions

1. Italy was one of the founders of the European Economic Community (now the EU). Do you think all of Europe should use the euro? Why or why not?

2. The term *bella figura* means good image, which is important to Italians. Do you think we have become too image conscious? In what ways?

3. In Italy the family is the center of the social structure and provides a stabilizing influence for its members. Who or what is a stabilizing influence in your life?

4. In Italy a bottle of fine wine is a typical gift to give a hostess. What is your favorite gift to give a hostess?

5. Milan is one of the fashion capitals of the world. Who is your favorite designer?

6. Marco Polo set out from Venice on his voyage to China. What is the longest trip you have taken? What hardships have you encountered on a trip?

7. About 75 percent of the Italian peninsula is mountains, with the Alps separating the country from France, Switzerland, and Austria. Which of these four countries would you most like to visit, and why?

8. Bologna stands out as one of the many beautiful cities of Italy. The Bolognese have given us tortellini, lasagna, mortadella, and spaghetti. What is your favorite pasta dish?

9. Some famous Italian inventions are the thermometer, eyeglasses, the typewriter, ketchup, the fork, the mechanical clock, and the radio. Which of these inventions has had the biggest impact on our society?

Suggested Menu

Appetizer	Tomato Bruschetta
Salad	Spinach Salad with Pine Nuts
Side Dish	Spaghetti Squash with Broccoli and Zucchini
Entrée	Penne with Fresh Tomatoes and Spicy Basil Pesto
Dessert	Tortoni

Appetizer

Tomato Bruschetta

- 3 cups diced tomatoes
- 1 cup chopped fresh basil
- ½ cup extra-virgin olive oil, divided
- 4 garlic cloves, minced and divided
- 1 teaspoon salt
- 1 teaspoon freshly ground pepper
- 1 large loaf crusty Italian bread, cut into 12 (¼-inch-thick) slices

Preheat the oven to 350 degrees. In a medium bowl, add the tomatoes, basil, ¼ cup olive oil, half the minced garlic, salt, and pepper. Toast the bread slices for 5 minutes, or until golden. Rub the remaining minced garlic against the slices of toasted bread—the crisp bread will act like a grater, wearing down the garlic as the bread is flavored. Drizzle the 12 slices of bread with the remaining ¼ cup olive oil. When ready to serve, top the bread slices with a spoonful of the tomato mixture, and drizzle with a little additional olive oil.

Makes 6 servings.

Spicy Goat Cheese Tartlets

10 ounces prepared pie crust
3 cups uncooked beans, for crust weights
7 ounces goat cheese
½ cup heavy cream
1 teaspoon salt
1 teaspoon freshly ground pepper
1 teaspoon crushed red pepper flakes
½ cup minced orange zest
½ cup paper-thin sliced fresh ginger
Fresh dill for garnish

Preheat the oven to 375 degrees. Roll out the dough to ⅛-inch thickness. Cut the dough to fit 12 small tart pans (use fluted mini-brioche molds if you want scalloped edges), and press the dough firmly into the pans. Place ¼ cup beans in each crust, bake for 15 minutes, and remove the crusts from the pans. Combine the goat cheese, cream, salt, pepper, and crushed red pepper; spoon into the crusts. Garnish with orange zest, ginger slices, and dill.

Makes 12 servings.

Ricotta and Goat Cheese Crostini

¾ cup part-skim ricotta
¾ cup goat cheese
2 tablespoons Dijon mustard
1 tablespoon extra-virgin olive oil
2 tablespoons chopped fresh basil

1 teaspoon hot sauce
1 teaspoon salt
1 teaspoon freshly ground pepper
1 loaf crusty Italian bread, cut into 1⁄4-inch-thick slices
5 sun-dried tomatoes packed in oil, drained, and julienned

Preheat the oven to 275 degrees. In a medium bowl, combine the ricotta, goat cheese, mustard, olive oil, basil, and hot sauce. Season with the salt and pepper, mix well, and lightly toast the slices of bread. Spread a small amount of the cheese mixture on each slice. Top with the sun-dried tomatoes.

Makes 6 servings.

Spinach Salad with Pine Nuts

1 tablespoon extra-virgin olive oil
2 garlic cloves, finely chopped
1 teaspoon lemon juice
6 cups fresh spinach
½ teaspoon salt
½ teaspoon freshly ground pepper
1 tablespoon toasted pine nuts

Heat the oil in a large sauté pan over medium heat. Add the garlic and lemon juice, and sauté for 1 minute. Turn the heat to high, and add the spinach, salt, and pepper. Wilt the spinach, tossing with tongs to coat the leaves with the hot oil mixture. Toss in the pine nuts.

Makes 6 servings.

Caprese Salad

16 slices tomato, divided
16 slices fresh mozzarella cheese, divided
16 fresh basil leaves, divided
2 tablespoons coarse sea salt
2 tablespoons freshly ground pepper
½ cup extra-virgin olive oil
½ cup balsamic vinegar

On each of four plates, place one slice of tomato, and top with a basil leaf and slice of mozzarella cheese. Repeat, making four layers on each plate. Sprinkle with the salt and pepper. Drizzle with the olive oil and balsamic vinegar.

Makes 4 servings.

Spaghetti Squash with Broccoli and Zucchini

❖❖❖

2 pounds spaghetti squash
1 cup broccoli flowerets
1 cup sliced zucchini
1 cup sliced fresh mushrooms
1 cup sliced carrots
1 garlic clove, minced
2 teaspoons extra-virgin olive oil
1 tablespoon skim milk
½ cup part-skim ricotta cheese
1 tablespoon grated Parmesan cheese
1 teaspoon butter
¼ teaspoon salt
1 teaspoon Italian seasoning
½ teaspoon freshly ground pepper

Wash the squash, and cut in half lengthwise; discard the seeds. Place the squash cut side down in a Dutch oven, and add 3 inches water. Bring the water to a boil, and cover and cook for 20 minutes, or until the squash is tender. Drain the squash and cool. Use a fork to scoop out the spaghetti-like strands. Measure 4 cups of the squash strands. Steam the broccoli, zucchini, mushrooms, and carrots for 7 minutes, or until tender. In a large bowl, combine the squash and the steamed vegetables, tossing gently. Cover to keep warm. In a medium saucepan, heat the olive oil and sauté the garlic. Add the milk, ricotta, Parmesan, butter, salt, Italian seasoning, and pepper to the saucepan. Cook over low heat, stirring constantly, until the mixture is hot. Toss the sauce into the vegetables gently.

Makes 6 servings.

Entrée

Baked Ziti with Roasted Eggplant

2 cups peeled and cubed eggplant
6 tablespoons extra-virgin olive oil, divided
2 garlic cloves, minced
1 (35-ounce) can plum tomatoes (do not drain)
1 teaspoon salt
1 teaspoon black pepper
1 teaspoon crushed red pepper flakes
6 cups water
1 pound ziti
1 cup torn fresh basil leaves, plus extra sprigs for garnish
1 cup grated Parmesan cheese
1 cup ricotta
6 ounces fontina cheese, sliced
1 cup bread crumbs
Basil sprig

Preheat the oven to 400°. Place the eggplant on a baking sheet lined with parchment paper, and drizzle with 3 tablespoons olive oil. Place in the oven and roast for 25 minutes, flipping once so that the cubes cook evenly.

In a large saucepan over medium-high heat, warm the remaining 3 tablespoons olive oil. Add the garlic and sauté for 2 minutes. Add the tomatoes with their juice, salt, black pepper, and crushed red pepper. Bring the mixture to a boil, and simmer for 10 minutes. In a large pot, bring the water to a boil. Salt the water, add the ziti, and cook until al dente. Drain the pasta, add it to the sauce, and toss. Remove the eggplant from the oven, and add it to the pasta along with the basil. Gently stir in the Parmesan and ricotta, and transfer the mixture to a large baking dish. Top with the fontina slices and bread crumbs, and bake at 350° until the cheese is slightly golden, about 25 minutes. Garnish with a basil sprig.

Makes 6 servings.

Entrée

Lemon Fettuccine

❖❖❖

- 4 cups water
- 1 teaspoon salt
- 2 cups shelled fresh peas
- 3 tablespoons unsalted butter
- 1 teaspoon freshly ground pepper
- 2 tablespoons grated lemon zest
- ⅔ cup heavy cream
- 1 pound fresh egg fettuccine

In a large pot, bring the water to a boil, add the salt and peas, and boil for 3 minutes. Use a slotted spoon to strain the peas, and set them aside. Keep the water boiling. In a deep skillet over medium heat, warm the butter. Add the peas and season with salt and pepper. Add the lemon zest and heavy cream, and cook until the sauce comes to a boil and thickens. Add the fettuccine to the pot of boiling water, and cook until al dente. Drain the pasta, and add it to the skillet. Toss the pasta with the sauce to coat evenly.

Makes 6 servings.

Penne with Fresh Tomatoes and Spicy Basil Pesto

❖❖❖

- 6 cups water
- 2 teaspoons salt, divided
- 1 pound short penne

Basil pesto:

- 4 cups fresh basil leaves, plus an extra sprig for garnish
- 2 teaspoons crushed red pepper flakes
- 1 cup extra-virgin olive oil, plus extra
- 1 teaspoon minced garlic
- 1 teaspoon freshly ground pepper
- 1 cup cherry tomatoes, quartered

Bring a large pot of water to a boil. Add 1 teaspoon salt and the penne, and cook until al dente. In a food processor or blender, add the basil, crushed red pepper, olive oil, garlic, 1 teaspoon salt, and pepper. Purée the mix until smooth. Drain the pasta, and return it to the warm pot. Toss in the pesto. Transfer to a serving bowl, and garnish with the cherry tomatoes and a sprig of basil.

Makes 6 servings.

Pasta and Cannellini Beans Neapolitan

- ½ cup minced onion
- 2 garlic cloves, minced
- ½ cup extra-virgin olive oil
- 10 cups soaked cannellini beans
- 4 quarts water
- 2 celery hearts, sliced
- 2 cups diced tomatoes
- 10 fresh basil leaves, torn
- 8 ounces mezzi tubetti (short tubular pasta without lines)

Infused oil:

- ½ cup extra-virgin olive oil
- 9 fresh rosemary sprigs
- 15 fresh sage leaves
- 3 garlic cloves, crushed
- 1 fresh chili pepper
- 1 teaspoon salt
- 1 teaspoon freshly ground pepper

Sauté the onion and garlic in the olive oil in a large pot for 5 minutes over medium heat. Add the beans and 4 quarts water; bring to a gentle boil, and lower the heat to medium-low. Cook for 1½ hours, adding more water if necessary to keep the beans covered.

For the infused oil, heat the olive oil with the rosemary, sage, garlic, and chili pepper for 5 minutes over medium-low heat and strain. When the beans are cooked, add the celery hearts, tomatoes, basil, and mezzi tubetti to the pot; cook until the mezzi tubetti are done, about 10 minutes. Season with the salt and pepper, and drizzle each serving with the infused olive oil.

Makes 8 servings.

Chicken Arugula

❖❖❖

6 skinless, boneless chicken breasts
1 cup flour
5 garlic cloves, minced and divided
3 tablespoons butter
1½ cups Marsala cooking wine, divided
3 tablespoons extra-virgin olive oil
1¼ cups chicken broth, divided
20 mushrooms, sliced
4 cups (uncooked) arugula
1½ teaspoons salt
1 teaspoon freshly ground pepper
½ pound fresh mozzarella, cut in 6 thin slices
Fresh parsley sprigs for garnish

Place the chicken breasts between 2 pieces of wax paper and pound until thin; then drag the breasts through the flour. In a large skillet, sauté slightly more than half the garlic in melted butter until the garlic is just slightly browned. Add the floured breasts, and brown about 3 minutes on each side. Remove to a dish. On very low heat, add 1 cup wine, the olive oil, and 1 cup chicken broth. Add the remaining garlic, and stir with a wooden spoon for a moment. Add the sliced mushrooms, cook until tender, about 5 minutes. Preheat the oven to 350 degrees. Add the arugula, and cook on low until just limp. Mix gently. Stir in the remaining ½ cup wine and the remaining ¼ cup broth. Season with the salt and pepper. Simmer for a moment or two and remove from the heat. Top each cutlet with the mushroom and arugula mixture, and then top with slices of mozzarella. Bake at 350 degrees until cheese is melted. Garnish with parsley sprigs.

Makes 6 servings.

Variations: This recipe can be made with veal rather than chicken. And if you prefer, spinach can be used instead of arugula. Red roasted peppers or artichoke hearts can replace the mushrooms. Black cured olives, capers, or basil can also be added.

Recipe by JoAnne Lotorto

Tortoni

2½ cups heavy cream
1 teaspoon vanilla
1¼ teaspoons dark rum
¾ cup powered sugar
1 cup finely crushed coconut macaroons
2 egg whites
½ cup sliced almonds, toasted
8 maraschino or candied cherries

Fill muffin tins with liners. Whip the cream until moderately stiff. Add the vanilla, rum, and powered sugar. Continue to whip as the cream begins to hold stiff peaks. Slowly add the crushed cookies. In a separate bowl, beat the egg whites until stiff. Slowly fold the cream mixture into the egg whites. Scoop the mixture into the muffin tins until two-thirds full. Sprinkle the toasted almonds on top of each tortoni, and add a cherry. Place in the freezer for 2 to 3 hours, or until firm.

Makes 8 servings.

Japan

FOR THE JAPANESE, LIFE IS AN EXERCISE IN DISCIPLINE, AESTHETICS, AND ATTENTION TO PROCESS. How something is done is as important as the end result. Beauty is considered at all cost. Even the natural landscape in Japan offers an invitation to experience some of the world's most beautiful and magnificent scenery. Whether winter, spring, summer, or fall each changing season brings new images to behold.

The traditional Japanese diet is one of the healthiest in the world, including tofu, miso, sushi, green tea, and soba (noodles made from buckwheat flour). Historically, Japanese cuisine has been one of the greatest cuisines of the world. It is a delight to all senses—sight, smell, and taste.

We often think of Japan as a single island, but it is actually four large islands and thousands of smaller ones. The volcanic and mountainous terrain provide for lush forests and heavy rainfall, much of it from monsoons. Crop land is limited and primarily used for rice. As you would expect, fish, both fresh and preserved, plays a major dietary role in Japan.

As you experience this country you will come to appreciate the beauty for yourself. From sushi to the kimono, Japan is truly an art of its own. Enjoy the calm serenity that comes from drinking green tea and greeting friends with a bow.

Hostess Tips

- [ ] When you invite guests, encourage them to dress in Japanese costume (page 198).
- [ ] Call guests one week ahead to remind them of the date.
- [ ] Ask the guest who is preparing the appetizer to arrive early.
- [ ] Have your dish prepared ahead so you can meet guests at the door.
- [ ] Make copies of the matching quiz (page 203) for each guest.
- [ ] Prepare a list of Japanese phrases (page 196) for guests to refer to.
- [ ] Prepare a copy of the menu (page 205) for each place setting.
- [ ] Make copies of the dinner questions (page 204) and place at each setting.
- [ ] Visit your local library or music store for Japanese music (page 201) in the background.
- [ ] Provide chopsticks with the meal.
- [ ] Provide sake with dinner for those who wish to try it.
- [ ] Provide a hashi oki or wine cork for each place setting.
- [ ] If you are participating in a monthly dinner club, write the name of each course (appetizer, salad, side dish, entrée, dessert, or drink) on a separate index card and place the cards in a bowl so guests can draw for next month's party.
- [ ] Get your camera ready for eventful pictures!

Before Dinner

Greet your guests with a bow (page 202) and by saying *konnichiwa.* Ask guests to remove their shoes at the door. The shoes are turned around so that the toe faces the door after taking them off.

Offer your guests slippers. (Pedicure slippers are inexpensive and easy to find.)

Welcome guests and serve green tea with the appetizer. Do matching questions.

Dinner

Invite guests to be seated around the table. Hand around hot towels *(o-shibori)* to clean the hands.

Begin the meal by asking guests to repeat *itadakimasu* (ee-tah dah-kee mahs) meaning, "I humbly receive."

Serve all the dishes at once.

Invite guests to read and discuss the dinner questions. As the host or hostess, you are the discussion leader. Encourage each person to participate.

Serve sake with dinner if available.

After Dinner

Ask who would like dessert. Serve green tea with the dessert selection.

If you are participating in a monthly dinner club, invite guests to draw names of courses (appetizer, salad, side dish, entrée, dessert, or drink) from a bowl for next month's party, and decide who will host.

Ask your guests to join you in a farewell, saying *gochisosama deshita* (go-chee-soh sah-mah desh-tah), which means "it was a feast."

Greetings & Phrases

Hello	*Konnichiwa*
How are you?	*O-genki desu ka?*
Please (request)	*Onegai shimasu*
Please (offer)	*Dozo*
Thank you	*Domo arigato*
Excuse me	*Sumimasen*
Yes	*Hai*
No	*Iie*
Good–bye	*Sayonara*

Dining Etiquette & Table Settings

Japan is noted for its refined etiquette and sincere appreciation for the host. At the beginning and close of the meal two expressions are said out loud: *itadakimasu* at the beginning of the meal to express appreciation for the meal prepared, and *gochisosama deshita* after the meal to express gratitude for the meal and for the hospitality of the person who prepared it.

Most Japanese families have dining tables and chairs in their homes, but on formal occasions meals are enjoyed on a low table at which people kneel. Try serving your dinner on a low table with cushions provided for guests to sit on.

Soup is served in a small bowl with no rim. Soup is always to be drunk directly from the bowl and not eaten with a spoon.

Nearly all meals are accompanied by green tea. It is acceptable to add a little green tea to your rice bowl to clear up any remaining grains.

Everyone starts eating at the same time, usually after a speech or greeting.

Aesthetics are important in Japanese culture. Take time to admire the presentation of the food, the bowls, and the decorations at the table.

When it comes to using the chopsticks *(hashi)* never give or receive food directly from someone else's chopsticks; do not pull a plate toward you using your chopsticks; do not spear or stab food with your chopsticks. Use the chopsticks for picking up, catching, supporting, scooping, breaking up, and dividing the food. Never gesture using chopsticks, and do not pass food with your chopsticks to another person. When you are sharing from a communal plate or dish, turn your chopsticks round and use the opposite end to pick up the food and put it in your bowl.

It is acceptable to eat sushi with your fingers, rather than chopsticks.

It is perfectly acceptable to make a slurping noise when eating hot noodles. This is standard behavior in Japan, and Japanese maintain that inhaling air when eating hot noodles improves the flavor.

While resting during a meal, place your chopsticks on a chopstick holder, a *hashi–oki*. A *hashi–oki* is usually a ceramic rectangle about four centimeters long and is part of the individual place setting. You may use a wine cork in its place.

Place the rice bowl slightly to the left, and the soup bowl to the right of it. Place the side dishes next to the soup bowl. If using plates, begin with the largest plate in the middle and the two smaller ones to the side.

Geisha girl: Wear a long silk or satin cloak (or bathrobe) with a Japanese print. Use a long wide sash *(obi)* as the belt. Wear white cotton socks or stockings and thong sandals with wood platforms (or use flip-flops). Accessorize with a long black wig or put your hair up with silk flowers as accent pieces. Make-up should be white face paint or talcum power, pink eye shadow, black eyeliner, and dark lipstick. Don't forget your fan. You also can find geisha costumes at your local costume shop.

Karate gi: Karate is a combination of art, sport, and self-defense training. Wear a Kung Fu top, pants, and shoes (or black wrestling shoes). Accessorize with a colorful belt and headband. Or you could borrow a friend's gi or find one at your local costume shop.

Kimono: Kimonos are T-shaped, straight robes that fall to the ankle, with collars and full-length sleeves. The sleeves are usually very wide at the wrist. The sash is about fifteen feet long and about a foot wide and used as a belt. Accessorize with white stockings, flip-flop style sandals, and a black wig. Kimonos can be rented at your local costume shop.

Ninja: A Ninja is a spy, usually trained for stealth. A ninja costume should include a black tunic, a belt pouch, black pants, a mask, and boots. Accessorize with a ninja sword. You can find a Ninja costume at a costume shop.

Sumo wrestler: Sumo is a competitive contact sport where two heavy-set wrestlers face off in a circular ring. You can rent a sumo wrestling costume featuring a body suit with an attached hoop inside to simulate the bulky figure. Accessorize with a character wig and goatee. Inflatable sumo suits can also be rented.

Dojo Kun

Karate has a *dojo kun,* which is basically a set of guidelines for *karetekas* (karate students) to follow in everyday life, both in and out of the *dojo* (a class in which karate is taught).

- Seek perfection of character.
- Be faithful.
- Endeavor.
- Respect others.
- Refrain from violent behavior.

What Is Sake?

To the Japanese sake means any alcoholic beverage, but actually it is an alcohol fermented from rice. The process starts by grinding the rice down into a fine starch. From this point the starch is fermented into sugar, and then transformed into alcohol.

Unlike wine, sake rarely ages and is best enjoyed while still fresh; it has a high alcohol content ranging from 14 to 16 percent. Sake is graded on dryness, maturity, and depth.

Goji
(The original Godzilla movie)
Starring Akira Takarada and Momoko Kochi
Directed by Ishiro Honda, 1954

Memoirs of a Geisha
Starring Ziyi Zhang, Suzuka Ohgo and Ken Watanabe
Directed by Rob Marshall, 2005

Miyazaki's Spirited Away
Starring Rumi Hiragi, Miyu Irino, and Mari Natsuki
Directed by Hayao Miyazaki and Kirk Wise, 2001 (Animated)

Seven Samurai
Starring Takashi Shimura and Toshirô Mifune
Directed by Akira Kurosawa, 1956

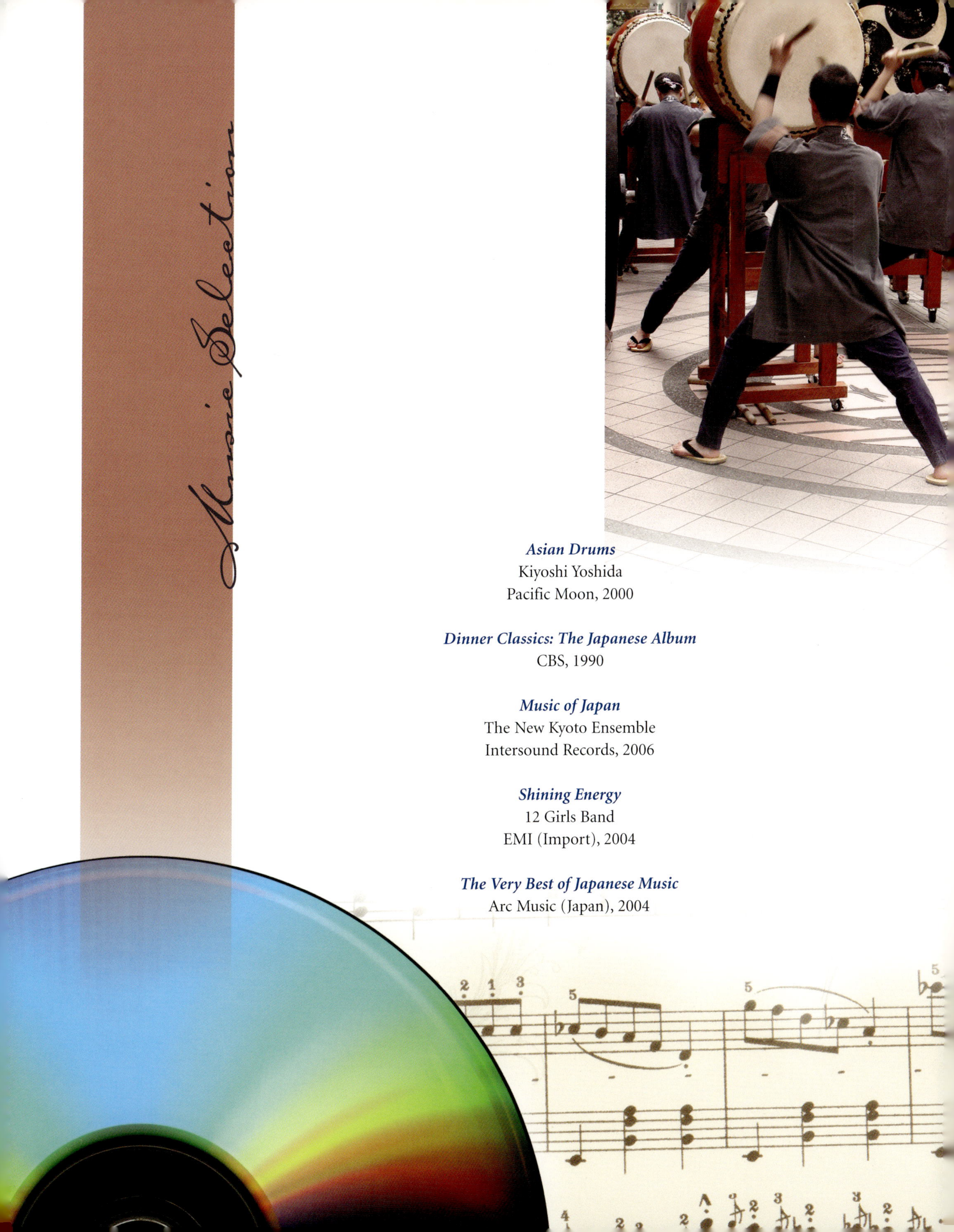

Music Selection

Asian Drums
Kiyoshi Yoshida
Pacific Moon, 2000

Dinner Classics: The Japanese Album
CBS, 1990

Music of Japan
The New Kyoto Ensemble
Intersound Records, 2006

Shining Energy
12 Girls Band
EMI (Import), 2004

The Very Best of Japanese Music
Arc Music (Japan), 2004

Bowing Etiquette

Bowing is a gesture of honor and respect, and can range from a small head nod to a long 90-degree bow from the waist. It can indicate apologies and gratitude, and express humility, sincerity, and remorse. Bowing is used in various traditional arts and religious ceremonies.

The basic bow is done with a straight back and eyes gazing downward. Males hold their hands at their sides while females clasp their hands in their lap. Generally, the longer and deeper the bow, the stronger the emotion and the respect expressed.

If your counterpart is of higher social status, you bow deeper and for a longer time. If the other person holds the bow for longer than expected (generally about two or three seconds), you should bow again, and you may receive another bow in return.

Icebreaker: Matching

Match the Japanese term on the left with the definition on the right.

1. _____	Tako	a.	calligraphy
2. _____	Tempura	b.	robes
3. _____	Bonsai	c.	vinegar-flavored rice topped with raw fish
4. _____	Shodo	d.	fluttering kites
5. _____	Wasabi	e.	food
6. _____	Origami	f.	female entertainer
7. _____	Tofu	g.	sumo wrestler
8. _____	Futon	h.	tea ceremony
9. _____	Sake	i.	art of flower arranging
10. _____	Sashimi	j.	straw mats
11. _____	Sushi	k.	coffee
12. _____	Cha	l.	covered with batter and fried
13. _____	Geisha	m.	art of dwarf trees
14. _____	Kimonos	n.	horseradish
15. _____	Tatami	o.	rice wine
16. _____	Ikebana	p.	soybean curd
17. _____	Rikishi	q.	raw fish
18. _____	Shabu-shabu	r.	cotton mattress
19. _____	Chanyou	s.	green tea
20. _____	Kohhi	t.	folding paper

ANSWER KEY

1-d, 2-l, 3-m, 4-a, 5-n, 6-t, 7-p, 8-r, 9-o,
10-q, 11-c, 12-s, 13-f, 14-b, 15-j, 16-i
17-g, 18-e, 19-h, 20-k

Dinner Questions

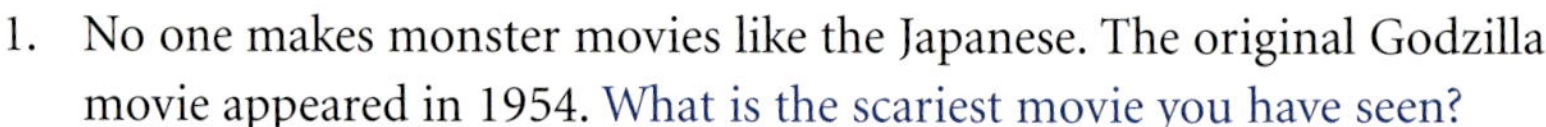

1. No one makes monster movies like the Japanese. The original Godzilla movie appeared in 1954. What is the scariest movie you have seen?

2. In Japan January 15 is "coming of age day" for 20-year-olds, the day they are officially adults. What were you doing at age 20?

3. About 1,500 earthquakes affect Japan every year. Not a day passes without at least a slight tremor somewhere in the country. Have you or someone you know experienced an earthquake? What was it like?

4. Kite flying was a popular court activity in the eighteenth century. Fluttering kites *(tako)* were sent aloft as prayers for good luck, prayers of thanksgiving, prayers for a child's health, or protection from evil. When did you last fly a kite? Share a kite story.

5. The Japanese are very detail oriented. From calligraphy to bonsai, origami to sushi, their work speaks of perfection. In what way are you a perfectionist?

6. It is believed that using chopsticks develops the dexterity of the fingers, which in turn stimulates the brain. When did you first use chopsticks? Demonstrate your brainpower by picking up something with your chopsticks now.

7. From ancient times until the mid-nineteenth century, rice was used as currency for paying taxes and wages. If you had to barter for exchange, what would you use?

8. In Japan the rule of thumb is to never kill the natural flavor of the ingredients. The ingredients work together to make harmony. What are your favorite flavors mixed together?

Suggested Menu

Appetizer	Chicken Teriyaki Skewers
Soup	Eggplant Miso Soup
Salad	Crunchy Japanese Salad
Side Dish	Vegetarian Sushi
Entrée	Miso Pork
Dessert	Green Tea Chocolate Cake
Beverage	Hot Green Tea

Chicken Teriyaki Skewers

❖❖❖

12 bamboo skewers
2 pounds chicken tenders

Marinade:

½ cup soy sauce
2 teaspoons vegetable oil
1 tablespoon sugar
2 teaspoons minced fresh ginger
1 teaspoon minced garlic
½ cup toasted sesame seeds
8 green onions, minced

In a large bowl, soak the bamboo skewers in water for at least one hour. Thread each bamboo skewer with the chicken tenders, and place the skewers in a deep glass dish. Preheat the broiler. In a medium bowl, combine the soy sauce, oil, sugar, ginger, garlic, sesame seeds, and green onions. Pour the marinade over the skewers, and let sit for 30 minutes. Place the marinated skewers on a baking sheet. Broil the skewers for 4 minutes, and turn them over and broil until the chicken is fully cooked. Serve on the skewers.

Makes 6 servings.

Eggplant Miso Soup

❖❖❖

8 cups water
4 tablespoons miso paste
2 cups julienned eggplant
1 cup cubed tofu
1 cup julienned carrots
2 cups spinach leaves
½ cup sliced mushrooms
6 green onions, minced

Boil the water in a large saucepan. Add the miso, and boil until completely dissolved. Lower the heat to a simmer, and add the eggplant, tofu, carrots, spinach, and mushrooms. Cook until the vegetables are tender. Sprinkle with the green onions and serve.

Makes 8 servings.

Crunchy Japanese Salad

2 packages chicken flavor ramen noodles, broken up
4 tablespoons sesame seeds
½ cup slivered almonds
3 cups grated cabbage
4 green onions, chopped
½ cup grated carrot
½ cup bean sprouts

Dressing:
½ cup vegetable oil
3 tablespoons rice vinegar
2 tablespoons sugar
1 teaspoon salt
½ teaspoon pepper
1 ramen seasoning packet

Preheat the oven to 350 degrees. On a large baking sheet, place the broken ramen noodles, sesame seeds, and almonds. Bake for about 7 minutes, and cool. In a large bowl, combine the cabbage, green onions, carrots, and bean sprouts. Fold in the toasted ramen noodles, sesame seeds, and almonds. In a small bowl, whisk together the oil, vinegar, sugar, salt, pepper, and seasoning packet. Drizzle the dressing over the salad, and gently toss.

Makes 6 servings.

Miso Spinach Salad

7 cups water
1 teaspoon salt
3 (6-ounce) bags fresh baby spinach
1 teaspoon mirin (see note)
1 teaspoon dashi (see note)
½ teaspoon sugar
½ teaspoon fresh lemon juice
¼ teaspoon minced lemon zest
8 ounces firm tofu, cubed
1 tablespoon toasted white sesame seeds

In a large saucepan, bring the water and salt to a boil. Using tongs, transfer the spinach leaves into the boiling water, and cook for about 2 minutes. Transfer the spinach to a colander, and press the excess water out of the blanched spinach leaves. Transfer the spinach to a large bowl, and fluff with a fork. In a medium bowl, add the mirin, dashi, sugar, lemon juice, and lemon zest. Whisk until well combined, add the tofu, and gently coat the tofu with the mixture. Spoon the tofu dressing over the spinach and toss. Sprinkle the sesame seeds over the salad to serve.

Makes 6 servings.

Note: Mirin is cooking wine made from fermented rice, and dashi is a fish and sea vegetable broth. You can find them in the ethnic aisle in your grocery store or in an Asian market.

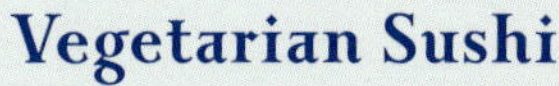

Vegetarian Sushi

2½ cups mayonnaise
1¼ cups Dijon mustard
2 (1-ounce) packages roasted seaweed (20 sheets)
8 cups cooked Sushi Rice (recipe follows)
4 cups julienned avocado, divided
4 cups julienned cucumber, divided
4 cups julienned radishes, divided
4 cups julienned carrot, divided
4 cups julienned zucchini, divided
2 cups toasted sesame seeds
2 cups soy sauce, divided
2 (10-ounce) jars pickled ginger
2 (1.5-ounce) tubes wasabi paste

Tools:
Bamboo sushi mat
Plastic wrap

In a small bowl, combine the mayonnaise and mustard. Wrap the bamboo sushi mat in plastic. Lay 1 sheet roasted seaweed on top of the mat, and spread 1 cup cooked sushi rice with your hands until the seaweed evenly covers the mat. Spread a little less than ½ cup of the mayonnaise and mustard mixture over the rice. Add 1 cup of the julienned avocado, cucumber, radishes, carrots, and zucchini in a strip along the bottom of the bamboo mat with the bamboo facing lengthwise. Roll the mat and press the ingredients together evenly, keeping the plastic on the outside of the roll. Repeat this entire process until you have eight rolls. Cut each roll into eight slices and serve on eight individual plates; top each cut roll with toasted sesame seeds. Divide the soy sauce into eight ¼-cup measures, and serve each roll with one serving of soy sauce, about 2 ounces of the pickled ginger, and 1 teaspoon of the wasabi paste.

Makes 8 servings.

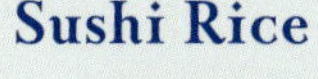

Sushi Rice

8 cups sushi rice
8 cups water
1 cup rice vinegar
½ cup sugar
¼ cup salt

Pour the rice into a large bowl, rinse with cold water, squeeze the water out of the rice, and drain. Repeat the rinsing process until the water is clear, and let soak for 30 minutes. Transfer the rice to a large saucepan, add 8 cups water, and cover. Bring to a boil, and reduce to a simmer for 15 minutes. Do not uncover the rice. Let it stand for 15 minutes.

In a medium saucepan, combine the vinegar, sugar, and salt, and heat until the sugar and salt are completely dissolved. Cool. Transfer the cooled rice to a wooden bowl with a wooden spatula. Move the rice around, and separate the clumps with a spatula. Fold in the cooled vinegar mixture, and fan out the rice while combining the two. Cover with a damp towel until ready to serve.

Makes 8 servings.

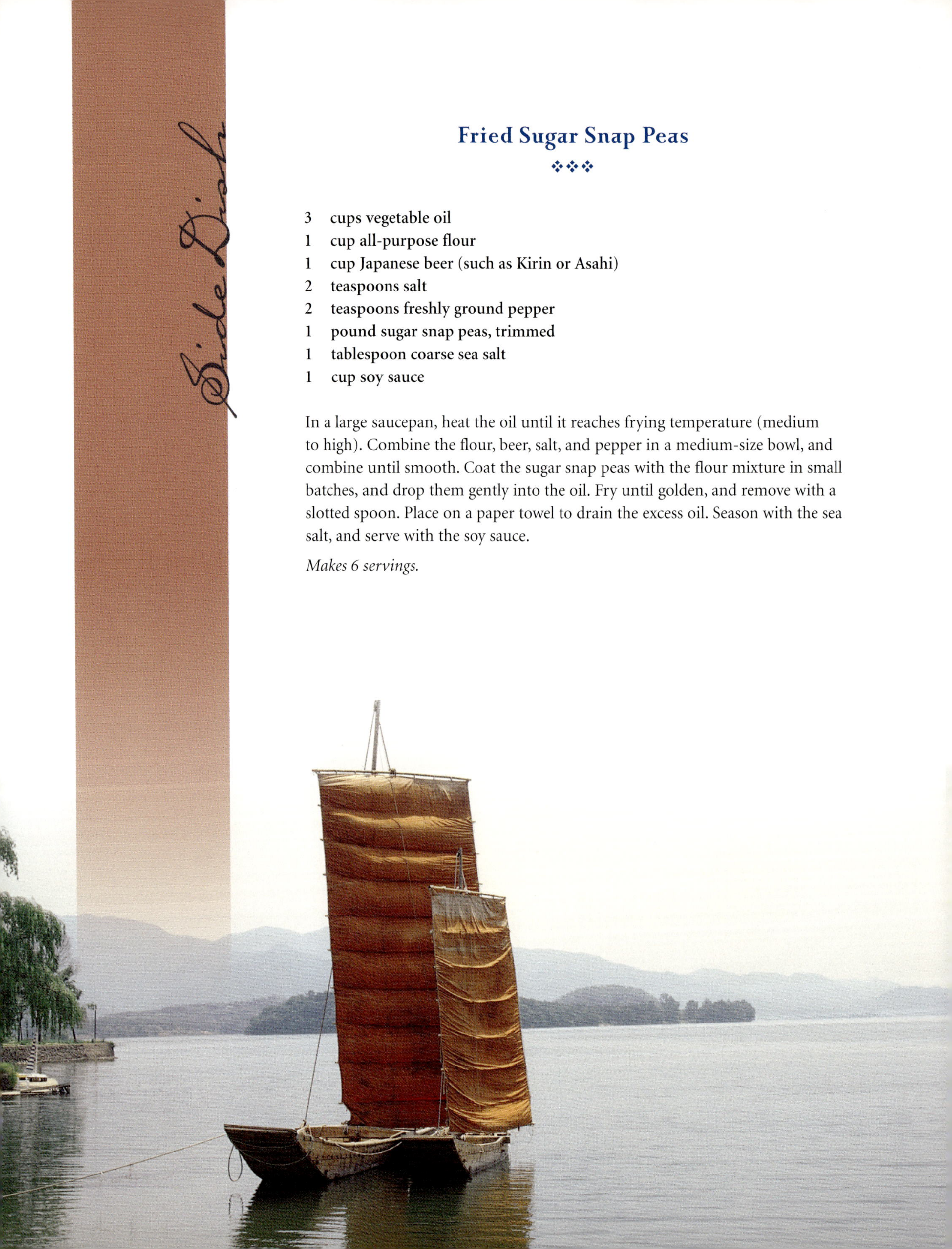

Fried Sugar Snap Peas

- 3 cups vegetable oil
- 1 cup all-purpose flour
- 1 cup Japanese beer (such as Kirin or Asahi)
- 2 teaspoons salt
- 2 teaspoons freshly ground pepper
- 1 pound sugar snap peas, trimmed
- 1 tablespoon coarse sea salt
- 1 cup soy sauce

In a large saucepan, heat the oil until it reaches frying temperature (medium to high). Combine the flour, beer, salt, and pepper in a medium-size bowl, and combine until smooth. Coat the sugar snap peas with the flour mixture in small batches, and drop them gently into the oil. Fry until golden, and remove with a slotted spoon. Place on a paper towel to drain the excess oil. Season with the sea salt, and serve with the soy sauce.

Makes 6 servings.

Japanese Eggplant

- 3 tablespoons vegetable oil
- 4 cups 1-inch-thick eggplant slices
- 2 teaspoons minced garlic
- ¼ cup sliced red onion
- 2 cups water
- 2 tablespoons sugar
- 3 tablespoons soy sauce
- 3 tablespoons mirin (see note, page 208)
- 2 teaspoons dashi (see note, page 208)
- 1 teaspoon crushed red pepper flakes
- ⅓ cup julienned fresh ginger
- ⅓ cup chopped cilantro

Heat the oil and brown the eggplant on both sides in a large saucepan over medium heat. Add the garlic and red onion, and sauté for 3 minutes. Add the water, sugar, soy sauce, mirin, dashi, crushed red pepper, and ginger; simmer for 10 minutes. Remove the eggplant, transfer to a shallow dish, and cover. Bring the sauce to a boil, and reduce by half. Pour the sauce over the eggplant, and garnish with cilantro.

Makes 6 servings.

Miso Pork

❖❖❖

Marinade:

2 cups water
½ cup soy sauce
1 cup white miso (see note)
1½ tablespoons ketchup
¼ cup firmly packed brown sugar
2 tablespoons minced garlic
1 tablespoon minced fresh ginger

Pork:

2 pounds pork cutlet [8 (4-ounce) cutlets]
2 tablespoons sesame oil
1 teaspoon coarse sea salt
1 teaspoon freshly ground pepper

In a 9 x 13-inch glass dish, combine the water, soy sauce, miso, ketchup, sugar, garlic, and ginger. Marinate the pork cutlets, covered, in the refrigerator for 30 minutes. Preheat the oven to 400 degrees. Heat the sesame oil in a large skillet, and sear the marinated pork cutlets for 3 minutes on each side. Pour the remaining marinade into a small saucepan, and bring to a boil. Place the pork back into the glass dish, and pour the marinade over the top. Bake for 15 to 20 minutes, or until the pork is fully cooked and a meat thermometer reads 165 degrees. Season with the salt and pepper. Let rest for 5 minutes before serving.

Makes 8 servings.

Note: White miso comes from the Kyoto region of Japan and has a sweeter taste and a smoother texture than darker miso. Look for white miso at your local Asian market.

Ginger Miso Salmon

❖❖❖

2 tablespoons rice vinegar
3 tablespoons white miso (see note, page 212)
3 tablespoons mirin (see note, page 208)
3 tablespoons soy sauce
2 tablespoons minced fresh ginger
6 (6-ounce) salmon fillets
2 tablespoons black and white sesame seeds
2 tablespoons minced green onions

In a glass baking dish, blend together the rice vinegar, miso, mirin, soy sauce, and ginger. Add the salmon, cover, and marinate for 1 hour in the refrigerator. Preheat the oven to 350 degrees. Remove the marinated salmon from the refrigerator, and bake for 20 minutes, or until fully cooked. Transfer to six individual plates, and sprinkle the salmon with the black and white sesame seeds and green onion.

Makes 6 servings.

Green Tea Ice Cream

1½ cups whole milk
2½ cups heavy cream
2 tablespoons matcha (see note)
10 egg yolks
1½ cups sugar
1 vanilla bean, split and seeds scooped out

Special equipment:
Ice cream maker

Bring the milk and heavy cream to a boil in a large saucepan. Add the matcha, and remove from the heat. In a large bowl, whisk together the egg yolks, sugar, and vanilla bean seeds. Add the egg mixture to the saucepan with the tea and cream mixture. Cook until it has an eggnog consistency. Let cool and cover; chill for 1 hour. Transfer to the ice cream maker to freeze.

Makes 6 servings.

Note: Matcha is powdered Japanese green tea. You can find matcha at most Asian markets or online at www.matchasource.com

Green Tea Chocolate Cake

1 cup softened butter
2 cups granulated sugar
2 whole eggs
2 egg yolks
2 tablespoons matcha (see note, page 214)
½ cup milk
2½ cups all-purpose flour
1½ teaspoons baking powder
½ cup semisweet chocolate chips
1½ cups dark chocolate chips

Preheat the oven to 350 degrees. In a large bowl, cream together the butter and sugar. Add the 2 whole eggs one at a time, and stir in the yolks. In a small bowl, add the matcha and milk, and whisk until well combined. Add the matcha mix to the butter mixture. Add the flour and baking powder, and fold until well combined. Add the semisweet chocolate chips, and gently fold into the batter. Pour the batter into a greased and floured Bundt pan. Bake for 22 minutes, or until a toothpick comes out clean. Let the cake cool in the pan for 15 minutes. Invert the pan on a rack, remove the cake, and allow it to cool completely. Place the dark chocolate chips in a small, microwave-safe bowl. Microwave, uncovered, on medium-high for 1 minute. Stir until smooth. If necessary, microwave for an additional 15 seconds until completely melted. To serve, slice the cake, place the slices on a dish, and drizzle with the melted chocolate.

Makes 8 servings.

STANDING ON THE TIP OF SPAIN YOU ARE ABLE TO GAZE INTO A WHOLE NEW WORLD: Morocco is just across the Strait of Gibraltar and easily accessible by boat. Upon arrival in the old city of Marrakech, you may choose to visit Djemaa el Fna, the main square, for dinner. If you are traveling in the fall, keep in mind Morocco practices Ramadan, a month of prayer and fasting during the daylight hours. (It falls on a different calendar month each year, but is usually in September or October.) You may find your surroundings quite somber but rest assured that after the sun has set the square begins to take on a life of its own. There is singing and dancing, celebration and laughter. The cities of Tangiers, Fez, and Marrakech all boast colorful bazaars and balmy nights.

Eating is both a practical and a social ritual, with the midday meal the main meal. Women virtually do all the cooking in this very traditional country. With a strong Arab influence, it is not uncommon for Moroccans to eat using the first and third fingers and a piece of bread as a utensil. Moroccan cooking is rich in spices that enhance, not hide, the flavor of the food. Some commonly used spices are cinnamon, black pepper, ginger, cayenne pepper, and cumin, to name a few.

MOROCCO

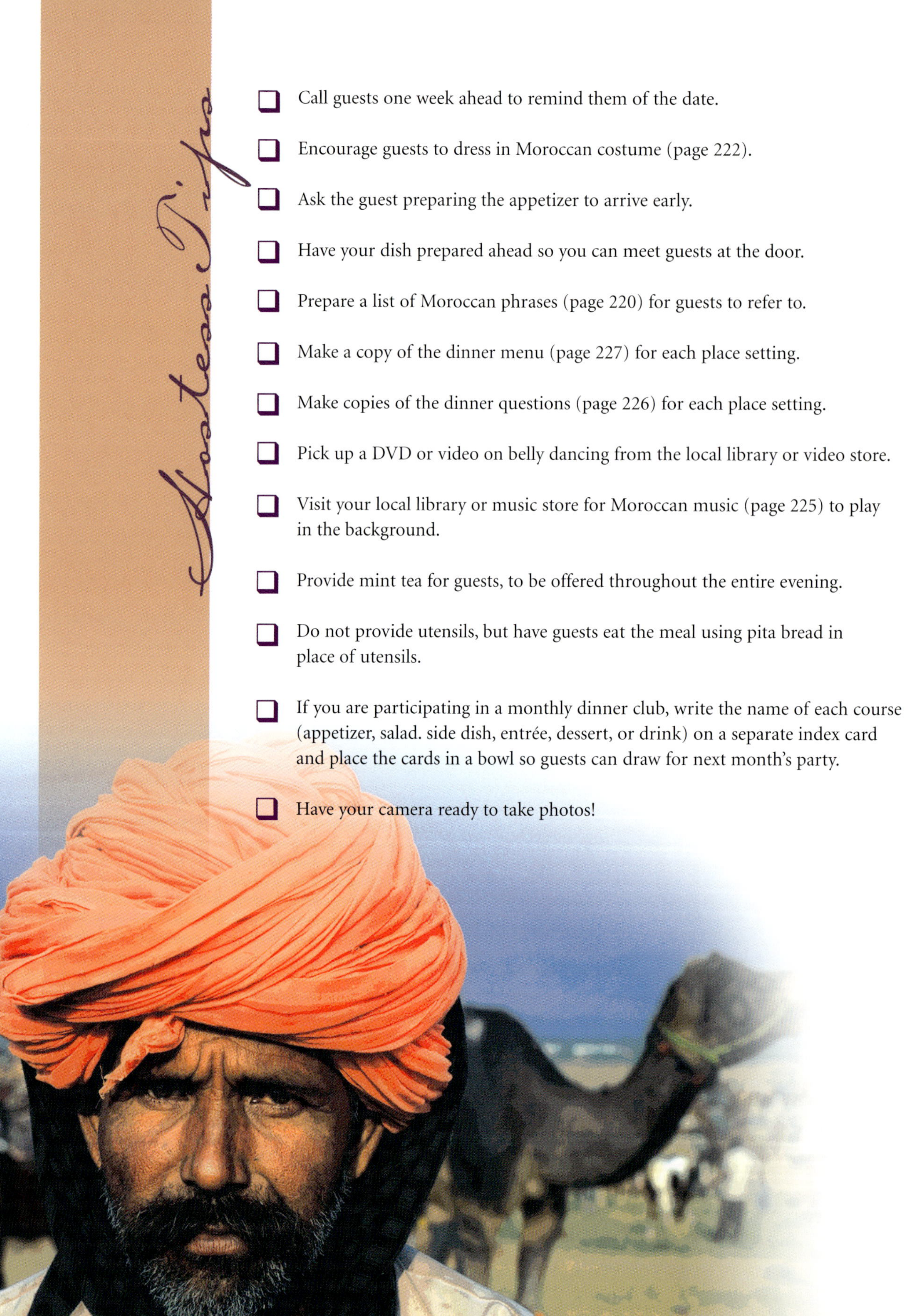

Hostess Tips

- ❑ Call guests one week ahead to remind them of the date.
- ❑ Encourage guests to dress in Moroccan costume (page 222).
- ❑ Ask the guest preparing the appetizer to arrive early.
- ❑ Have your dish prepared ahead so you can meet guests at the door.
- ❑ Prepare a list of Moroccan phrases (page 220) for guests to refer to.
- ❑ Make a copy of the dinner menu (page 227) for each place setting.
- ❑ Make copies of the dinner questions (page 226) for each place setting.
- ❑ Pick up a DVD or video on belly dancing from the local library or video store.
- ❑ Visit your local library or music store for Moroccan music (page 225) to play in the background.
- ❑ Provide mint tea for guests, to be offered throughout the entire evening.
- ❑ Do not provide utensils, but have guests eat the meal using pita bread in place of utensils.
- ❑ If you are participating in a monthly dinner club, write the name of each course (appetizer, salad. side dish, entrée, dessert, or drink) on a separate index card and place the cards in a bowl so guests can draw for next month's party.
- ❑ Have your camera ready to take photos!

Before Dinner

Greet the guests at the door, and offer them mint tea. Invite them to enjoy the appetizer and discuss costumes. Have Moroccan music playing in the background.

After the appetizer is served, play a belly dancing DVD or video, and ask guests to join in the belly dancing.

Invite guests to move into the dining area. If you have a low table guests can eat at, set cushions on the floor for them to sit on. Cover the table with a bright, brocaded cloth, and give your guests towels to cover their knees.

Dinner

Using an attractive pitcher (silver if possible) filled with warm water that is scented with cologne or perfume, approach each guest with a towel over your left arm and carrying a small basin. Pour a little water over their finger tips and catch the water in the basin.

Encourage guests to use pita to soak up juices and sauces and also to wipe their hands and mouth if necessary.

If serving kebabs, provide additional small plates. The salad may be served as a separate course or served with couscous.

Serve the couscous on a large platter. Guests may either use a large spoon to serve themselves or scoop small balls of couscous from the platter with their fingers and place them directly into their mouths. Encourage your guests to try to roll the couscous into a ball.

Serve slices of melon, watermelon, or cantaloupe speared with toothpicks on a platter (no individual plates) after the couscous.

Invite guests to read and discuss the dinner questions. As the host or hostess, you are the discussion leader. Encourage each person to participate.

After Dinner

When you have finished dinner, ask guests to stay seated while you clear the table.

Begin serving the dessert along with mint tea. It is customary to drink a minimum of three tiny glasses of tea at the close of a meal. Consider using juice glasses.

If you are participating in a monthly dinner club, invite guests to draw names of courses (appetizer, salad, side dish, entrée, dessert, or drink) from a bowl for next month's party, and decide who will host.

Repeat the hand washing. After tea has been served, bring in a tiny incense burner and light it on the table.

Greetings & Phrases

Hello (Peace be to you)	*Salamu lekum*
How are you?	*Labass?*
Please	*Afek*
Thank you	*Shoukran*
Yes	*Iyeh*
No	*La*
Good-bye	*Besslama*

Traditional Cooking

You will not find measuring utensils or electrical appliances in most Moroccan kitchens. Ingredients are measured by experience and taste. Moroccan girls begin their culinary education at a very early age.

Moroccan homes have their heaviest meal at midday. Breakfast is not considered an important meal, and dinner is to be light and refreshing.

The women of the house begin making the midday meal in the morning, and it may take up to four hours to prepare. From freshly grinding spices to chopping vegetables, they consider these preparations an act of love and respect for their family and guests.

The midday meal may start with *bistilla* (a crisp pastry rolled very thin and filled with chicken), followed by beef or lamb kebabs. Then a *tajine* (spicy stew) of chicken or meat may be served with *khubz* (flat bread). *Batinjaan* (eggplant salad) may be served as the next course, followed by couscous, the national dish made from semolina wheat. The meal may end with slices of peeled melon, honey and almond pastries, and a glass of mint tea.

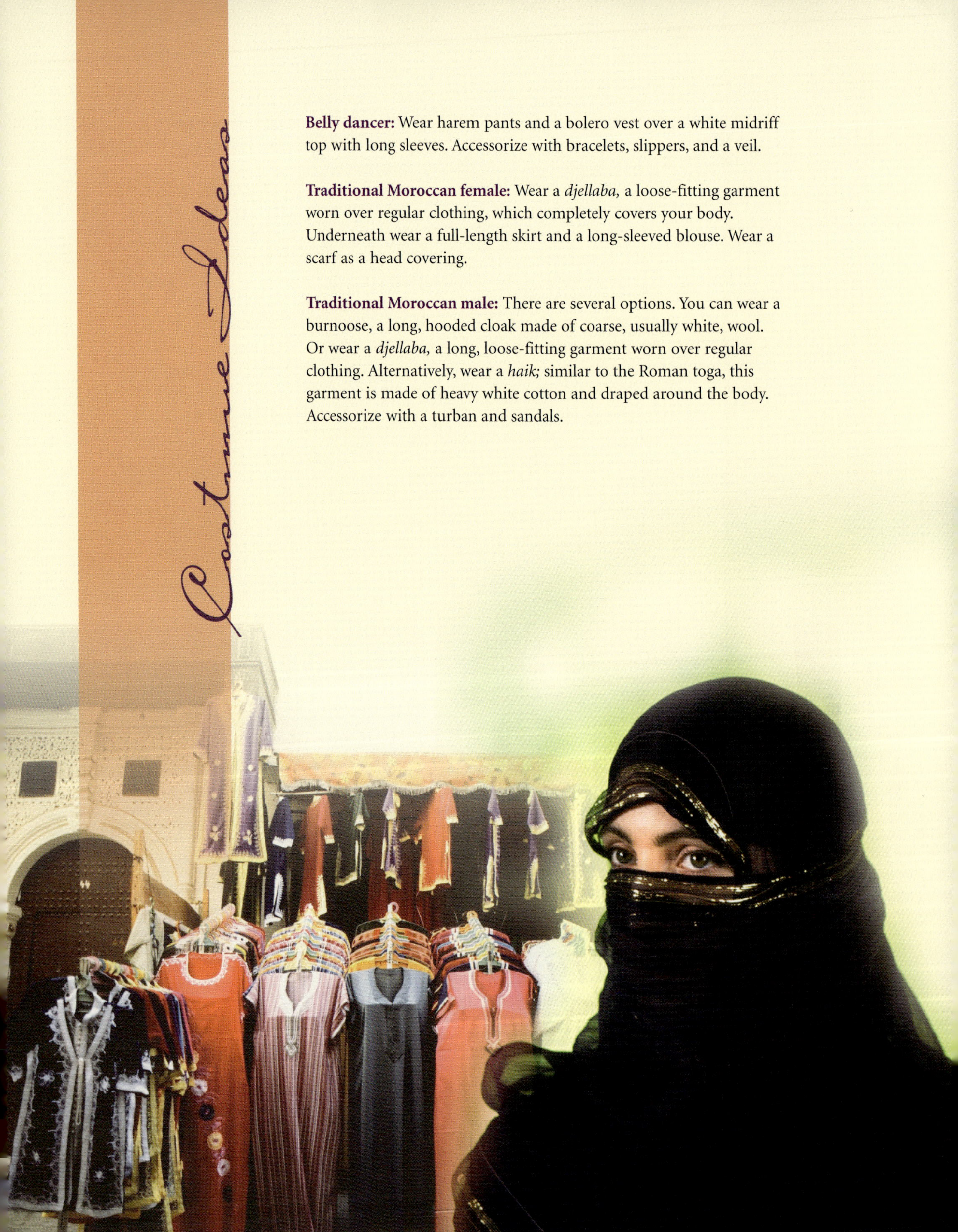

Costume Ideas

Belly dancer: Wear harem pants and a bolero vest over a white midriff top with long sleeves. Accessorize with bracelets, slippers, and a veil.

Traditional Moroccan female: Wear a *djellaba,* a loose-fitting garment worn over regular clothing, which completely covers your body. Underneath wear a full-length skirt and a long-sleeved blouse. Wear a scarf as a head covering.

Traditional Moroccan male: There are several options. You can wear a burnoose, a long, hooded cloak made of coarse, usually white, wool. Or wear a *djellaba,* a long, loose-fitting garment worn over regular clothing. Alternatively, wear a *haik;* similar to the Roman toga, this garment is made of heavy white cotton and draped around the body. Accessorize with a turban and sandals.

Icebreaker: Belly Dancing

Belly dancing is the new wave in exercise and relaxation for both men and women. Belly dancing consists of isolated movements of the abdomen, hips, upper torso, head, and hands. To truly appreciate this type of dance, you must be willing to become uninhibited and completely relaxed.

Belly dancing was thought to be a sacred act and was performed as a gift or offering. The belly was seen as the cup or chalice of life and therefore highly revered. Throughout its thousands of years of existence, different variations of belly dancing have evolved. Belly dancing has been used for various reasons such as, entertainment, childbirth preparation, ritual, exercise, bonding, and celebration.

Some belly dancing moves:

Shoulder circles: begin by making small circles with your shoulders.

Swimmer arms: lift your arms parallel with your shoulders and swim backwards.

Snake arms: allow arms to flow freely as a snake.

Shoulder shimmies: rock shoulders back and forth.

Figure eight: slowly move your head in a figure eight.

Hip circles: rotate hips back and forth as in a hula-hoop.

Pelvic tilt: slowly rotate hips in the yoga cat and cow move.

Figure 8: rock hips back and forth in a figure eight.

Shimmy hips: vigorously shake hips in a horizontal motion.

You can find great websites that teach belly dancing or check your local library for a DVD or video.

The key to truly enjoying this type of dance is in allowing yourself to be completely relaxed and self-confident. Many women find this an excellent way to reconnect with their femininity and self-worth.

Arabian Nights
Starring Mili Avital, Alan Bates, and James Frain
Directed by Steve Barron, 2000

Casablanca
Starring Humphrey Bogart and Ingrid Bergman
Directed by Michael Curtiz, 1943

Jewel of the Nile
Starring Michael Douglas, Kathleen Turner, and Danny DeVito
Directed by Lewis Teague, 1985

Morocco
Starring Gary Cooper and Marlene Dietrich
Directed by Josef von Sternberg, 1930

The Mummy
Starring Brendan Fraser and Rachel Weisz
Directed by Stephen Sommers, 1999

Road to Morocco
Starring Bing Crosby, Bob Hope, Dorothy Lamour,
and Anthony Quinn
Directed by David Butler, 1943

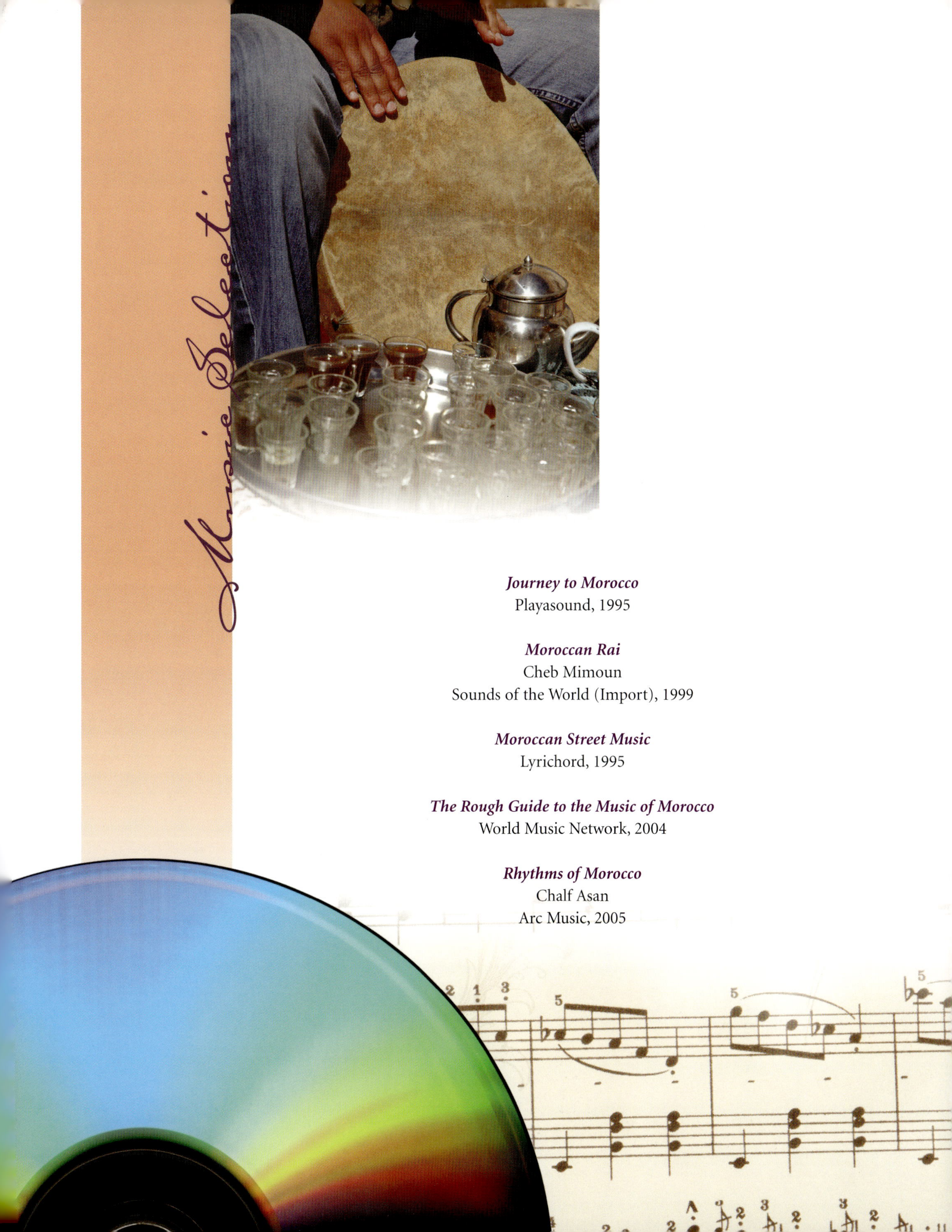

Music Selections

Journey to Morocco
Playasound, 1995

Moroccan Rai
Cheb Mimoun
Sounds of the World (Import), 1999

Moroccan Street Music
Lyrichord, 1995

The Rough Guide to the Music of Morocco
World Music Network, 2004

Rhythms of Morocco
Chalf Asan
Arc Music, 2005

Dinner Questions

1. Morocco is a country of many cultures, and has been occupied by French, Germans, Spanish, Berbers, and Arabs. Although located at the northwest corner of the African continent, black Africans are not native to Morocco. What country or countries did your ancestors come from?

2. King Hassan II describes Morocco as "rooted in Africa, watered by Islam and rustled by the winds of Europe." What would be the best three words to describe you?

3. Morocco is used as a setting for many Hollywood films, the most famous being *Casablanca.* However, the film was actually shot in Hollywood. What famous movie was actually filmed in Morocco? Hint: It was in the Sahara.

4. Muslim culture plays a major role in the homes of Morocco: private and public life are quite separate, with the home to be seen only by family and close friends. When a woman marries, she goes to live with her husband's family. Do you live close to family? Would you like to? Why or why not?

5. The art of henna began with the daughter of the prophet Muhammad, founder of Islam. She decorated her hands and feet with lacy geometric patterns to look like lace gloves. Once the pattern dries, it lasts for weeks. The henna paste is made from the henna plant. Do you or did you ever have a tattoo? Would you get one?

6. Most Moroccan meals include couscous, a grain from semolina, finely ground before it is cooked. It is often served with chicken, lamb, or seafood. The grain has the same role in Moroccan food as rice does in Chinese food. Do you prefer rice or couscous?

7. Moroccans believe in the power of the color blue to ward off evil spirits. The country is full of doorways and windows that are painted blue.
Do you believe in a protective power?

8. Morocco is 99 percent Muslim and observes the month of Ramadan, which calls for abstinence from food and drink through out the daylight hours. Have you ever fasted for physical or spiritual purposes? Share your story.

ANSWER KEY
3. Lawrence of Arabia.

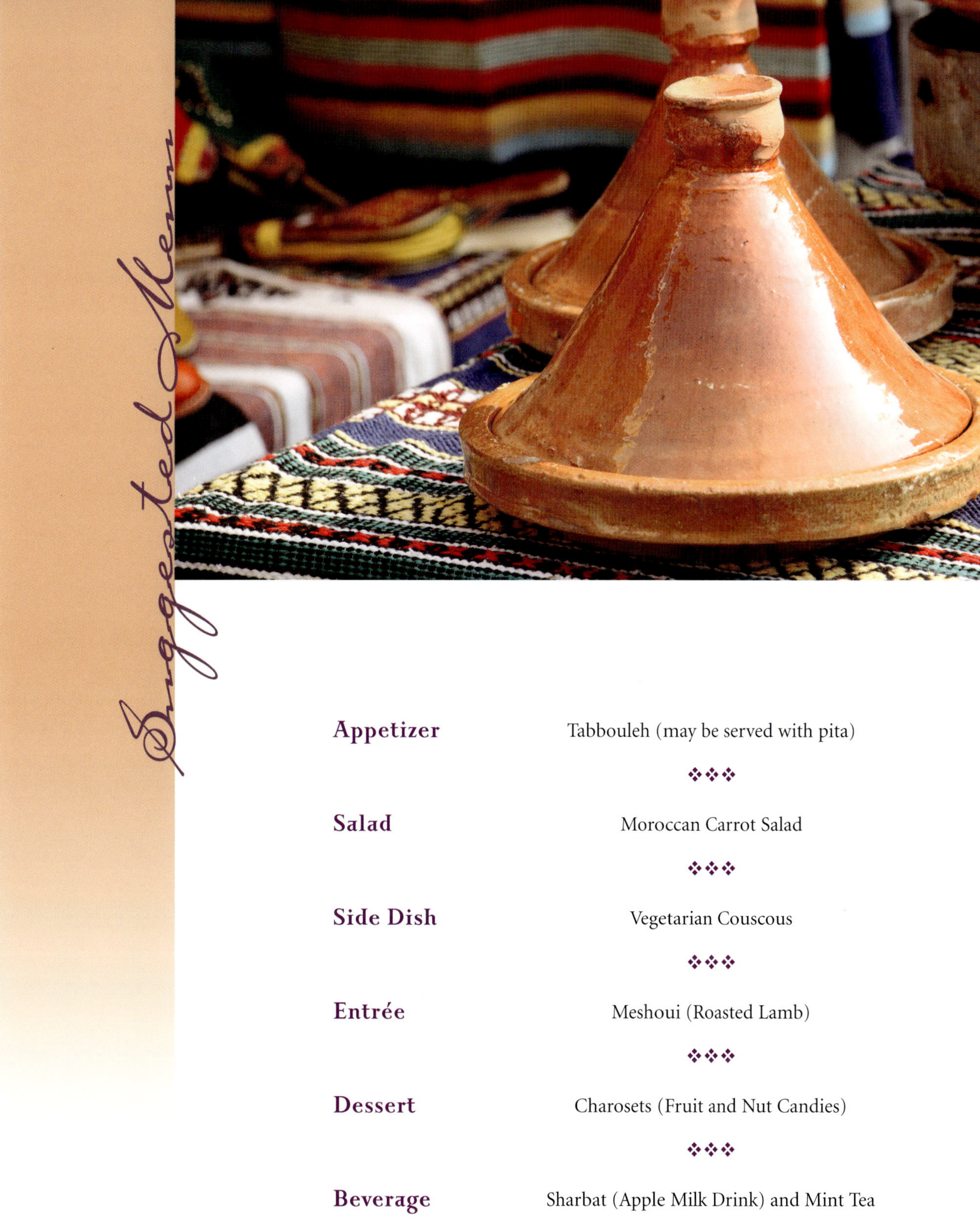

Suggested Menu

Appetizer	Tabbouleh (may be served with pita)
Salad	Moroccan Carrot Salad
Side Dish	Vegetarian Couscous
Entrée	Meshoui (Roasted Lamb)
Dessert	Charosets (Fruit and Nut Candies)
Beverage	Sharbat (Apple Milk Drink) and Mint Tea

Appetizer

Tabbouleh

1 cup bulgur wheat
3 cups cold water
2 cups diced tomatoes
1 cup diced cucumber
½ cup grated carrot
1 cup chopped spinach leaves
½ cup chopped green onions
⅓ cup chopped fresh mint
2 cups chopped fresh parsley
1 teaspoon freshly ground pepper
1 teaspoon salt
½ cup lemon juice
¼ cup olive oil

Put the bulgur wheat and cold water in a large bowl, and soak for 45 minutes. Drain in a fine strainer. Return the bulgur to the bowl, and add the tomatoes, cucumber, carrot, spinach, green onions, mint, and parsley; toss lightly. Refrigerate for 1 hour, and add the pepper, salt, lemon juice, and olive oil. Toss until well combined, and serve.

Makes 6 servings.

Spinach Hummus

❖❖❖

2 (15-ounce) cans chickpeas
1 cup chopped spinach leaves
⅔ cup tahini
½ cup lemon juice
2 tablespoons olive oil
5 garlic cloves, chopped
¼ cup chopped cilantro
2 teaspoons chili powder
1 tablespoon salt
¼ cup chopped fresh parsley
¼ cup toasted pine nuts

In a food processor or blender, place the chickpeas, spinach, tahini, lemon juice, olive oil, garlic, cilantro, chili powder, and salt; blend into a paste. Transfer to a serving dish, and sprinkle with chopped parsley and toasted pine nuts.

Makes 6 servings.

Salad

Mixed Orange Salad

❖❖❖

- ½ cup extra-virgin olive oil
- ¼ cup red wine vinegar
- ¼ cup orange juice
- 1 teaspoon salt
- 1 teaspoon freshly ground pepper
- ½ teaspoon ground cinnamon
- 1 tablespoon honey
- 1 pound mixed salad greens
- ½ cup thinly sliced red onion
- ½ cup thinly sliced radishes
- ½ cup shredded carrots
- ½ cup golden raisins
- 2 cups mandarin oranges
- 1 cup slivered almonds

In a medium bowl, whisk together the olive oil, vinegar, orange juice, salt, pepper, cinnamon, and honey. In a large bowl, add the salad greens, red onion, radishes, carrots, and raisins. Pour the dressing over the salad, and toss well. Serve the salad on individual salad plates, and top with the mandarin oranges and almonds.

Makes 6 servings.

Moroccan Carrot Salad

❖❖❖

2½ cups shredded carrots
½ cup dark raisins
1 tablespoon minced garlic
¼ teaspoon crushed red pepper flakes
1 teaspoon ground cumin
1 teaspoon paprika
¼ teaspoon ground cinnamon
½ teaspoon freshly ground pepper
1 teaspoon salt
1 tablespoon olive oil
1 tablespoon honey
⅓ cup lemon juice
1 tablespoon chopped fresh parsley

In a large bowl, toss the carrots, raisins, garlic, crushed red pepper, cumin, paprika, cinnamon, pepper, and salt. In a small bowl, whisk together the olive oil, honey, and lemon juice. Pour the mixture over the carrot salad and toss. Sprinkle with the parsley, refrigerate, and serve cold.

Makes 6 servings.

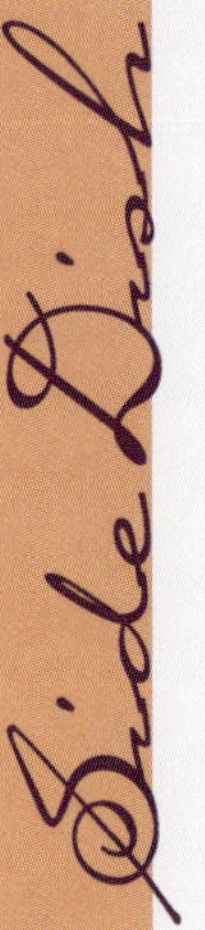

Spicy Spaghetti Squash

❖❖❖

4 pounds spaghetti squash
2 tablespoons butter
2 tablespoons olive oil
3 garlic cloves, minced
¾ cup canned chickpeas
2 teaspoons chili powder
1½ teaspoons ground cumin
1 teaspoon ground coriander
¼ teaspoon cayenne pepper
¼ teaspoon nutmeg
½ teaspoon salt
2 tablespoons chopped fresh cilantro
½ cup toasted pine nuts

In a large saucepan, bring 5 cups water to a boil. Slice the squash in half, remove the seeds, and boil for 20 to 25 minutes. In a small saucepan, heat the butter and olive oil, and sauté the garlic. Add the chickpeas, chili powder, cumin, coriander, cayenne pepper, nutmeg, and salt. When the squash is fully cooked, remove it from the water, and use a fork to remove the squash flesh. Add the squash to the small saucepan, and combine well. Remove the squash from the heat, transfer to a serving bowl, and top with the cilantro and pine nuts.

Makes 8 servings.

Vegetarian Couscous

2 tablespoons olive oil
½ cup diced onion
½ cup shredded carrots
½ cup shredded zucchini
1 cup cubed sweet potato
1 cup vegetable broth
1 (15-ounce) can chickpeas
½ teaspoon ground cinnamon
½ teaspoon ground turmeric
¼ teaspoon ground cumin
1 pound uncooked couscous
½ cup dark raisins
½ cup slivered almonds
½ cup chopped cilantro

In a large saucepan, heat the oil, and sauté the onion, carrot, zucchini, and sweet potatoes for 7 minutes. Add the broth, and bring to a simmer. Add the chickpeas, cinnamon, turmeric, and cumin; cook for an additional 7 minutes. Cook the couscous according to the package directions. Add the cooked couscous, raisins, and almonds to the vegetable mixture, and stir until well combined. Top with the cilantro and serve.

Makes 6 servings.

Entrée

Moroccan Meatloaf

❖❖❖

1½ tablespoons olive oil
1 cup diced onion
4 tablespoons minced garlic
1½ pounds ground lamb
2 eggs
3 tablespoons bread crumbs
½ cup chopped fresh parsley
½ cup chopped fresh mint
1 teaspoon ground cumin
1 teaspoon ground cinnamon
1½ teaspoons salt
½ teaspoon freshly ground pepper
1 package pita bread
2 cups sliced cucumber
2 cups Spinach Hummus (recipe on page 229)
2 cups chopped tomatoes
1 cup sliced red onion
2 cups plain yogurt

Preheat the oven to 400 degrees. In a medium skillet, heat the olive oil, and sauté the onion and garlic. Transfer to a large bowl, and add the lamb, eggs, bread crumbs, parsley, mint, cumin, cinnamon, salt, and pepper. Combine the mixture with your hands, and place in a large loaf pan, but do not compact the meatloaf. Bake for 30 to 40 minutes, or until cooked thoroughly. When the meatloaf is done, let it rest for 30 minutes. Place the pitas on a rack in a warm oven until lightly toasted. Remove from the oven, and stuff the pitas with a ½-inch slice of the meatloaf and the desired amount of cucumber, hummus, tomatoes, red onion, and yogurt. Serve with couscous.

Makes 8 servings.

Meshoui (Roasted Lamb)

❖❖❖

Rub:

½ cup olive oil
2 teaspoons chopped garlic
1 teaspoon ground ginger
½ teaspoon ground turmeric
1 tablespoon paprika
1 tablespoon salt
1 tablespoon pepper

Lamb and vegetables:

1 (4-pound) leg of lamb
½ cup chopped onion
½ cup chopped carrot
¼ cup chopped celery
1 cup chopped tomatoes
1 cup water

Sauce:

2 tablespoons tomato paste
3 cups water
½ cup chopped almonds, blanched

Preheat the oven to 350 degrees. Combine the olive oil, garlic, ginger, turmeric, paprika, salt, and pepper. Rub the seasoning mixture over the leg of lamb, and place it in a roasting pan. Add the onion, carrot, celery, and tomatoes, and cook for 20 minutes. Add the water and cover. Cook for 1 hour and 20 minutes, or until a meat thermometer reads 160 degrees. Set the meat aside, covered. Pour the drippings from the roasting pan into a medium saucepan. Add the tomato paste and 3 cups water. Simmer for 15 to 20 minutes, skimming off the grease. Arrange the lamb with vegetables on a serving platter, top with the chopped almonds, and serve the sauce on the side.

Makes 8 servings.

Moroccan Chicken

½ cup olive oil
1 cup diced onion
1 tablespoon minced garlic
6 skinless, boneless chicken breasts, cubed
1½ cups diced tomatoes
3 tablespoons ground cumin
1½ tablespoons ground coriander
2 teaspoons ground cinnamon
¼ teaspoon cayenne pepper
1 teaspoon paprika
5 saffron threads
1½ cups water
4 russet potatoes, peeled and cubed
1 cup peas
1 cup chopped carrots
1½ teaspoons salt
1 teaspoon freshly ground pepper
1 cup diced red bell pepper
¼ cup chopped fresh parsley

Heat the olive oil, and sauté the onion and garlic in a large stockpot. Add the cubed chicken, tomatoes, cumin, coriander, cinnamon, cayenne pepper, paprika, saffron, and the water. Cook at a simmer, covered, for 1 hour. Add the potatoes, peas, carrots, salt, and pepper, and cook another 20 minutes. When done, transfer to a serving dish, and sprinkle with the red bell pepper and parsley.

Makes 6 servings.

Charosets (Fruit and Nut Candies)

- ½ cup chopped pitted dates
- 4 dried figs, chopped
- ¼ cup golden raisins
- ¼ cup dark raisins
- ¼ cup chopped dried apricot
- ½ cup chopped walnuts
- ¼ cup blanched almonds
- 1 teaspoon honey
- ¼ teaspoon minced fresh ginger
- 2 tablespoons grape juice

Combine the dates, figs, golden raisins, dark raisins, apricots, walnuts, almonds, honey, ginger, and grape juice in a large bowl. Spread the mixture out on a large glass dish, and press evenly into the dish with greased hands. Refrigerate for 2 hours. Cut into 1-inch cubes to serve.

Makes 12 servings.

Dessert

Couscous Pudding

❖❖❖

¾ cup water
½ cup uncooked couscous
1 tablespoon unsalted butter
½ large banana, chopped (about ½ cup)
1 tablespoon (packed) golden brown sugar
1½ cups plus 2 tablespoons chilled whipping cream
5 tablespoons sweetened cream of coconut (see note)
1 tablespoon Triple Sec
½ cup minced candied pineapple
1½ cups peeled and diced fresh pineapple

Bring the water to a boil in a heavy, medium saucepan over high heat. Stir in the couscous, and remove from the heat. Cover and let stand until the water is absorbed, about 15 minutes. Fluff the couscous with a fork. Melt the butter in a small, nonstick skillet over medium-high heat. Add the banana and sugar, and sauté until the banana is soft, about 1 minute. Cool.

Using an electric mixer, beat the whipping cream in a large bowl until soft peaks form. Fold in the cream of coconut and Triple Sec. Reserve 6 tablespoons whipped cream mixture for topping. Fold the candied pineapple, couscous, and banana into the remaining whipped cream mixture in a large bowl. Divide the mixture among six parfait glasses or dessert bowls. (The dessert can be made 4 hours ahead. Cover the whipped cream mixture and puddings separately to refrigerate.) Top each pudding with some of the reserved whipped cream mixture. Sprinkle each with the fresh pineapple to serve.

Makes 6 servings.

Note: Sweetened cream of coconut is available in the liquor section of most supermarkets.

Beverage

Sharbat (Apple Milk Drink)

4 red delicious apples, peeled and chopped
4 teaspoons orange blossom water (see note)
3 cups cold milk
⅔ cup orange juice
3 tablespoons sugar

In a blender or food processor, combine the chopped apples, orange blossom water, milk, orange juice, and sugar. Purée until almost liquid. Refrigerate for 2 hours. Serve very cold with ice.

Makes 6 servings.

Note: Orange blossom water is distilled water that contains oils of the orange blossom. It complements the flavor of foods by adding a hint of citrus. You can find orange blossom water in some supermarkets, Middle Eastern markets, or online at www.lotusblossomwatergardens.com.

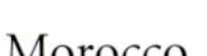

Barer-Stein, Thelma. *You Eat What You Are: People, Culture and Food Traditions.* Buffalo, NY: Firefly Books, 1999.

Bellinger, Martha Fletcher. *A Short History of the Drama.* New York: Henry Holt and Company, 1927.

Chang, Kwang-chih (editor). *Food in Chinese Culture: Anthropological and Historical Perspectives.* New Haven: Yale University Press, 1977.

Chao, Buwei Yang. *How to Cook and Eat in Chinese.* New York: The John Day Company, 1945.

Chen, Pearl Kong, Tien Chi Chen, and Rose Tseng. *Everything You Want to Know about Chinese Cooking.* Woodbury, NY: Barron's, 1983.

Cuisine Cuisine. "Basic Indian Spices and Ingredients." http://www.cuisinecuisine.com/BasicIndianSpices.htm.

Cuisine Cuisine. "Introduction to Indian Cuisine." http://www.cuisinecuisine.com/IndianCuisine.htm.

Cuisine Net. "Japanese Cuisine." http://www.cuisinenet.com/digest/region/japan/index.shtml.

Cuisine Net. "Moroccan Food." http://www.cuisinenet.com/glossary/morco.html.

Devine, Elizabeth and Nancy L. Braganti. *The Traveler's Guide to Asian Customs and Manners.* New York: St. Martin's Griffin Press, 1998.

Devine, Elizabeth and Nancy L. Braganti. *The Traveler's Guide to European Customs and Manners.* New York: Meadowbrook Books, 1984.

Devine, Elizabeth and Nancy L. Braganti. *The Traveler's Guide to Latin American Customs and Manners.* New York: St. Martin's Griffin Press, 2000.

Greeka.com. "Greece Traditions: Information about the Customs and Traditions of Greece." http://www.greeka.com/greece-traditions.htm.

Lahcen's Moroccan Cooking. "The Art of Moroccan Cuisine, A Culture of Eating, Drinking, and Being Hospitable." http://fescooking.com/?page_id=24.

Masson, Kari. "Table Etiquette in France." About.com: French Travel. http://gofrance.about.com/od/culture/a/tablemanners.htm.

Mothershead, Alice Bonzi. *Dining Customs Around the World.* Garrett Park, MD: Garrett Park Press, 1982.

Pazzaglia, Alice Ann. "Italian Table Etiquette." http://www.virtualitalia.com/recipes/etiquette.shtml.

Parkinson, Rhonda. "Chinese Cuisine." About.com: Chinese Food. www.chinesefood.about.com.

Paris.org. "Place de la Concorde; Obélisque de Luxor." www.paris.org/Monuments/Concorde/.

Ramano, Katherine. *The Italian Cookbook.* California: Nitty Gritty Productions, 1973.

Rosario, Danielle. "Exploring the Culture of Little Havana." A Learning Community Project (School of Education, the College of Arts and Science and Eaton Residential College, University of Miami). http://www.education.miami.edu/ep/LittleHavana/Cuban_Food/cuban_food.html.

Savarin, Anthelma Brillat. *The Physiology of Taste or Meditations on Transcendental Gastonomy.* London: Boni and Liveright, 1926.

Tannahill, Reay. *Food in History.* New York: Stein and Day Publishers, 1973.